brand ROYALTY

HOW THE WORLD'S TOP 100 BRANDS THRIVE & SURVIVE

matt haig

KOGAN PAGE

London and Philadelphia

Publisher's note

Every possible effort has been made to ensure that the information contained in this book is accurate at the time of going to press, and the publishers and author cannot accept responsibility for any errors or omissions, however caused. No responsibility for loss or damage occasioned to any person acting, or refraining from action, as a result of the material in this publication can be accepted by the editor, the publisher or the author.

First published in Great Britain and the United States in 2004 by
Kogan Page Limited
Paperback edition 2006
Reprinted 2007, 2008

120 Pentonville Road
London N1 9JN
United Kingdom
www.kogan-page.co.uk

525 South 4th Street, #241
Philadelphia PA 19147
USA

ISBN-10   0 7494 4826 1
ISBN-13   978 0 7494 4826 4

British Library Cataloguing-in-Publication Data

A CIP record for this book is available from the British Library.

Library of Congress Cataloging-in-Publication Data

Haig, Matt.
   Brand royalty : how the world's top 100 brands thrive & survive / Matt Haig. – Pbk. ed.
   p. cm.
   Includes bibliographical references and index.
   ISBN 0-7494-4826-1
   1. Brand name products—Management.   I. Title.
HD69.B7H346 2006
658.8'27—dc22

               2006020806

Typeset by JS Typesetting Ltd, Porthcawl, Mid Glamorgan
Printed and bound in India by Replika Press Prt Ltd

Contents

Introduction

Being good in business is the most fascinating kind of art.

(Andy Warhol)

Branding is now the most important aspect of business. Whether the business is a bank or a toy shop, it is the brand itself that will dictate whether it succeeds or fails. Brand success equals business success. That may seem a simple equation, but identifying what exactly makes a brand work is pretty tricky, as no two brands are the same.

In fact, the whole point of branding is to make a product or a business look distinct from its competition. Therefore, looking for a single magic brand formula that encompasses all successful brands seems like a bad idea. By focusing on 100 of the most successful brands, the difference between them becomes astoundingly clear.

The simple ready-made solutions of the brand gurus start to unravel. You look at Hoover or Gillette or Coca-Cola and you think 'Ah yes, of course, the secret to a successful brand is to invent a completely new type of product.' And then you look at Mercedes-Benz or Nike or Pepsi and realize you can build a successful brand around someone else's invention.

You then think that maybe the secret to a successful brand is to be associated with one type of product or service. You look at brands such as Rolex, Kleenex, Wrigley's, Colgate, Moët & Chandon, Hertz and Bacardi and you think: 'At last! That's it! That's the secret!

One type of product per brand!' And then your heart sinks as you think of Yamaha and Caterpillar and Virgin, all of which produce widely different types of products.

Ultimately, the examples in this book are successful not because they conform to a neat little set of laws that apply to all brands but because they follow their own individual path with confidence. Successful brands are similar in that they all have a clear vision, but that vision is never the same.

It is precisely this lack of universal conformity that turns branding, and the business it generates, into the 'fascinating kind of art' Andy Warhol once spoke about.

The brand as religion

While branding may be an 'art', it also owes a debt to religion. Indeed, you could easily be fooled into thinking that many brands want to be mini-religions in themselves. Looking at 100 brands therefore starts to feel like looking at 100 very different religious cults. Consider the following characteristics:

- *Faith*. Like religions, brands want people to have faith in what they have to offer. This faith ideally leads to life-long devotion and belief in the brand's authenticity. Think of the attempts to position brands as 'the real thing' (Coca-Cola) or the 'truth' (Budweiser's 'true' slogan).
- *Omnipresence*. Successful brands want to be everywhere, and many have already achieved this aim. For example, the golden arches of McDonald's are now more recognized around the globe than the crucifix.
- *Gurus*. Successful brand managers are no longer called 'captains of industry'. They are 'gurus' to be worshipped devoutly by customers and employees alike. Religions were often founded by bearded men with enigmatic smiles who initiated virgin worship. Today we have Richard Branson.

- *Goodness.* Religion preaches good will to all people. 'Conscience' brands such as The Body Shop, Cafédirect and Seeds of Change also appeal to our philanthropic instincts.
- *Purity.* Brands, like religion, often centre around the pursuit of purity. Sometimes, as in the case of Evian and malt whisky, it is all about the purity of the product. More often, it is about the purity of the message, stripping a whole brand identity to a one-sentence strapline or a singular image.
- *Places of worship.* It is no longer enough for brands to be sold in a shop; they now have their own places of worship. Disneyland was the first, arriving in the 1950s, but in the 21st century brand temples are everywhere. Consider the numerous Nike Towns where trainers are displayed on pillars rising from the ground. Or think of state-of-the-art car showrooms on the Champs-Elysées in Paris, complete with interactive games, wine bars and restaurants.
- *Icons.* Iconic figures from the world of sport or entertainment attract the kind of devotion once reserved for saints and prophets. Celebrities such as Tiger Woods, David Beckham and P Diddy not only endorse brands, but are brands themselves with a market value most companies can only dream of.
- *Miracles.* Religion promises the miraculous. Even when the 'M' word isn't mentioned, it is implied. From the multicultural nirvana offered by Benetton to the promise of a new body on the cover of a fitness DVD, consumers are asked to choose not only between products, but also between competing miracles.

The 100 choices

A brand is an identity. The process of branding is therefore the process of creating and managing that identity. The 100 brands included in this book are those I feel have managed this process the most successfully.

It is inevitable that people will question a number of the choices of brands in this book. There will be people wondering why I haven't included brands such as Pizza Hut or Honda or Canon or Citibank or Marlboro or KFC. There will be other people wondering why I have included Oprah Winfrey and *Cosmopolitan* and Cafédirect. I want to make one thing clear from the start. The brands in this book are not necessarily the most profitable in the world (although many of them are, and all of them have generated huge financial success).

In choosing the 100 brands, I have tried to pick examples that best illustrate the broad nature not only of branding, but also of success. As Henry Ford once said, 'a business that makes nothing but money is a poor kind of business'. Success can be measured in dollars, but it can also be measured in time. After all, brands that have been around for over a century clearly have something to teach us.

Success can also be about change. Some of the brands in this book have pursued objectives that don't necessarily have a dollar sign in front of them. Some have revolutionized working conditions or the way a business communicates with its customers. Some have been instrumental in changing the way millions of people live and work, whether it be through bringing a new technology to the masses (as Henry Ford did with the automobile) or by giving them easier access to information (Reuters, CNN, Google).

Others have challenged the very definition of branding itself. For a hundred years, sports stars have been helping to endorse brands, but only recently have sports professionals such as Tiger Woods been considered global brands in their own right.

So some of the choices may be controversial, but it is hoped that each will shed a slightly different light on what is now the most significant of all business subjects.

CHAPTER I

Innovation brands

Business has only two functions – marketing and innovation.

(Peter F Drucker)

It is no coincidence that many of the biggest brands are also some of the business world's biggest innovators. Through the invention of a new product category or the radical change of an old one, a brand becomes more than a machine for making money. It becomes an influencer on society, changing the nature of everyday life.

Of course, innovation is not for the faint-hearted. Human beings are conservative creatures. They like what they know. When something new comes along – be it the automobile or Elvis Presley or the internet – people start to get anxious. As the psychologists tell us, change indicates that time moves on and therefore reminds us of our own mortality. We don't want to die, so we are resistant to change. It therefore makes sense that the younger we are the more we are willing to try something new, because death tends to be far from our minds.

It takes a brave or foolish company to see the long view, as very few radically new products are an instant success. People appreciate innovations in hindsight, rarely as they happen. Success happens slowly, through word of mouth or media endorsement, but, once the market has started to accept the idea, the innovator becomes the spokesperson for the category invented.

In some cases – such as Hoover and Xerox – the brand becomes so associated with its innovation that its name becomes synonymous with the product. In other cases – such as Sony – the brand is responsible for so many radically new types of products that the name is associated with innovation itself.

Either way, there is no denying that innovation is a high-stakes game. Researching and promoting a new product costs a lot of money, and can lead to spectacular failure. That said, when brand innovators make it, they make it big. After all, it's easier to lead if you've made the first few steps alone.

1　Adidas: the performance brand

All truly great brands are innovators, and Adidas is no exception. Adolph 'Adi' Dassler, the man originally behind the Adidas brand, is widely considered to be the founder of the modern sporting goods industry.

When he was a teenager, growing up in a Germany that had been economically devastated by World War I, he helped his family make house-slippers from left-over military bags. But Dassler's real love was sport, and particularly soccer, so in 1920 he started making sports shoes. He contacted various doctors, trainers and sports coaches to gain their input, and drew on his own personal athletic experience. From the start, his emphasis was on each shoe's 'performance' for a particular sport, and so he created different types of shoe according to the activity – such as running or tennis or soccer.

This well-researched approach quickly earned him an international reputation. Still in his twenties, he was dubbed the 'equipment manager of the world'.

Adidas shoes were worn in the Olympics as early as 1928. Athletes loved them. Indeed, athletic performance seemed to improve visibly with the arrival of Adidas. When Jesse Owens dazzled the crowds (and dismayed a furious Hitler) by winning four gold medals in the 1936 Berlin Olympics, he was wearing Adidas running shoes. So was Armin Hary, when he became the first athlete to run the 100-metre sprint in 10 seconds.

Dassler kept Adidas ahead through constant innovation and his determination to design shoes catering for each sport's demands. Take soccer. Dassler realized that standard soccer boots weren't sufficient if the pitch was damp. He therefore came up with the idea of studs that could be screwed into the base of each boot, ensuring greater control and accuracy for players. It was with these new boots that the German team sailed to victory in the 1954 World Cup.

As well as soccer studs, Dassler was also the first to come up with spikes in running shoes to enhance the grip as athletes ran around the track.

He also wanted to make sure his shoes were made with the best possible material for their specific use. He conducted thousands of tests on any materials that could provide a possible benefit, including the skin of sharks and even kangaroos. His most successful experiment ended with the creation of nylon shoes.

Dassler wasn't just a good innovator. He also had a brain for marketing. He knew that if Adidas was going to have completely different shoes for different sports there would have to be an element of unity. In 1949, he therefore came up with the idea of putting three stripes on the side of his shoes so everyone would be able to tell they were Adidas just by looking at them. It wasn't until 1996, however, that the three stripes became the Adidas corporate logo.

Today, Dassler's legacy lives on. It still focuses on the sports performance aspect of its products (which now extend to all sportswear). However, it also acknowledges that its market has moved beyond athletes. Indeed, Adidas is now a fashion brand as much as a sports brand. Ever since 1986, when Run DMC's hip-hop anthem 'My Adidas' became a massive worldwide hit, the brand has enjoyed a cool image. Today, Adidas is still embraced by the hip-hop community, with stars like Missy Elliott keeping it high in the fashion stakes.

The challenge for Adidas has been how to balance street credibility with sports performance. Rather than try to combine both together, Adidas has set up different divisions – Sport Performance, Sport Heritage and Sport Style. The Sport Performance division focuses on functionality and innovation, the way Adidas has always done. The Sport Heritage range of Adidas originals with an 'old-school' feel showcases the brand's rich history (these are the ranges loved by the hip-hop community). Adidas Sport Style is aimed directly at the fashion-conscious consumer, and produced with fashion designer Yohji Yamamoto. The Sport Performance division is the bulk of Adidas's market, representing 70 per cent of overall sales. Sport Heritage is currently at around 25 per cent and Sport Style at 5 per cent.

In terms of marketing, Adidas still concentrates on the major sports events, being an official sponsor of the Soccer World Cup and sponsoring individual sports stars like David Beckham (who is an Adidas 'spokesperson' with a $161 million life-long contract) and US basketball star Tim Duncan.

It is also looking for future stars through its various youth sports projects such as Adidas America's ABCD camp, a basketball skills workshop for top high-school athletes. This camp, which has helped teenagers Shaquille O'Neal and Patrick Ewing become sports icons, perfectly illustrates Adidas's multifunctional approach to business. Firstly, there is the great PR potential involved with such a project. Then there's the sponsorship angle. The camp is a key part of Adidas's strategy to attract top athletes for endorsement deals. It is also the perfect testing ground for new products, as the company can gauge the responses of the future basketball stars.

So this is Adidas: a brand that is looking both forward and back. It is on the lookout for future trends and talent, while never forgetting its own history – even promoting its own history through the Sport Heritage division.

It may now be partly overshadowed by Nike, but Adidas is unlikely to fade away anytime soon. It is a brand that retains credibility, in the worlds of street fashion and sport, by being proud of its past and confident of its future, and by staying innovative. In fact, I'd argue that Adidas benefits from its second-place status. While Nike gets all the criticism for its business practices, the associations of Adidas remain firmly on sports. Also, it is easier to be the number two sports brand than, say, the number two software brand.

Branding, like sport, appeals to our tribal instinct. And the tribalism of branding is never stronger than in the sportswear market. Nike and Adidas are two tribes that depend on each other in the same way as a soccer or a basketball team needs someone to play against. An Adidas sports shoe doesn't just say 'Adidas'; it also implicitly says 'not Nike', just as a Nike shoe says 'not Adidas'. Nike and Adidas may hate each other's guts, but the aggressive competition has ultimately made them both stronger.

The Adidas brand certainly doesn't seem to be panicked by Nike into making any wrong decisions. Although advertising and sponsorship are a key part of Adidas's marketing strategy, they have never been at the expense of the products. Staying true to Adolph Dassler's original intentions, the performance of the products remains as important as the performance of the brand.

Secrets of success

- *Innovation.* Studs for soccer boots; spikes for running shoes; nylon soles: these are just three of the innovations that helped build the Adidas brand.
- *Performance.* As an athlete himself, Adolph Dassler never neglected the performance of his products. He always looked for new ways to improve athletic standards through the use of Adidas equipment.

- *Competition*. Sportswear is as tribal as sport itself. Therefore it will never be a one-brand market. Adidas has stuck to its own gameplan and has thrived in competing with other brands such as Nike and Reebok.
- *History*. Unlike other sports brands, Adidas keeps its history alive through its Sports Heritage division. Far from making the brand seem stuffy and outdated, its 'old-school' ranges are considered the most fashionable among the hip-hop community.
- *Key influences*. Hip-hop stars like Run DMC and Missy Elliott, and sports stars such as David Beckham have helped give the brand street and sport credibility.

Fact file

Website: www.adidas.com

Founded: 1928

Country of origin: Germany

Brand fact 1: Adidas produces approximately 60 new footwear designs each year.

Brand fact 2: The company spends 13 per cent of total group sales on marketing.

Brand fact 3: Adidas is the second largest company in the sporting goods industry.

---

2 Sony: the pioneer brand

Sony was founded in 1946 by Akio Morita and Masaru Ibuka. Originally, it was a radio repair firm, but by the 1950s it was producing its own Sony-branded products.

Sony quickly developed a reputation in its native Japan for innovative products such as the first effective transistor radio (in 1958) and the first all-transistor TV (1960). These innovations helped the firm expand throughout Asia, and then to the United States and Europe. In 1961, it became the first Japanese company to be listed on Wall Street.

Throughout the decades, Sony has led the way, producing one innovative product after another. In 1971, it created the world's first colour video recorder. A few years later it created another revolutionary product: the Walkman. On its launch in 1979 few within the industry took the Walkman seriously. It was seen as a gimmick that would probably die an early death. In fact, it went on to become the most popular consumer electronics product in history, and has led to newer versions such as the CD Walkman and MiniDisc. Sony has achieved similar success in other areas with its TVs, videos, DVDs, hi-fis and game consoles (the Sony Playstation).

Of course, being an innovator has its risks, and Sony has had one notable flop, having been the company behind the ill-fated video format Betamax, which I have written about in detail elsewhere (in *Brand Failures*).

However, Sony has been smart enough to realize that hardware is only one side of the consumer equation. In the book *Cool Brand Leaders* (Knobil (ed), 2003), Sony is singled out for its ability to see the larger picture: '[The] ability to identify and act on consumer and industry trends has served Sony well over the years. It was arguably the first global electronics corporation to recognise the importance of synergy – the interface between hardware and content.'

In 1988, Sony bought CBS records and the following year it acquired Columbia Pictures Entertainment. Sony Music Entertainment is now one of the largest players in the music industry, and Sony Pictures Entertainment has produced massive blockbusters such as the Charlie's Angels franchise.

Sony is, without doubt, one of the world's healthiest brands. Part of this health is down to what Akio Morita (who led the company until he resigned in 1993 after suffering a brain haemorrhage while playing tennis) referred to as the brand's 'pioneer spirit'. The other part is due to successful marketing. Sony's marketing philosophy is very different to that of many other companies, especially in the West, as the secrets of its success reveal.

Secrets of success

- *A distrust of market research*. As a true pioneer, Sony has often been wary of market research. The Walkman, which was Akio Morita's own invention, would certainly not have been invented if it had been dependent on market research. 'I do not believe that any amount of market research could have told us that it would have been successful,' said Morita, adding: 'The public does not know what is possible. We do.'
- *Innovation*. Sony is *the* innovation brand and looks set to remain so in the future, with its new focus on 'connectivity' – the meeting of computing and home entertainment. The products it is coming up with certainly seem as innovative as ever. For instance, Sony launched the world's first Walkman phone in 2005.
- *A belief in buzz*. When the Walkman first appeared in Japan, Sony workers walked the streets of their native Tokyo with Walkmans strapped to them, creating a valuable buzz. When the MiniDisc was launched in the UK, postcards advertising the product were placed in trendy bars and clubs.
- *A belief in people*. People are important to Sony. The human element is never neglected in its advertising (hence the recent slogan 'Products for People'). It always finds a way to make technology accessible and friendly. This belief in people extends to the employees themselves. 'Never break another man's rice bowl' was Morita's motto. Morita also believed it was better to sacrifice a profit than lay off employees in a recession.

Fact file

Website: www.sony.net

Founded: 1946

Country of origin: Japan

Brand fact 1: Sony's first product was a rice cooker.

Brand fact 2: Before the Walkman became a worldwide brand name it was introduced as Soundabout in the United States, Stowaway in the UK and Freestyle in Australia.

Brand fact 3: Sony Playstation 2 dominates the game console market with 70 per cent of global sales.

---

3 Hoover: the synonymous brand

Hoover is, in the truest sense, a household name. It is also, in the English language, a household verb. 'Could you hoover the carpet?' is a phrase that inspires lethargic grunts almost anywhere in the English-speaking world.

The reason the brand became so synonymous with the product was because it invented the category. Or, more accurately, Murray Spangler did. Murray was a relation of William H Hoover's wife. Unlike William, Murray didn't have his own company. In fact, he was a janitor at a department store who spent his working life sweeping dusty floors. Bad enough, you might think, but poor Murray also suffered from chronic asthma. To make his job easier, he experimented with bits and pieces he had lying about at home – a metal box, a broom, a pillow case, a fan – and came up with a device that sucked the dust particles away as he swept. He then approached William and asked if he was interested in manufacturing the device. After his wife had tested and approved the product, Hoover bought the patent in 1908.

With the help of various free-trial offers, the 'suction sweepers' became a success, and word spread across the United States and Canada. Hoover then decided to give up selling the products he had originally based his business on, as leather harnesses for horses and carts were struggling due to the rise of the automobile. The company then devoted all its energies to vacuum cleaners. It is ironic that the company was nearly killed by the rise of one new technology, and saved by the invention of another.

The brand succeeded even further after William H Hoover's death in 1932, and continued to lead the way in the market it had started. It has expanded into other categories of household products, such as washing machines and refrigerators, but the name remains synonymous with the vacuum cleaner.

In recent years the brand has faced tough competition from the British company Dyson, which revolutionized the market with its patented cyclone system. Hoover has fought back by patenting its own equivalent new system, called the Wind Tunnel. This may have been necessary to stop Dyson from sucking up its market share, but the perception in terms of the Hoover brand is negative as it turns the brand leader into a brand follower.

That said, Hoover remains by far the most recognized name within the category. Whether a perceived lack of innovation and extensions into other categories will eventually weaken the brand remains to be seen.

Secrets of success

- *It invented the category.* The market for vacuum cleaners didn't exist before Hoover. It is therefore the natural leader.
- *Home improvement.* New products only work if they offer a visible improvement on the way things were done before. The invention of the vacuum cleaner provided a clear step up from the broom.

- *Try before you buy*. Free 10-day trials in the early 20th century were key to Hoover's market dominance in North America.

Fact file

Website: www.hoover.com

Founded: 1908

Country of origin: USA

Brand fact 1: Hoover is America's number one name in vacuum cleaners and the leading manufacturer of floor care appliances.

Brand fact 2: The first vacuum cleaners were sold in 1908 when only 10 per cent of homes were wired for electricity.

Brand fact 3: The first Hoovers were imported to Britain in 1912.

Brand fact 4: WH Hoover unwittingly realized that demonstrations sold stock. He said, 'I would stock up hardware stores with cleaners, go out two months later and find none of them moved. I would get busy and demonstrate them to housewives and move the stock.'

---

4 Xerox: the research brand

In branding, there are no pure success stories and there are no pure failure stories. Usually, successes and failures coexist within the same brand, and Xerox is no exception.

When Xerox – a name associated with paper copiers – decided to launch IBM-style office data systems it ended up with one of the largest brand failures of all times, at least in financial terms. Another disaster was the Telecopier, the company's early version of a fax machine. However, the reason these ventures failed is exactly the same reason why Xerox is a success. Xerox is associated with one category, the category it invented – paper copiers.

The Xerox brand first became massive in 1959 with the launch of the Xerox 914, the world's first automatic plain-paper copier. *Fortune* magazine two years later called this machine 'the most successful product ever marketed in America'. From the 914 onwards, Xerox has been inextricably associated with copiers, and has led the field with advanced and innovative products. In fact, innovation is key to the company's success and is exemplified by its emphasis on technological research. For instance, in 1970 it set up the Xerox Palo Alto Research Center, or Xerox PARC as it has become known.

However, in terms of the Xerox brand, the research centre has been a rather mixed blessing. As well as producing undeniable advancements in copier technology, it was also behind Xerox data systems and the Telecopier. Xerox also has its own university – the Xerox Document University in Virginia.

Of course, research is important to just about all technology brands, and nobody can accuse Xerox of falling short on these grounds. What people have accused Xerox of is the wrong focus. 'Xerox... lost focus on their base business,' writes Jack Trout, in his book *Big Brands, Big Trouble* (2001), 'thus allowing competition to take away their most important customers.' 'When Xerox tried to put its powerful copier name on computers, the result was billions of dollars in losses,' write Al and Laura Ries, in *The 22 Immutable Laws of Branding* (1998).

Xerox is singled out by such leading advocates of branding, because it spent a long length of its history trying to change its identity in people's minds. This ambition and its futility were evident in an advert for Xerox computer services, which said: 'This is not about copiers.' The fact that the word 'copiers' was included shows that Xerox acknowledged the problem it faced. Xerox was about one type of product, copiers. It was not, like IBM, about a broader concept such as computer technology.

As inventors of the copier category, it has been stuck with that single association. Xerox has been able to use that association and build a $20 billion empire on the back of it. And it is the Xerox name itself, rather than the research and new products, that is the most powerful part of the brand. Now that it has decided to focus on what it does best rather than finance ambitious new directions, the brand will grow even more powerful.

It is remarkable to think that the name could be even bigger if its ambition had been a little bit smaller.

Secrets of success

- *First mover*. Xerox was the first in a new category when it launched its Xerox 914 copier.
- *PR*. As the first in a new category, it was able to generate valuable PR as the US media sought to document the technological breakthrough Xerox had made.

Fact file

Website: www.xerox.com

Founded: 1906 as the Haloid Company; named Xerox in 1961

Country of origin: USA

Brand fact 1: Xerox has 60,000 employees around the world.

Brand fact 2: From 1939 to 1944, Chester Carlson, a New York patent attorney and the inventor of xerography, had his work turned down by twenty companies including IBM, Kodak and General Electric. It wasn't until 1959 that the first convenient office copier using xerography was launched.

Brand fact 3: Earth-friendly design and manufacturing saved Xerox more than $2 billion in 10 years from 1991 to 2001.

- *Research.* Through its research centre and university, Xerox remains at the cutting edge of technological research.
- *Name.* Xerox is a short, distinctive name that has become synonymous with the copiers it manufactures. As such, it is hard for competitors to eat into the company's market share, even when it makes a few wrong turns.

5 American Express: the integrity brand

American Express has a significant history. In 1850, it was launched as an express freight company, and its reputation grew during the American Civil War when it transported supplies to the eventually victorious Union army. In the 1880s, American Express still shipped physical cargo, but it also moved into finance, transferring funds from the new wave of Europeans settling in America to their families back home. In 1891, American Express invented the traveller's cheque, revolutionizing the travel and finance industries simultaneously.

Fast-forward to 1958. American Express launches its second major innovation – the American Express card. Like the traveller's cheque, this famous piece of green plastic liberated people. Not just travellers, but consumers. The American Express card enabled people for the first time to do their shopping without having to carry cash in their pocket.

It was a charge card and, as such, wasn't available to everybody. The American Express card therefore became the ultimate status symbol – a convenient social shorthand for 'I have a great credit rating'.

American Express had started the move away from the grubby realities of handling cash in the 1880s through its funds transfer. The charge card moved society – or at least a certain strand of society

– one step further away from notes and coins (hard finance) towards the cleaner, more mysterious world of plastic (soft finance).

The card, as a symbol of status, not only liberated people but helped to define them. Throughout the second half of the 20th century, American Express's advertising campaigns portrayed the card as a signifier of prestige or even as a symbol of membership to an exclusive club ('Membership has its privileges' was one famous slogan). Business leaders such as Richard Branson starred in adverts, promoting American Express membership.

Today, although the company is now a 'financial supermarket' (in its own phrasing, 'a diversified worldwide travel, financial and network services company'), it is still best known for its pieces of plastic.

However, in recent years the connotations of the American Express brand, and its cards, have undeniably changed. It has moved from an exclusive to an inclusive brand. Its charge cards have been joined by credit cards that are less symbols of status and more a practical convenience. People now use American Express cards to pay for such mundane things as groceries and even their rent. Through advertising aimed at retail customers, it has successfully dusted down its image and shaken off old-fashioned connotations of prestige and membership. After all, unlike in the 1950s, the whole world is now run on plastic.

Although the move from 'prestige' to 'populist' is always a tricky one, American Express's long-established and respected reputation for financial integrity and security has made the transition easier than it is for most brands. Its stated goal to become 'the world's most respected service brand' is now back on track.

Secrets of success

- *Foresight.* Its introduction of traveller's cheques and charge cards showed remarkable foresight, and has set the world on its long journey towards a cashless economy.

- *The ability to evolve.* From its origins as a freight company to its current 'financial supermarket' status, the American Express business has proved able to adapt to changing lines. So too has the brand: its recent move from an aspirational image to the mass market has strengthened its position as one of the world's few super-brands.

Fact file

Website: www.americanexpress.com

Founded: 1850

Country of origin: USA

Brand fact 1: Nearly 80 per cent of American Express's revenues are US generated.

Brand fact 2: American Express is the world's number one travel agency.

Brand fact 3: American Express publishes magazines such as *Food & Wine* and *Travel & Leisure*.

---

6 L'Oréal: the individuality brand

Successful brands have two stages. There is the innovation stage and the consolidation stage. To become a global leader from nothing a brand needs to innovate first and consolidate later. There is no way a new brand can become the leader in a category with advertising alone. It needs to offer the world something new – something significant enough to generate PR and word of mouth.

Think of Gillette, with its safety razor. Or Nike, with its rubber outer sole for running shoes. These innovations revolutionized the market and gave the brands the step-up they needed to get started. Then they could consolidate their achievements by advertising.

Other brands – such as Sony – are constant innovators. In such cases, the innovation and consolidation phases are simultaneous. Without innovation, however, there would be nothing to consolidate.

Even a brand like L'Oréal, which is now more about expanding and capitalizing on what it's already got, originally started as a revolutionary brand. It started with one man, Eugene Schueller. He was a talented chemical engineer, living in Paris. In 1907, he invented the first synthetic hair dye. In 1908, he turned his invention into the basis of his business, the French Company for Inoffensive Hair Dyes (renamed L'Oréal the following year).

Initially, it was a one-man operation, with Eugene sacrificing sleep so he could make hair dyes all night and tour Parisian hair salons all day, selling his products. The consolidation phase was already under way. Following a small investment from an accountant he got a bigger apartment and his first employee in 1909. He also started to advertise in the hairdressing magazine, *La Coiffure de Paris*. By 1934 L'Oréal was large enough to buy the French company Monsaron. This gave Eugene the perfect platform from which to launch the second major L'Oréal innovation – the first mass-market shampoo without soap. However, rather than call it L'Oréal shampoo, he gave it a new brand name, Dop.

This set the pattern for the rest of the century: acquisitions and the creation of new brands in different product categories. In the 1960s, the company bought Lancome and Garnier, and created Guy Laroche perfumes. Today, it is behind most of the leading perfume brands, such as Ralph Lauren, Lancôme and Giorgio Armani. It is also the market leader in cosmetics, owning the Maybelline brands alongside its own L'Oréal ranges.

The secret of its success is in keeping each of its brand identities distinct. Maybelline, for instance, is associated with a young and punchy New York personality, despite being owned by the French company. Indeed, L'Oréal has earned itself a reputation as the

'United Nations of beauty' owing to the various separate identities housed within one global company. According to a cover story in *Business Week* magazine ('L'Oréal: The Beauty of Global Branding', 28 June 1999), L'Oréal's secret is its ability to convey the 'allure of different cultures' through its many products:

> Whether it's selling Italian elegance, New York street smarts, or French beauty through its brands, L'Oréal is reaching out to more people across a bigger range of incomes and cultures than just about any other beauty products company in the world. That sets L'Oréal apart from one-note marketers such as Coca-Cola, which has just one brand to sell globally.

As L'Oréal's British-born CEO Lindsay Owen-Jones has said, 'We have made a conscious effort to diversify the cultural origins of our brands.' For example, when the company bought Maybelline for $758 million in 1996, L'Oréal deliberately accentuated its US origins, launching new sub-brands such as Maybelline Miami Chill and setting TV ads in Manhattan. The strategy worked. Maybelline's sales doubled by 2003, and it is a far bigger brand outside the United States than it was before the takeover.

L'Oréal has proved that giving brands clearly defined national identities does not place limits on their international success. By adding personality to the brand, this strategy in fact has the opposite effect.

Another interesting thing about L'Oréal is that it is not scared about self-cannibalization. As the company owns so many brands in similar or identical markets they obviously risk eating into each other's sales. L'Oréal has grown so big it has become its own competition. But Owen-Jones says he deliberately wants to create a tension between his marketing teams. 'A charged atmosphere is exactly what I'm looking for,' he told *Business Week*.

He therefore set up another headquarters in New York, a 'counter-power' separate from the company's base in Paris. Such measures have stopped any complacency setting in, even in sectors where L'Oréal dominates the market. It has experienced top-line growth above its rivals for over a decade, but Owen-Jones says he is 'never satisfied' and never convinced his company is winning. Such internal competition inevitably leads to an intensely creative environment.

To make sure the various brands don't blur into one, L'Oréal has not only accentuated national identities, but has also stripped itself down. It now solely focuses on five core areas – hair care, hair colour, colour cosmetics, fragrances and skin care. It has also, under Owen-Jones, narrowed the focus on to a smaller number of global brands. These brands range from mass-market names such as Maybelline to luxury brands such as Helena Rubinstein. They retain strong, individual identities because there is no need for L'Oréal to create one brand that is all things to all people.

Perhaps the broadest brand within the company's stable is the L'Oréal brand itself. It has been targeted at both sexes for a variety of products. Its identity, in keeping with Eugene Schueller's original idea, is French sophistication matched with scientific expertise. The L'Oréal brand is positioned not just as products we can use, but as personal rewards the consumer deserves. The L'Oréal slogan 'Because you're worth it', which has been spoken by celebrities such as Ben Affleck and Jennifer Aniston in TV ads recently, sums up the brand's identity. Like the whole company itself, it condenses the universal into the personal. It is speaking directly out to individuals and entire markets simultaneously, because the two cannot be separated.

Indeed, 'individuality' is perhaps the word that sums up L'Oréal's entire strategy. Each brand retains its individuality along with its own name. This way, L'Oréal has been able to have the best of both business worlds. It has been able to keep brands strong while stretching its reach, resisting the temptation to bundle them all into a homogeneous whole under the L'Oréal banner.

Although there are examples (Virgin, Yamaha, Sony) where brands have successfully kept hold of their name as they've plunged into new markets, there are plenty more examples where such strategies have failed. What L'Oréal has shown is that, in a world where markets are increasingly fragmented, success lies in creating various individual brands rather than one catch-all identity.

Secrets of success

- *Innovation.* Great brands are launched by innovation, not advertising. That can come later.
- *Individuality.* L'Oréal uses different brands to attract different markets. It is unlike other global brands in that no 'God complex' seems to be at work, and L'Oréal shows no desire to create the world in its own, singular image.
- *Personality.* Because L'Oréal has different brands for different markets, it is not scared to exaggerate their personality. With other brands the tendency is to water their identity down as they expand.
- *Consolidation.* L'Oréal does not launch new brands just for the sake of it. It capitalizes on the brands it has already built up or acquired through carefully targeted markets.

Fact file

Website: www.loreal.com

Founded: 1907

Country of origin: France

Brand fact 1: L'Oreal is the world leader in cosmetics..

Brand fact 2: L'Oreal develop more than 3,000 formulas each year.

Brand fact 3: 3.3 per cent of L'Oreal sales are invested in cosmetics and dermatology each year.

Brand fact 4: L'Oreal sells 85 of its products every second.

- *Nationality.* Many brands play down their nationality for fear of alienating foreign markets. L'Oréal, on the other hand, exaggerates the national or regional identities and even places them next to the brand name. Think of 'Maybelline New York' or 'L'Oréal Paris', for instance.

7 Durex: the safe brand

Durex has been producing condoms since 1929. Since then it has become the undisputed market leader, partly due to its long series of innovations. For instance, in 1957 it invented the world's first lubricated condom.

Its name is designed to suggest its three 'guiding principles' – DUrability, REliability and EXcellence. These principles ensure that Durex conducts rigorous tests to assess the durability and quality of its products before they enter the market. The condoms are even rolled in blotting paper to check for the tiniest leakages and the latex undergoes 'stretch tests'.

As such, it has become a brand intrinsically associated with safe sex. In the 1980s, its products became more widely available as the growing threat of AIDS led to more open public debate about sex. The Durex brand was made available in supermarkets and bars as well as pharmaceutical chains.

The brand has successfully turned into a leading sex authority, with its annual Durex Global Sex Survey, which not only provides market research, but is also used by various agencies to help develop programmes promoting sexual health issues.

Social responsibility is a big part of the Durex brand, and the company invests millions of dollars every year to emphasize the realities of AIDS. It also produces health media such as the *International Barrier Protection Digest* and the website durexhealthcare. com.

By becoming a sex health ambassador, in terms of both its products and its research, Durex has become intrinsically associated with the issue of safe sex in people's minds and therefore remains a long way ahead of the global market.

Secrets of success

- *Durability.* Durability, reliability and excellence remain the brand's guiding principles.
- *Responsibility.* For a product associated with safe sex and sexual health, responsibility should not be a brand add-on. Indeed, Durex has brought the issue of responsibility into the heart of its business, combining market and health research, and promoting awareness of sexually transmitted diseases.

Fact file

Website: www.durex.com

Founded: 1915 as London Rubber Company; named Durex in 1929

Country of origin: UK

Brand fact 1: Durex were the first to provide lubricated condoms and the first non-latex condoms.

Brand fact 2: Durex is the market leader in more than 40 countries.

Brand fact 3: The Durex brand accounts for 26 per cent of the world's 4 billion condom market, making it the number one condom brand in the world.

8 Mercedes-Benz: the prestige brand

In January 1886, Karl Benz, a 41-year-old German engineer, patented the world's first automobile powered by an internal combustion engine.

A year before, his fellow German, Gottlieb Daimler, had built the first land vehicle ever to use an internal combustion engine – a motorcycle. In 1886, Daimler topped Benz's achievement by building the first four-wheeled automobile (Benz's vehicle had been a three-wheeler). Although the two men were only about 70 miles apart, they never met to work together on their inventions.

Forty years later, the companies both men set up – Daimler's Daimler-Motoren-Gesellschaft and Benz's Benz & Co – would merge. The resultant brand of cars, Mercedes-Benz, has become the most well-known prestige brand in the world. Although in recent years it has shifted slightly downmarket with vehicles such as the A-Class, a relatively affordable sub-compact hatchback, it has stayed true to its pioneering heritage.

For instance, in 2002 the new Mercedes-Benz E-Class became the market leader partly due to innovations such as an electro-hydraulic braking system, patented 'sensotronic' brake control and an 'Electronic Stability Program' that ensured better handling in emergency situations.

Even the cheaper A-Class represented a completely new type of car, which boasted lots of inside space despite its short design. Indeed, the car looked so different that Mercedes-Benz started running advertisements for it months in advance in Europe, to get people accustomed to the idea. It worked. The car has been a phenomenal success across Europe.

The trouble is, Mercedes-Benz has spent most of its history establishing itself as a prestige brand. Obviously, it has to be subtle about it. It couldn't call itself 'Mercedes-Benz, the prestige car', because people don't want to own up to their superiority complexes. They'd much rather pretend they were buying a car for another reason – engineering, say. Mercedes-Benz has therefore built a brand that focuses on engineering, even though the implicit intention has been to create a prestige brand. This is a clever strategy. It means Mercedes-Benz can appear consistent, even as it moves slightly downmarket. Cheaper cars such as the A-Class and M-Class are also legitimately sold on the basis of quality engineering.

However, while this strategy works in the short to mid-term, the longer view may be different. After all, prestige is ultimately about price, not engineering. The cheaper cars are popular because they are a way of buying into a prestige brand, but there is an obvious law of diminishing returns. The more cheaper cars that are sold, the less prestigious the brand becomes. Therefore product success could, paradoxically, equal brand failure.

Fact file

Website: www.mercedes-benz.com

Founded: 1924

Country of origin: Germany

Brand fact 1: The Mercedes-Benz logo represents the company's original aim to provide small powerful engines to travel on land, sea and air.

Brand fact 2: Mercedes-Benz has introduced a number of advanced technologies to cars – such as fuel injection and anti-lock braking systems.

Brand fact 3: Gottlieb Daimler, one of the founders of Mercedes-Benz, also introduced the world's first motorized taxi in 1897 (complete with taxi meter).

Secrets of success

- *Innovation.* Innovation is a natural quality you would expect from the company associated with the invention of the car.
- *Price.* Historically, its high prices have helped Mercedes-Benz become a prestigious brand.
- *Prestige.* People who drive a Mercedes-Benz like to feel superior. Whether they continue to feel superior when everyone can afford one remains to be seen.

9 Nescafé: the instant brand

Nestlé's Nescafé is the leading brand of instant coffee. It was also the first. Like many brand innovators, Nescafé was a result of intensive research – seven years of research to be precise, taking place in Swiss laboratories in the 1930s. The Brazilian government had approached coffee expert Max Morgenthaler at the start of the decade asking him to find a way of reducing its coffee surpluses by producing a cheaper coffee, which could be made by adding water.

Over the years it has kept the emphasis on innovation, introducing pure soluble coffee (1952) solely using roast coffee beans, freeze-dried soluble coffee (with the launch of Gold Blend in 1965) and coffee granules (1967). In 1994 it invented the 'full aroma' process, which improved the quality of instant coffee.

Such innovations have made sure that Nescafé has remained the world's leading coffee brand. It is also the second most valuable brand in the entire drinks sector, behind Coca-Cola, with around 3,000 cups of Nescafé drunk every second.

However, innovation isn't the only factor. Nescafé has had to work hard at maintaining its position with successful advertising aimed at specific markets. It has been singled out as an expert in adding value *between* brands. For example, in the UK Nescafé and Nescafé Gold Blend are two different products but both serve to boost the overall Nescafé brand through implied endorsement of each other.

Secrets of success

- *Research*. Seven years of intensive research went into the original Nescafé product.
- *Innovation*. That 'I' word again. Nescafé is yet another brand that shows that if you invent a market you are the natural leader within it.
- *Added value*. The various Nescafé brands fall roughly into the 'popular' and 'prestige' brackets, but both types of product are promoted in such a way that they add to, rather than diminish, the appeal of other Nescafé products.

Fact file

Website: www.nescafe.co.uk

Founded: 1938

Country of origin: Switzerland

Brand fact 1: 3,000 cups of Nescafe are drunk every second.

Brand fact 2: Nescafe is owned by Nestle, the number one food producer.

Brand fact 3: Nescafe was the staple drink of the US armed forces during World War II.

---

10 Toyota: the big-picture brand

In 2003, Toyota overtook Ford to become the world's second car maker, falling behind only General Motors in terms of sales volume. The Japanese car giant now has 11 per cent of the world car market, selling around 7 million cars a year.

Part of this success can be attributed to various advertising campaigns aimed at a younger market, and revamping old models like the Corolla. However, another key to its success has been its switch from being a follow-the-crowd kind of company to being something of an industry pioneer. For instance, it has become an ambassador for environmentally friendly vehicles. In 1997, Toyota became the first car manufacturer to sell a mass-produced 'hybrid' vehicle. Hybrid cars combine an internal combustion engine with an electric motor, making them more fuel-efficient and therefore more eco-friendly than traditional models. Toyota's president Fujio Cho has stated that 'development of eco-friendly cars is a key to our future growth strategy'.

Often when companies promote a new type of product or technology they make the mistake of confining it to their own brand. Think of Apple's determination to keep its operating system to its own computers, or Sony's reluctance to license out Betamax technology to other manufacturers. You only have to think of Microsoft's operating system or the VHS format to realize that the technologies that become the most popular are those that can be shared between companies, not confined to one individual brand. Fortunately, Toyota has not taken a protective or defensive attitude with its eco-cars. In 2002 it struck a deal with rival Nissan to share information and discuss the joint development of environmentally friendly technology.

This ability to see the bigger picture is evident throughout Toyota. Indeed, it currently seems less like a standard car manufacturer and more like an organization trying to change the future of driving. In recent years, it has come up with various innovations. For example, it has developed a 'self-parking' car, which uses electronic sensors to avoid obstacles and guide it into spaces.

Although self-parking, eco-friendly cars still represent only a fraction of Toyota's business, well-known models such as the Corolla reflect a brand with its eye firmly on the future. Having already overtaken Ford, it could soon be the most popular car maker in the world.

Secrets of success

- *Mission*. Toyota has switched from being a boring old car manufacturer to one with a broader mission, reflected by its partnership with Nissan to develop environmentally friendly vehicles.
- *Innovation*. Innovations such as 'self-parking' and hybrid cars have gained the company a lot of valuable PR, and positioned Toyota as a forward-thinking brand.

Fact file

Website: www.toyota.co.jp

Founded: 1937

Country of origin: Japan

Brand fact 1: Toyota started out in 1933 as the automobile department of Toyoda Automatic Loom Works, Ltd.

Brand fact 2: Toyota has the best overall miles per gallon ratings of any full-line car maker.

Brand fact 3: Toyota produces more than 5.5 million vehicles per year, equivalent to one every six seconds.

CHAPTER 2

Pioneer brands

The start of the 20th century was a period of radical change. New theories and inventions were exploding the old world order. Einstein's theory of relativity challenged traditional certainties with its conclusion that time and space weren't absolute, as previously thought, but relative to the speed of light. This meant, in the words of author Felipe Fernandez-Armesto (2003), that 'commonsense perceptions vanished as if down a rabbit-hole in Wonderland'.

But Einstein wasn't the only one transforming the way people perceived reality. In 1900, the publication of Sigmund Freud's *The Interpretation of Dreams* popularized his idea of a human unconscious where all our motivations are buried. This questioned the notion of a coherent mind, where thoughts are under our own control, just as Einstein was to question the idea of a coherent universe.

These theories coincided with revolutionary new techniques and inventions. In 1901, the first wireless broadcast took place. In 1903, the Wright brothers flew their aeroplane. Plastic was introduced in 1907. The major inventions of the late 1800s, such as the car and the telephone, were now appearing everywhere.

Society was changing faster than ever before, and the shock of the change was evident in the new types of art emerging from the canvases of Picasso, Braque, Mondrian and Kandinsky. Artists were no longer representing a straightforward 'reality', because the very idea of a straightforward reality suddenly seemed ridiculous.

The changing nature of society, politics and technology (changes that would take a devastating turn for the worse in 1914) was also reflected in the business world. The arrival of the Ford Model T showed how technological advances could be harnessed to benefit society as a whole. Pioneers such as William Wrigley and William Kellogg were taking the power of advertising to new levels with innovative, wide-reaching campaigns.

The new era of skyscrapers and jazz music was also the era of mass production and advertising and Coca-Cola. This electronically powered age led to bigger business ambitions than ever before, as the world seemed to be becoming ever smaller. As early as the 1880s the businessman Henry Heinz was able to say that his market was 'the world'. It is this broadening of business ambition, more than changes in technology and production and media, that is the ultimate legacy of the pioneering brands included in this section.

11   Heinz: the trust brand

In the 19th century, very few brands were thinking global. Heinz was an exception. 'Our market is the world,' said its Pittsburgh-born founder Henry Heinz, shortly after its launch in 1876 (actually, it was a relaunch, because he had set up an earlier food business, selling grated horseradish, seven years before).

During the 1880s, Henry Heinz got on a boat to Europe with cases stacked full of Heinz produce (including bottles of tomato ketchup, which was one of the very first Heinz products). He stopped off in London and visited a variety of shops and food halls, one of which was the very grand and highly respected Fortnum and Mason store, the most famous shop in Victorian London. Heinz was not intimidated. He walked into the opulent hall and asked to see the food purchaser. Once the purchaser had sampled Heinz's produce he was in no doubt. 'I think, Mr Heinz, we will take the lot,' he told him, probably not realizing his words would be quoted over a century later.

Heinz salesmen soon ventured further afield to sell the product in every corner of the inhabited world. They were famously devoted to their boss, who always made sure his employees were cared for. His factories were visited by business people from across America, who had heard about their clean, safe and friendly working environment.

Henry Heinz died in 1916 but his business remained in family hands until 1965, under the control of his son Howard and then his grandson Jack, both of whom helped to establish Heinz as a good-quality and trustworthy brand.

Henry had come up with the bizarre but highly successful slogan '57 Varieties'. (It was bizarre because at the time Heinz in fact had 60 product varieties and the slogan remained as the range expanded further.) Howard and Jack may not have had the same knack for sloganeering, but they were just as ambitious, stretching the Heinz brand into areas such as baby food, beans and soups. In 1946, Jack Heinz turned the empire into a public company.

Today, under the leadership of William Johnson, the company's sixth CEO in nearly 130 years, the brand has probably outgrown even Henry Heinz's ambitions. Its goods are available in almost every country in the world. It employs nearly 50,000 workers. It is still the number one product in a lot of categories (could there ever be a more successful ketchup?). The company is now worth billions of dollars. And the '57 Varieties' have become 5,000.

Secrets of success

- *Trust*. Heinz is the most trusted of food brands. Even after the company slipped out of family hands, trust remained the core brand value.
- *Loyalty*. Linked with trust is the issue of loyalty. Tony O'Reilly, the fifth boss of Heinz, famously gave his 'acid test'. The test was whether someone 'intending to buy Heinz tomato ketchup in

a store, finding it to be out of stock, will walk out of the store to buy it elsewhere or switch to an alternative product'.

- *Heart*. Heinz has never ignored the human element. 'Heart power is better than horse power' was Henry Heinz's favourite maxim. Even today, you will hear few complaints from the company's devoted workforce. It is telling that Heinz was the largest global brand to have been left out of Naomi Klein's scathing attack on the inhuman aspects of globalization, *No Logo* (2002).
- *Ambition*. Heinz was one of the earliest global brands, and that it remains one of the biggest is testimony to sustaining ambitious values.

Fact file

Website: www.heinz.com

Founded: 1869

Country of origin: USA

Brand fact 1: The Heinz brand was valued at over $7 billion in 2004.

Brand fact 2: Heinz sells 650 million bottles of ketchup each year.

Brand fact 3: Heinz makes 11 billion packets of ketchup and dressings each year. That's at least two packets for every person on earth.

---

12 Kellogg's: the familiarity brand

Like Coca-Cola and many other major food brands, the first Kellogg's products were used for medicinal and health purposes.

Indeed, the very first Kellogg's product – corn flakes – began life at the Western Health Reform Institute, a rather strange organization based on the idea of purifying the soul through a grain-based diet. The institute was the subject of Alan Parker's 1988 movie *The Road to Wellville*, where it was depicted almost as a religious cult. Dr John Harvey Kellogg was the chief physician there from 1876 and, along with his brother William, pioneered the breakfast cereal as a means of preventing digestion problems.

It was William who proved the more entrepreneurial of the two, and in 1906 he set up the Battle Creek Toasted Cornflake Company to start mass-producing the product they had invented. However, it wasn't just the cereal that was toasted. In 1907 a fire destroyed the company's wooden premises and William had to start again.

Once he was over his initial setback, the company, which changed its name to Kellogg's, grew rapidly on the back of intensive advertising campaigns. Indeed, in the early 20th century, the brand was the most ambitious advertiser the world had ever known, with an advertising budget of $1 million by 1911, and creating the largest sign the world had ever seen, installing it in New York's Times Square (which has never looked the same since).

The aim was to make the word logo 'Kellogg's' as familiar as possible. It therefore became the main subject of adverts and was printed on every box of cereal. Even before any other Kellogg's cereals were introduced, the word 'Kellogg's' was always as important as the words 'Corn Flakes'.

Throughout the last century, Kellogg's achieved its aim by becoming one of the most familiar brands on the planet. Its individual brands such as Rice Krispies and Special K became household names in their own right, but consumers were never in any doubt about who produced them. This concentration on the Kellogg's brand – a brand built on values of taste, trust and health (from the 1940s the cereals were fortified with vitamins) – meant that consumers were willing to opt for the familiarity of Kellogg's over cheaper equivalents.

Kellogg's has therefore become the expert on umbrella branding. Each individual brand of cereal supports, and is supported by, the Kellogg's name. This distinguishes Kellogg's from competitors such as General Mills (makers of Cheerios) and Philip Morris Post (makers of Shredded Wheat), where the name of the specific cereal is all that matters.

Secrets of success

- *Price elasticity.* Years of investing in the promotion of the Kellogg's name have meant it can raise its prices above those of competitors. However, in recent years, Kellogg's has tested what economists call the 'price elasticity of demand' to the limit. For instance, when it started charging US consumers over $5 for a box of cereal (Apple Jacks) sales started to slide.
- *Familiarity.* The familiarity of the Kellogg's name has turned it into the ultimate example of successful 'umbrella branding', as it adds value to all its products.

Fact file

Website: www.kelloggs.com

Founded: 1906

Country of origin: USA

Brand fact 1: Kellogg products are manufactured in 19 countries and marketed in more than 160 countries around the world.

Brand fact 2: Kellogg is the world's leading producer of cereal, with projected annual sales of more than US $9 billion.

Brand fact 3: In 1906, Kellogg's put a full-page ad in the July issue of the *Ladies' Home Journal.* This resulted in sales leaping from 33 cases to 2,900 cases per day.

---

13 Colgate: the total brand

In 1873, nearly 70 years after William Colgate had founded the company, Colgate introduced its first toothpaste. Up until that time, the company had concentrated on selling starch, candles and scented soap. The first Colgate toothpaste was an aromatic cream sold in jars. The real breakthrough though came in 1896, when Colgate made the first collapsible toothpaste tube, making the act of cleaning teeth a lot easier and more hygienic.

Although Colgate merged with another successful brand, Palmolive soap, in 1928, the identity of the toothpaste remained as strong as ever. In fact, the merger helped the brand expand further outside its native United States.

The main threat to the brand has been its chief rival, Crest. Crest was the first toothpaste to introduce fluoride in 1955. When it became clear that fluoride really did prevent cavities, Colgate added fluoride in 1964.

However, cavities didn't stay the main dental issue. As fluoride became added to the water supply in many key markets, cavity prevention was overtaken by other dental problems, such as tartar control and gingivitis protection. In the 1990s Colgate became the first toothpaste to tackle the 'big three' – cavities, tartar and gingivitis – with the launch of Colgate Total. As consumers had become increasingly confused by ever-expanding toothpaste ranges, they welcomed a product that made their life simpler by offering a total solution.

This combined with earlier innovations such as improved 'MPF' fluoride, the Blue Minty Gel toothpaste (the first to target 9- to 14-year-olds) and the 1984 introduction of the pump action toothpaste dispenser.

Colgate has long been the leader in the global market, but the totality claim of Colgate Total has also helped it return to the US number one spot after 30 years in Crest's cavity-fighting shadow.

Secrets of success

- *Simplicity.* Colgate Total simplified a cluttered market, by giving the consumers an all-in-one solution.
- *Innovation.* Colgate has reconfirmed its leadership status by setting, rather than following, tooth care trends.

Fact file

Website: www.colgate.com

Founded: 1806

Country of origin: USA

Brand fact 1: Colgate is the number one seller of toothpastes and a world leader in oral care products.

Brand fact 2: Colgate does business in over 200 countries.

Brand fact 3: Colgate launched nearly 900 new products in the year 2000 alone.

---

14 Ford: the volume brand

The Ford Model T, available 'in any colour so long as it's black', is the most significant vehicle in automobile history. When it rolled off the assembly line in 1908, the Model T (or 'Tin Lizzie') wasn't the first car that had been built. Nor was it the fastest or the most beautiful. Yet it was the most revolutionary.

Through this car Henry Ford had achieved his dream of building 'a motorcar for the great multitude'. Unlike the car manufacturers who had gone before, Ford didn't focus his dream solely on performance, but on popularity. Before the Model T, cars were the ultimate playthings for the very rich. What Ford managed to do with the Model T (after 19 previous experimental models, from A to S) was to turn the car into a vehicle for the masses.

The revolution was based on radical economics. Instead of making money by raising the cost of the product, and therefore raising profit margins, Ford realized he could make more money by increasing sales volume and *lowering* prices and profit margins. When the Model T came to an end in 1927, over 15 million models had been sold and a Ford car was being produced every 24 seconds. The automobile age and the era of mass production had well and truly arrived.

Everything was about the economics of volume. Even the limited choice of colour was a result of Ford's desire to speed up the assembly line process. He seemed to realize that, when it came to a product as genuinely useful and revolutionary as the car, supply increased demand.

In the years and decades following the Model T, Ford followed the same populist principles, whether designing cars, vans or trucks. It became a brand of the people and responded to people's concerns. For example, when road accidents first became a major issue in the 1930s, Ford became the first car manufacturer to introduce safety glass.

Ford also responded to the desire for better-looking cars, with the introduction of purely ornamental design features such as car fins in the 1940s. This emphasis on design peaked in the 1960s with the arrival of the Ford Mustang, the second most significant car in the company's history. The Mustang signified the move towards designing expensive sports cars for a younger generation. Its attractive design and state-of-the-art engine made it a contradiction in terms: a status symbol that almost everyone could afford. As a result, it sold millions.

Ever since, Ford has dominated the market with models such as the Cortina, the Mondeo, the Escort, the Fiesta, the Explorer, the Taurus and many others. It has remained popular, despite other companies offering products in the same categories at equivalent prices. This is not only because it was the first to popularize these categories (sports car, work van and so on), but also because it continues to emphasize the quality of its products. An emphasis on high quality, combined with high volume and low prices, has led to Ford's current status as the most ubiquitous brand on the road.

Secrets of success

- *Volume.* Low sales volume and high profit margins was the original formula for car manufacturers. Ford reversed the formula and changed the industry for ever.
- *Populism.* From the Model T to the Mustang and the Mondeo, Ford has aimed its cars at the widest possible market.
- *Pioneer spirit.* Ford didn't invent the car, but it has invented different types of car, with pioneering models such as the Mustang, Cortina and Transit.
- *Quality.* Ford's advancement of safety features, engine design and manufacturing materials has justified its emphasis on quality, and its models have often been voted 'car of the year' by the automotive press.

Fact file

Website: www.ford.com

Founded: 1903

Country of origin: USA

Brand fact 1: Ford was launched from a converted wagon factory, with US $28,000 cash from 12 investors.

Brand fact 2: In 1914, Ford doubled pay to US $5 a day, and cut shifts from 9 hours to 8, setting high employee standards.

Brand fact 3: Malcolm X used to be an assembly worker at Ford.

---

15 Goodyear: the leadership brand

In the nineteenth century a man called Charles Goodyear invented the process of vulcanization. This had nothing to do with *Star Trek*. Instead, it was the complex process that transformed rubber into something that could be used for a variety of practical purposes. As well as tyres, he also created rubber boots and rubber clothes (hats, vests and ties).

The trouble was, Goodyear was an innovator, not a businessman. The Goodyear family nearly starved to death while Charles concentrated on one failing rubber factory after another, amassing a crippling amount of debt. The food he and his family ate had largely been fished from the river by Charles himself.

You see, although vulcanization was one of the key commercial and technological breakthroughs of the 19th century, Goodyear, one of history's Homer Simpsons, had been slow to patent it. This meant he was in and out of court trying to stop businesses exploiting his breakthrough. And even by the time he died in 1860 he had failed to capitalize on his own achievements.

Forty years later, however, Frank Seiberling did capitalize on Goodyear's achievements, and acknowledged those achievements by naming his company after him, that being the Goodyear Tire and Rubber Company. Unlike the life of the eponymous hero behind it, the Goodyear brand's life has been relatively trouble-free. In 1901, only three years into operation, Henry Ford started using Goodyear rubber tyres on his cars. Throughout most of the last century Goodyear grew and successfully sustained its position as the number one brand of tyres, through various alliances with leading car manufacturers.

It was only in the 1980s that Goodyear started to lose its grip (metaphorically speaking) on the market. Its market share started to dwindle as the competition heated up. In 1988, the Japanese tyre company Bridgestone Corporation purchased Goodyear's rival

Firestone. Goodyear's sales slipped further in the 1990s, and the company responded by axing employees (including over 2,800 in one year).

However, by the end of the millennium things were turning back around. In 1997, the company embarked on a brave investment plan that involved building two new factories. In 1999, it followed Firestone's example and joined forces with a massive Japanese tyre company when it formed an alliance with Sumitomo Rubber.

That same year, the quality of Firestone tyres was placed under scrutiny after a series of customer complaints and traffic accidents, causing the National Highway Traffic Safety Administration to recall 6.5 million Firestone tyres on primarily Ford Explorers. This was followed by a very public dispute between Ford and Firestone over who was to blame.

Of course, this only helped reaffirm Goodyear's status as the leading tyre brand, a position it firmly holds on to today.

Secrets of success

- *Trust.* There are few products where trust is a life-and-death issue, but the tyre category is one of them.

Fact file

Website: www.goodyear.com

Founded: 1898

Country of origin: USA

Brand fact 1: Goodyear has plants in 28 countries.

Brand fact 2: Goodyear's first plant was bought with a US $3,500 down payment using money Frank Sieberling borrowed from his brother-in-law.

Brand fact 3: Goodyear is the world's largest tyre company.

- *Longevity.* Goodyear has built its trust through longevity – it is now over 100 years old.
- *Leadership.* Goodyear's advertising campaigns promote the fact that it is the leading tyre brand, with straightforward slogans such as 'Number One in tyres'. As it is the leader, people assume it's the best and buy Goodyear tyres. As a result, it stays the leader and people buy even more Goodyear tyres.

16 Gillette: the shaving brand

Boston, USA, 1895. A 40-year-old man working on the waterfront has an idea for a new safety razor. The man is called King Camp Gillette. That is not his only problem. He also has to trek around the banks and businesses of his native city finding money to fund the Gillette Safety Razor Company before he is able to trial the product among the public.

Getting the money takes a while, as investors were as reluctant to plough money into an untested project as they are today. In fact, King Camp is 48 by the time his company is able to start producing razors and blades. Even when production starts he finds it hard to calm his investors' nerves. In its first year of operation, the Gillette Safety Razor Company sells a grand total of 51 razor sets and 168 blades: hardly the making of a global enterprise.

Then, in 1904, something happened. Sales picked up. News of this razor that didn't cut your chin started to spread like stubble rash. In one of the biggest word-of-mouth phenomena of all time, the demand curve shot up. The following year Gillette sold over a quarter of a million razors, and even more blades. It opened an office in London and a European manufacturing plant based in Paris. Even in the age of viral marketing, sales jumping from 51 units to 250,000 in the space of two years would be pretty reasonable.

The reason why such phenomenal growth occurred is, with hindsight, quite understandable. Gillette revolutionized the market. It didn't invent shaving. But it did come up with an entirely new product: a product, moreover, that could be used every day by every man, and that offered a definite and identifiable improvement on what had gone before.

And what's more, the growth continued. By 1915, the company was selling 7 million blades a year. In 1917, Gillette razors were used by over 3 million members of the US army.

Around this time, King Camp, unable to believe his luck, decided he needed a rest. He headed west to California and spent the rest of his life as a social theorist. He died in 1932.

Throughout the 20th century Gillette expanded to become a leading global brand. It launched shaving foam in 1953 (which some business theorists refer to as the perfect brand extension as it's used with the original product). It launched other brands, including Right Guard deodorant. It came up with radical new products such as the Trac II (a twin-bladed razor launched in 1971), the Sensor Shaving System (1990) and the Mach 3 triple-bladed razor (1998), which remains the bestseller today.

The company also had a lengthy shopping list of other companies it wanted to acquire, buying Braun, Oral-B, Waterman and Parker Pens. In 1996, there was also a major merger with Duracell.

It is now ranked within the world's top 10 most valuable brands and still produces the most popular shaving products.

Secrets of success

- *Testosterone.* When advertising to men, Gillette has always promoted the masculine values of its brand. Gillette razors aren't just *for* men. They define men. In Gillette adverts men are heroes, fathers and lovers, and smile rugged grins above a soft-rock soundtrack. 'The best a man can get' is the slogan, signifying quality and masculinity in six words.

- *Innovation.* 'Good products come out of market research. Great products come from research and development.' So says Gillette former CEO Alfred Zeien. And he should know. His company has succeeded through creating brand-new products that are both pioneering and incredibly popular, from King Camp's first safety razor to the Mach 3.

Fact file

Website: www.gillette.com

Founded: 1901

Country of origin: USA

Brand fact 1: Gillette is driven by the conviction that 'There is a better way to shave and we will find it.'

Brand fact 2: In 1904 Gillette received the first US patent on the safety razor and sales soared to 90,000 razors and 12 million blades.

Brand fact 3: Gillette introduced the first women's razor, Milady Décolletée, in 1915.

---

17 Kleenex: the disposable brand

Brands change. They evolve. They metamorphose into something new. So do products.

Normally this change is initiated by the company itself, on a whim, or as a result of extensive market research. Sometimes though it happens naturally. The product stays exactly the same, but it becomes used in a way the company hadn't anticipated.

Take Kleenex. The Kleenex tissue began life in the 1920s as a make-up remover, which was more cost-effective than the cloth towels that women had previously used. The screen icon Jean Harlow, among other celebrities, helped promote the brand for this use and it became a big seller.

In the late 1920s, however, Kimberly-Clark (the company that owned Kleenex) started to realize why the tissues were so popular. The company was inundated with letters from customers who said they used the tissues for colds. The previous description for the tissues had been 'sanitary cold cream remover'. This was now exchanged for 'the handkerchiefs you can throw away'. People may have already invented this use, for themselves, but Kleenex was the first brand to capitalize on it.

As the first in the category, it was the first to dominate it. Kleenex has consequently become a generic noun as much as a brand name, and it is recognized in over 180 countries.

Having been the inventor of the facial tissues category in the 1920s, which became the 'disposable handkerchief' category in the 1930s, Kleenex kept on innovating. It was the first brand to introduce perforated cartons, upright cartons, pocket tissues, coloured tissues, printed tissues, paper towels, 'man-size' tissues, eyeglass tissues, junior tissues, 'purse pack' tissues, scented tissues, three-layer tissues, 'bundle pack' tissues and travel tissues. The innovations have continued into the 21st century, with the introduction of Kleenex with lotion, menthol Kleenex and Kleenex Ultra Soft.

All these innovations have helped Kleenex maintain its position as one of the few truly global, billion-dollar brands.

Secrets of success

- *Consumer insight*. Ever since Kleenex first changed its identity to become a 'disposable handkerchief', it has been alert to the needs of its customers. According to parent company Kimberly-Clark, 'customer insight' is the key factor that sets its brands such as Kleenex and Huggies apart.

- *New variations.* The Kleenex product has been varied and reinvented almost continually over the last eight decades. Such variations inject new life into the brand without extending it into inappropriate categories. As a result, Kleenex is still solely associated with tissues.

Fact file

Website: www.kleenex.com

Founded: 1924

Country of origin: USA

Brand fact 1: In the 1920s many famous actresses proclaimed Kleenex tissues contributed to their clear complexions.

Brand fact 2: In 1957, a Kleenex tissue promotion for a Perry Como record album resulted in album sales of 330,000.

Brand fact 3: The Kleenex brand is recognized by families in more than 150 countries.

---

18 Wrigley: the new thinking brand

As with the Kleenex 'disposable handkerchief', it was the customers who dictated the direction of the Wrigley brand.

When the 29-year-old William Wrigley set up his Chicago-based business in 1891, his main product wasn't chewing gum but Wrigley's Scouring Soap. He was a firm believer in customer incentives – 'something for nothing', as he put it. He therefore decided to offer a free packet of baking powder whenever someone bought the scouring soap. Soon, however, he realized that the incentive product was more popular than the original product, so he switched from selling soap to selling baking powder. Maintaining his belief in customer incentives, he started offering two free packets of chewing gum with every packet of baking powder. And yet again, Wrigley let his customers dictate his business direction.

In 1892, when he realized the chewing gum was more popular he made it the sole focus of his company. He introduced his famous Wrigley's Juicy Fruit and Wrigley's Spearmint varieties in 1893 and worked hard to establish his place in the market. As there were already companies established in the market, he had a tough job.

However, Wrigley had a natural gift for marketing. He decided to focus on what he believed to be his best product – Wrigley's Spearmint – at the expense of other Wrigley's gum products.

Like William Kellogg and Henry Heinz, he was one of the early experts in advertising, with his successful 'tell 'em quick and tell 'em often' approach. In 1907, the business community fell into a slump, and advertising was suddenly seen as a foolish waste of money by many companies. However, Wrigley decided to take a risk and actually increased his advertising expenditure that year, with ads for Wrigley's Spearmint plastered all over New York. While other brands suddenly concentrating less on advertising seemed to vanish, Wrigley's was everywhere.

The strategy paid off, and in 1908 Wrigley began advertising across the United States. By 1910 Wrigley Spearmint was chewed by more American mouths than any other gum.

While Freud was in the process of changing the way we viewed the human mind, Wrigley was in the process of changing the way advertisers got inside that mind. In 1911, over 50 years before the official rise of abstract advertising, Wrigley created an ad depicting a beautiful young woman above the line: 'The Girl with the Wrigley Eyes'.

Wrigley was helping to change the marketing worldview at the same time as Freud, Picasso and Einstein were fracturing worldviews in psychology, art and science. The 'command-and-control', utilitarian principles of the 19th-century industrialists were completely disregarded by Wrigley, who had a very creative approach to business.

In 1915 he sent free samples of Spearmint gum to every single one of the 1.5 million people listed in the US national telephone directory. That same year, he rewrote the Mother Goose rhymes to include mentions of his brand and gave 14 million copies away for free. Wrigley also helped revolutionize employee relations, being one of the first US bosses to give his workers a two-day weekend.

Of course, Wrigley remains something of an unsung hero, certainly nowhere near as revered as the two Henrys – Ford and Heinz. However, his creative, consumer-centric business ideas provide one of the missing links between the industrial era and the age of marketing.

His son Philip inherited his business courage. During the Second World War, Wrigley stopped catering for the US domestic market to supply gum to the army. Before it vanished from the shelves, Philip devised an advertising campaign his father would have been proud of: a simple picture of an empty packet of Wrigley's Spearmint gum and the slogan 'Remember this Wrapper'. They remembered. When the brand returned in 1945 it exceeded its pre-war popularity.

In 1961, Philip's son William took over and turned Wrigley's into a global brand, setting up facilities in the Philippines, France, Kenya, Taiwan, China, India, Poland and Russia. Today, the brand is sold in over 150 countries, and sub-brands such as Hubba Bubba and Orbit have also grown in popularity.

The Wrigley family remain in charge of the brand, with the founder's great-grandson Bill Wrigley boldly adapting the brand to the new marketing era. He has launched various new brands and has made over the packaging of the early products – including his great-grandfather's beloved Spearmint.

Secrets of success

- *New thinking.* William Wrigley's new business thinking made him a pioneer of marketing and transformed his products into a well-loved brand.
- *Consumer focus.* Wrigley wasn't afraid to change direction. As a result he turned a freebie into the basis of a multimillion-dollar brand.
- *Courage.* Withdrawing from the US market during the Second World War was one of the most courageous brand decisions and proved that absence can make brands, if not hearts, grow stronger.

Fact file

Website: www.wrigley.com

Founded: 1891

Country of origin: USA

Brand fact 1: Wrigley has 14 manufacturing factories worldwide: three in North America, four in Europe, one in Africa, and five in the Asia Pacific region.

Brand fact 2: Wrigley brand gums are available in 150 countries worldwide.

Brand fact 3: Most of Wrigley's advertising budget goes to TV.

Brand fact 4: Retail sales of chewing gum in the United States total more than US $2 billion. That averages out to more than 190 sticks of gum per person every year. The Wrigley Company has just slightly less than half of all chewing gum sales.

CHAPTER 3

Distraction brands

The days when the economy was dominated by agriculture are long gone. Those of industry are nearly over. Economic life is no longer geared chiefly to production. To what then is it geared? To distraction.

(John Gray, *Straw Dogs*, 2002)

Contemporary philosophers and novelists have identified that leisure and distraction are becoming the driving economic forces of modern society. In his novel *Cocaine Nights* (1996), JG Ballard even anticipated a 'future without work':

People will work, or rather some people will work, but only for a decade of their lives. They will retire in their late thirties, with fifty years of idleness in front of them... A billion balconies facing the sun.

Cocaine Nights is, of course, a piece of fiction, but the rise of what has been termed a 'leisure society' is a reality in many regions of the world, even without a population enjoying 'fifty years of idleness'.

People no longer want simply to be clothed, cleaned and fed; they want to be distracted and entertained. Rather than make our own entertainment, the way our grandparents did, we'd now prefer to buy our entertainment ready packaged.

Distraction brands used to be the preserve of the very young, who were catered for by toy manufacturers such as Mattel or by entertainment brands such as Disney. Now, however, there is no age distinction. Adults are no longer ashamed to indulge in childlike escapism, whether it be through Harry Potter or by watching the latest Disney movie. Just as more and more people are seeking to stay young by having plastic surgery or botox injections, so more people are buying into brands that would have once seemed too trivial or juvenile to get their attention.

Distraction brands have always been with us. It's just that everybody now wants to be distracted, not just the kids. After all, as the world continues to descend further into war and violence, it is no wonder that brands that offer a temporary escape are ever more popular.

19 MTV: the youth brand

According to whom you believe, MTV is responsible for various things: the birth of the music video; the arrival of reality TV; the relaunch of Ozzy Osbourne's career; the diminishing attention span of its audience. But there is one thing all agree on: MTV is a branding phenomenon. According to *Vanity Fair*, the MTV logo is 'one of the most instantly identifiable on the planet'.

Founded in 1981 by a group of like-minded pop music lovers, it quickly became an iconic symbol of 80s youth. Michael Jackson videos such as 'Billie Jean' and 'Thriller' broke the mould, and raised the standard of content MTV was able to broadcast. In 1985, Sting (singing backing vocals on the Dire Straits track 'Money for Nothing') gave voice to a generation when he declared: 'I want my MTV.' Years later, MTV continues to be referenced by musicians in tune with the zeitgeist (it gets a name-check on every Eminem album, for example).

MTV is now a truly global brand. It is available in 400 million homes in 166 countries. Unlike some other global brands, however, MTV always tries to accommodate the specific tastes of each local audience. So in India, alongside Christina Aguilera and Justin Timberlake, there are videos of local bhangra artists.

However, MTV is no longer just about music. Indeed, the main MTV channel hardly ever plays music at all. Instead it has broadcast groundbreaking shows such as the reality TV show *The Real World*, the award-winning animation series *Beavis and Butthead*, *Celebrity Deathmatch*, *Jackass*, *Cribs*, *Wildboyz*, *Rich Girls* (documenting the daily life of Tommy Hilfiger's teenage daughter Ally) and *The Osbournes*. Following its launch in 2002, *The Osbournes* became one of the most talked-about shows on the planet.

Of course, the main task for any youth brand is to keep up with its ever-changing, ever-segmenting and ever-diversifying audience. MTV has managed to do this by not treating its viewers as a homogeneous mass with similar tastes. Just as it adapts its content to each geographic market, it also accommodates the taste of each niche. For instance, in the UK there are now five MTV channels – MTV, MTV Hits (for pop music), MTV 2 (for rock and alternative music), MTV Base (playing r 'n' b and hip-hop) and MTV dance (which, as you'd expect, plays dance music).

The other problem faced by that of any youth brand is that the audience eventually outgrows you. MTV has managed to find a solution to this dilemma by setting up VH1, a music channel aimed at a slightly older and calmer viewership. Then there are sub-brands such as VH1 Classic (for those of its audience old enough to remember the 60s and 70s) and VH2 (playing rock and alternative songs that have stood the test of time).

Such successful strategies have kept MTV ahead of the music TV market – a market they created – and, so long as they keep the emphasis on breaking new ground, the brand's future seems assured. People still want their MTV.

Secrets of success

- *Diversity.* Music tastes differ between and even within markets. MTV has acknowledged this diversity by broadcasting localized content and by providing niche channels.
- *Relevance.* MTV knows it has to stay relevant to its audience. This relevance extends beyond music to its TV shows, which quickly develop the necessary 'must-see' factor and treat social issues that concern its viewers. It has produced documentaries and concerts to promote awareness of the AIDS epidemic, and in Europe has even aired a debate with Tony Blair regarding his decision to go to war in Iraq.
- *Trend setting.* MTV sets trends. It doesn't follow them. As Naomi Klein says, 'MTV International has become the most compelling global catalog of the modern branded life.' Of course, Klein is saying this as a criticism. But MTV would probably receive the statement as a compliment.
- *Umbrella branding.* The genius of MTV is that, while it broadcasts individual shows or videos, viewers are always

---

Fact file

Website: www.mtv.com

Founded: 1981

Country of origin: USA

Brand fact 1: MTV is available in 400 million homes in 166 countries.

Brand fact 2: MTV is owned by the leading global media company, Viacom.

Brand fact 3: MTV led to Michael Jackson's *Thriller* album selling more than 800,000 copies in a week.

conscious they are watching MTV (thanks, in part, to the logo being continuously displayed in the corner of the screen). 'As far as we were concerned, MTV was the star,' says Tom Freston, one of the channel's founders. In other words, the medium became the brand message.

20 Harry Potter: the story brand

Harry Potter is a publishing phenomenon, but it is also a branding phenomenon. Indeed, it is no longer possible to think of Harry Potter solely as a series of books. There are the movies, for a start. Then there are the Harry Potter toys. The Harry Potter sweets. The Harry Potter pyjamas. In fact, there have been hundreds of products around the world.

Of course, there was a time when a lead character from a popular book wasn't viewed in this way. After all, no one ever referred to Huckleberry Finn as a 'brand'. Now, though, books are as related to the modern world of marketing as any other commercial industry. Publishers seek to establish a brand identity for their authors by producing similar covers for each book they write.

For books where there is an easily identifiable lead character, such as Bridget Jones or Harry Potter, the branding opportunities are immense. In the case of Harry Potter, these opportunities have been successfully exploited to create one of the greatest examples of word-of-mouth marketing ever.

Now, obviously, any marketing success has to be – in part at least – down to the product itself. (As every business studies student is aware, the five Ps of marketing are: Product, Price, Place, Promotion and People.) And there can be no denying that JK Rowling's books are exceptional products. In an age of TV, Nintendo, Gameboy and Pokemon the Harry Potter books have – in the words of novelist

Jeanette Winterson – 'given children their childhood back'. They have created a magical world centred around Hogwarts School of Witchcraft and Wizardry that is every bit as wonderful as CS Lewis's Narnia or JRR Tolkien's Middle Earth.

When Rowling started writing the series in 1990, she could not possibly have imagined that the books would go on to sell tens of millions of copies worldwide, and go on to make her the richest woman in Britain (ahead of the Queen).

However, as well as Rowling's natural gift for storytelling, her publisher's natural gift for marketing has also helped. Indeed, Rowling's UK publisher Bloomsbury was the only one to spot Harry Potter's original potential. Three other publishers – Penguin, Transworld and HarperCollins – had turned it down.

The first book in the series, *Harry Potter and the Philosopher's Stone*, was published on 30 June 1997, and was instantly bought by US publisher Scholastic. By Christmas of that year, the buzz had started, and the book had sold 30,000 copies in the UK. This, combined with the publicity generated by the winning of the Smarties Book Award, fuelled further interest from publishers across the globe.

By the time the second book – *Harry Potter and the Chamber of Secrets* – appeared in 1998, the word-of-mouth interest was so strong that it instantly topped the bestseller charts in the UK, knocking John Grisham off the top-spot.

Two more Harry Potter books appeared over the next two years, and then the Warner Brothers movie of *Harry Potter and the Philosopher's Stone* (or *Harry Potter and the Sorcerer's Stone* as it is known in the United States) appeared in November 2001. The movie, directed by Chris Columbus, made over $300 million in the United States over two months, and achieved equivalent success worldwide. Sequels were already being made.

From then on, there has been no stopping the Harry Potter brand. The movies have helped sell the books and the books have helped sell the movies, while both have managed to sell the plethora of spin-off merchandise.

Of course, the rise of Harry Potter has not been free from the odd spell of trouble (no pun intended). Rowling has had the originality of her work thrown into question after a Pennsylvanian author took legal action, claiming that the Potter books plagiarized an earlier book called *The Legend of Rah and the Muggles* (1984). This book included a character called Larry Potter.

Then, there are those who have considered Harry Potter to be a corrupting influence on children. In October 1999, some parents in the United States grouped together and accused Rowling of depicting 'sheer evil'. Two years later, there were book burnings in New Mexico where Harry was referred to as 'the devil'. A preacher based in Maine publicly shredded hundreds of copies of *Harry Potter and the Chamber of Secrets* on the day of its release. A primary school teacher in Georgia was harassed by the anti-Potter brigade, and was told to stop reading pupils the books because of their supernatural content.

And has any of this damaged the Harry Potter brand? Not in the slightest. In truth, it has probably helped, because all these stories have done is add to the Harry Potter hype, and gathered it even more column inches in newspapers. There is a lesson here for all brands.

The Harry Potter books are narratives. They are stories, with a heavy emphasis on plot. Put simply, a lot happens. However, there is another Harry Potter story, that of the brand itself, a story that started in 1990 when a young woman called Joanne Rowling got stuck on a train (British Rail, rather than the Hogwarts Express) and started to write some ideas down for a children's story.

Like the Harry Potter books themselves, the story of the brand has a magical quality. It is the story of how a single mother (the central protagonist of this narrative) became one of the highest-earning women in the world, and the initiator of Potter mania. Also, as with Harry Potter, there have been spectacular ups and downs (downs such as the various early rejection letters, and the squabbles with the church; ups such as movie deals and awards). There has even been a touch of John Grisham, with the 'Larry

Potter' court case and Warner Brothers' various legal cases against unofficial Potter sites.

I would argue that the story about the book has now become almost as important as the story within the book, in the making of the Potter brand. This is the lesson of all great brands. They have created their own mythology. Whether it's Henry Ford saying the customer can have any colour so long as it's black or Coca-Cola's Father Christmas adverts of the 1930s, the fact remains the same. Great brands create great stories. Harley-Davidson, Walt Disney, even Microsoft (super-geek student becomes richest man alive and takes over the planet): these aren't just successful brands. They are business legends. They include narrative structures most novelists would struggle to create.

Obviously, brand stories aren't always 100 per cent reality. There has to be some embellishment, some editing out of irrelevant details, even some mythologizing. In a way, that's the brand's purpose. That's its *raison d'être*. To create a legend that people want to buy into, whether it's hairy Hell's Angels with Harley-Davidson or five-year-olds with Harry Potter, the same principle applies. By buying a motorcycle or visiting Disneyland or reading JK Rowling, consumers aren't just making a choice based on the cheapest price or convenience. They are buying into a story and – in doing so – becoming part of the brand story itself.

Indeed, great brands *are* great stories. And while JK Rowling may nearly have finished the Harry Potter series, the story of the Harry Potter brand still has many chapters to come.

Secrets of success

- *Story-telling*. Harry Potter, along with Tolkien's *The Lord of the Rings* trilogy, is one of the most popular narratives of all time. It is an escapist fantasy that has almost universal appeal. However, the publicity and marketing machines at Warner Brothers and the various publishers of the book have been working on a different story – the rise and rise of the Harry Potter phenomenon itself.

- *Groundwork.* In 1997, JK Rowling was relentless in promoting the books and toured various independent and children's bookstores across the UK to spread the word.
- *Crossover appeal.* When JK Rowling first started to write Harry Potter, she envisioned it as a children's story. Quite quickly, though, it became clear that adults in touch with their inner child were also taking pleasure from the books. 'A friend saw a man on a train reading a copy behind his newspaper,' observed Rowling. 'And at signings adults are happy to admit that it's for themselves.' The publishers have successfully capitalized on this broad appeal by producing adult covers to avoid any embarrassment while people read the books on public transport.
- *Omnipresence.* Harry Potter has now joined the super-league of omnipresent brands. In 1997 the only way you encountered the

---

Fact file

Website: www.jkrowling.com

Founded: 1997

Country of origin: UK

Brand fact 1: JK Rowling's website attracted 220 million visits in an eight week period.

Brand fact 2: Seventeen thousand questions from all over the world were submitted to JK Rowling, during her hour-long web chat for World Book Day.

Brand fact 3: *Harry Potter and the Order of the Phoenix* became the fastest selling book of all time when it was published in hardback on June 21st 2003, and sold 1,777,541 copies in one day in the UK.

brand was by walking into a bookstore. Now, it is everywhere – in cinemas, supermarkets, toy shops, newspapers, sweet shops, video stores. You can read the book, watch the film, play the computer (or board) game, buy the action figures, eat the sweets or even buy the T-shirt.

21 Barbie: the escapist brand

Barbie is many things to many people. To feminists she is the Antichrist. To post-feminists she is an icon – a career woman with her femininity intact. To millions of little girls (and maybe even some grown-up boys) she is a fantasy figure. To Mattel, she is a money-making machine.

Okay, so here are the Barbie facts. She was created in 1959. She was invented by Ruth Handler, co-founder of Mattel, who named her after her daughter Barbara. The original idea was to create a fashion doll that would, according to Mattel, 'inspire little girls to think about what they wanted to be when they grew up'. She was an instant success, with 351,000 Barbie dolls sold in her first year.

She hit Europe in 1961, the same year she got a boyfriend, Ken. The first black and Hispanic Barbie dolls were introduced in 1980. She has had over 80 careers, including being a rock musician, a vet and even a palaeontologist. Her first pet was a horse. She has now had 43 pets, including a zebra. The bestselling Barbie doll was Totally Hair Barbie, who had hair down to her toes. Barbie's fashion collection includes designs by Gucci, Versace, Dolce & Gabbana and Givenchy. In the early 1990s, Barbie joined the military as Army Barbie, a medic sergeant enlisted in Desert Storm. She became a bona fide movie star in 1999 with a supporting role in *Toy Story 2*. In 2000, there was a Barbie presidential candidate with a political platform of opportunities for girls, educational excellence and animal rights.

And she remains as popular as ever. Indeed, every second, three Barbie dolls are sold somewhere in the world. She has been the major player in helping Mattel reach its strong position today, with the company's international sales currently averaging around $2 billion a year.

One of the most recent successes was Rapunzel Barbie. The long-haired doll, who wore a pink ball gown, was released on the same day in 2002 in 59 countries. This was the largest product launch in Mattel's history, but it paid off. The doll became a top 10 bestseller in the United States, Italy, Germany, France, Spain, the UK and across Asia. Rapunzel Barbie managed to make $200 million in its first year on sale. Rapunzel Barbie is interesting for lots of reasons. Firstly, and most trivially, she has long hair, just like Totally Hair Barbie. This means that the two bestselling Barbie dolls are also the two with the longest hair. Also, Rapunzel is a fairy-tale figure. Unlike most other Barbie incarnations, which have 'real world' jobs, such as air hostess or doctor, Rapunzel Barbie is pure fantasy. This could indicate a subtle change of direction from Barbie's status as a role model. As Rapunzel, Barbie gives up helping little girls to think about their future society, and instead provides a means of escaping reality.

In an age where women have long since broken through the glass ceiling, Barbie cannot fulfil the same role she had in the 1960s through to the 1980s. Having a high-flying career is no longer a fantasy for little girls. Perhaps Mattel is realizing that the fantasy now has to be purer, and not attached to any aspect of reality whatsoever. After all, children of the 21st century have so far proven to be obsessed with fantasy stories, from *Harry Potter* to *The Lord of the Rings*. Fantasy is simpler than reality, and more reassuring. And today, in many regions of the world, children need to feel reassured more than ever. Indeed, the interesting thing about Rapunzel Barbie is that children across the globe found her equally appealing.

A few years ago the doll wouldn't even have been marketed in Asia, where a blonde-haired, blue-eyed Barbie would have been viewed as inappropriate to the market. Barbie dolls sold in, say, Japan used to have Asian facial features, black hair and a Japanese dress sense. However, a radical change of thinking has occurred among the leading toy manufacturers, as a 29 April 2003 *Wall Street Journal* article headlined 'One-Toy-Fits-All' reported:

> Major toy makers are rethinking one of the basic tenets of their $55 billion global industry – that children in different countries want different playthings. The implications are significant for both kids and companies. In the past, giants such as Mattel, Hasbro Inc, and Lego Co produced toys and gear in a variety of styles. Increasingly, they are designing and marketing one version world-wide. This has led to a series of massive merchandising blitzkriegs, with companies deluging boys and girls around the globe simultaneously with identical dolls, cars and gadgets.

One of the reasons why Mattel has changed its strategy is because of its market research. In 2000, the company researched consumer reactions to its products in different markets and found that little girls in Asia liked the original blonde-haired Barbie just as much as little girls in the United States or Northern Europe did. In other words, they didn't seem to mind that Barbie didn't resemble them.

This returns to my earlier point. Barbie is no longer a career adviser. She is a fantasy. Little girls no longer believe they will grow up to be Barbie any more than little boys believe they are Harry Potter.

Mattel has recognized this fact, and is capitalizing on it very successfully. It can now broadcast similar adverts in every market, with equal success. It can use the same Barbie website and simply provide different language options. For the Rapunzel Barbie, Mattel even produced a computed-generated movie, called 'Barbie as Rapunzel', which was shown on TV and sold on DVD around the world.

Significantly though, Mattel updates the Grimm Brothers' fairy tale. In the movie, Barbie escapes her prison tower with the help of a magic paintbrush rather than a prince. The message for little girls is therefore simple. They do not need a handsome prince, or a fake-tanned Ken, to rescue them. They are in control of their own lives. So even in fantasy, Barbie's role-model credentials remain intact.

Secrets of success

- *Adaptability.* Barbie has remained the world's most popular doll for over 40 years by managing to stay up to date. Following the feminist movement of the 1970s her career options broadened a lot further than the 'fashion model' status she was originally born with. In the 21st century, she has become a fairy-tale figure and fits in with the golden age of children's fantasy we are living through.
- *Empowerment.* At first glance it is difficult to see how such a fantastically proportioned image of womanhood could empower

---

Fact file

Website: www.barbie.com

Founded: 1959

Country of origin: USA

Brand fact 1: Three Barbie dolls are sold every second.

Brand fact 2: Barbie is the number one girl's brand worldwide.

Brand fact 3: Today, an average American girl owns at least eight Barbies.

little girls. But place her next to her wimpy, neutered boyfriend, Ken (who was dumped for an Australian called Blaine in 2004), and consider her 80 different careers, and she suddenly seems to be winning the battle of the sexes. With Barbie, her exaggerated femininity becomes a badge of strength, rather than weakness. And besides, she makes more money than Action Man.

22 Disney: the nostalgic brand

Disney, the first major distraction brand, has seen its fair share of trouble. Up until recently its shareholders were increasingly unhappy with Disney's performance. They were disgruntled for various reasons, one being the breakdown of Disney's relationship with the digital animation company Pixar that partnered with Disney on *Finding Nemo* and *Toy Story*. Many blamed the strained personal relationship between Disney's former CEO Michael Eisner and Pixar CEO Steve Jobs for the split. Without Pixar, Disney's movie-making future looked a lot less healthy. And as the movies have traditionally been the spring from which all else flows, the magic kingdom of Disney had suddenly lost some of its sparkle.

However, at the moment, Disney remains one of the 10 most valuable brands in the world. And if, as some have suggested, it has become guilty of being trapped in its own history, it is hardly surprising. After all, what a history. Throughout the 20th century Disney was responsible for revolutionizing not only cinema, but children's entertainment. It was also the first of all experience brands.

Needless to say, the Disney story started with Walt Disney himself. Disney, however, was not an instant business success. Along with his brother Roy, Walt arrived in California in 1923. Having failed to get a job in the film industry, he set up his own small studio and, with Roy, set up an animation company under their own surname.

Disney's early projects, short films such as *Alice* (1924) and *Oswald the Rabbit* (1927), were not very successful. Then, in 1928, things changed. Walt Disney came up with a new character: a high-pitched mouse called Mickey, drawn as a series of circles (round nose, round ears, round eyes and so on). This circular style of drawing, which became one of their trademark styles, was suited to a brand that – both literally and metaphorically – depicted life with soft edges.

Mickey Mouse, who was originally called Mortimer Mouse (Walt's wife Lilly thought Mortimer sounded too pompous), made his debut in *Steamboat Willie*, a seven-minute tale of a mouse aboard his steamboat. It was a massive word-of-mouth success and spawned follow-ups such as *Plane Crazy* (Mickey aboard a plane).

The little mouse had spawned a giant. Riding high on Mickey's fame, Disney rose into world recognition during the 1930s. The key year was 1937. This was when *Snow White* was launched. Journalists questioned the wisdom of the first full-length, animated, Technicolor feature film. One newspaper even played with the title of a Mickey Mouse feature to come up with the says-it-all headline 'Plain Crazy'. But Disney's gamble paid off. *Snow White and the Seven Dwarfs* became an instant classic. More successes followed with *Pinocchio* (1940), the high-brow *Fantasia* (1940) and the biggest weepie of them all, *Bambi* (1942).

In 1955, Disneyland opened, and the brand now meant more than just movies. It was, in fact, the first true 'experience' brand. People could go and meet the characters they had seen on the silver screen. And 1955 was also the year when Disney moved into television, with *The Mickey Mouse Club*, which lasted for decades and became one of the most successful children's shows in history.

Meanwhile, the company continued to produce classic cinema, bringing the stories of Hans Christian Andersen (*Cinderella*),

JM Barrie (*Peter Pan*) and, of course, Rudyard Kipling (*The Jungle Book*) to life.

By 1971, the year Walt Disney World opened in Florida, Disney had managed to create an alternative world for children to escape into, both via the two giant theme parks and through the TV and cinema screens.

However, not all was right with the company. Walt had died in 1965. His brother Roy died shortly after the completion of Disney World. The giant company hobbled through the 1970s with few major cinema hits.

Things stayed the same until 1984, when Michael Eisner, former president of Paramount Pictures, became chairman and CEO of Walt's empire. He lifted the company's market value from $3 billion to almost $80 billion in two decades. Part of his initial success was in returning the brand to its core values, as represented by a tidal wave of successful animated movies such as *The Little Mermaid*, *Aladdin*, *The Lion King* and, with Pixar, *Toy Story*, *A Bug's Life* and *Finding Nemo*.

By the start of this century, Disney had expanded even beyond 'Uncle Walt's' wildest dreams. Today there are Disney Stores, Disney Channels on TV, cruise lines, an internet company (Buena Vista Interactive), various movie production companies, multiple theme parks (including Disneyland Paris and Animal Kingdom), Disney Villages and even a Disney sports team (the Mighty Ducks of Anaheim professional ice-hockey team).

The trouble is, brand extensions end up having a diminishing return. As father-and-daughter marketing gurus Al and Laura Ries write in *The 22 Immutable Laws of Branding* (1998), 'in the long term, expanding your brand will diminish your power and weaken your image... A brand becomes stronger when you narrow its focus.' There are certainly lots of examples where the 'Law of Contraction' (the second of the 22 laws) seems to be proved right. For instance, the Children's Supermart was a US company selling children's furniture and toys. It decided to stop selling furniture and concentrate on the toys, rebranding itself as Toys 'R' Us. It is now the leading toy shop in the United States.

There is no denying that Disney's expansions have fuelled growth. In 1984, the year Eisner joined, Disney signified a couple of nostalgic theme parks and a load of old movies. Today, it has become the second-largest media and entertainment company in the world, after AOL Time Warner.

The trouble is, if the hit movies dry up, the vast range of the Disney brand could start to signify incoherence. One way Disney has tried to find coherence is through its original brand mascot, Mickey Mouse. But even this caused criticism. Eisner's decision to bring back Mickey Mouse for a new generation of children has been derided by the media, as it was seen to signify the backward-looking nature of the brand while its rivals are constantly looking forward.

Another problem was Pixar. Pixar is the company Disney worked with on many of its big hits such as *Finding Nemo*, *Monsters Inc* and *Toy Story*. As David Yelland clarified in an article for *The Times* in November 2003: 'New kids on the block such as Hasbro, Pixar and HIT Entertainment have kidnapped the imagination of the world's children. . . Eisner's dilemma is interesting for all those interested in communications. His fear must be that Disney's central brand, its core message, might lose touch with its market – a disconnection that could prove disastrous.'

But with a new Disney CEO in 2005, Robert Iger, who has subsequently bought Pixar, it looks like Disney is already addressing some of the issues that plagued the company in the past. Even if its previous failures do have long-term consequences it is likely that Disney will remain a phenomenal brand, and just as capable of proving its critics wrong today as it did in 1937 with the launch of *Snow White*.

Secrets of success

- *Premium prices*. According to Martin Lindstrom, author of *Brand Child* (2003), Disney is an 'Olympic brand'. This is the strongest category of brand, and means it can charge premium prices. 'Disney theme parks, hotels, and merchandise command significantly higher prices than competitors' offerings,' says Lindstrom. 'Often Disney is able to charge two to three times more for their products than a generic version.'

- *Quality.* Obviously, Disney wouldn't be able to charge such high prices if it didn't offer quality products and experiences.
- *Crossover appeal.* 'From Disney's original focus on children, the brand has been extended to the full range of demographic groups, covering ages 8 to 80,' says Lindstrom.
- *It knows its competition.* When a brand is as broad as Disney, everyone is a potential competitor. 'Everybody seems to understand that content is important, and so there are a lot of people that are competing with us,' says Disney chairman and CEO Michael Eisner.
- *Global ambition.* 'Since the world is getting pretty small, we are looking to be everywhere,' says Eisner. 'A Disney theme park in China may not be a cash cow until our 150th anniversary, but it will probably happen a lot sooner.'

Fact file

Website: www.disney.com

Founded: 1923

Country of origin: USA

Brand fact 1: The Walt Disney company is the number two media conglomerate in the world behind Time Warner.

Brand fact 2: Disney owns the ABC network, 10 broadcast TV stations and 70 radio stations.

Brand fact 3: Walt Disney World is about the size of the city of Ottawa.

- *Populism.* Disney is the best brand populist. It has a knack of knowing what people will want, even before the people know it themselves. It even managed to turn the basis of Shakespeare's *Hamlet* into a movie blockbuster with *The Lion King.*
- *Reassurance.* From *Snow White* to *Pirates of the Caribbean,* Disney's central message has always been reassurance. As John Hench, one of the original Disney designers once explained: 'Walt's thing was reassurance... the message is, "You're going to be okay."' We all need to be reassured now as much as ever.
- *Cross-branding.* Look up 'cross-branding' in the dictionary and you should see a picture of Walt Disney. He practically invented the idea, taking characters from films and putting them in theme parks. Today, Disney works the other way around. Park rides such as *The Pirates of the Caribbean* and *The Haunted Mansion* have been converted into massive movie blockbusters.

CHAPTER 4

Streamlined brands

Customers want brands that are narrow in scope.

(Al Ries)

'The ability to simplify means to eliminate the unnecessary so that the necessary may speak,' wrote the German painter Hans Hofman in his essay on art *Search for the Real* (1994). This applies to the art of marketing as much as the art of painting.

Brands that have a complex, multifaceted identity rarely work. Of course, brands such as Yamaha and Virgin have a broad scope, but they are unified by simple brand attributes. The quality performance associated with Yamaha or the positioning of Virgin as a lively 'people's brand' personified by Richard Branson make up for the lack of cohesion between the products and services offered by both companies.

Generally though, the way a brand gains a clear identity is by narrowing its scope or by 'eliminating the unnecessary'. This goes against the business instinct. After all, most businesses try to expand their brand by adding to rather than subtracting from their original offerings. Think of all those food and drink companies that offer diet or fat-free versions of their original products.

When a brand has a strong customer base, the impulse is to broaden the brand to reach even more people. If you make a luxury car, for instance, you might want to reach new audiences by producing cheaper versions. However, as the brand broadens, the more confused the customer becomes.

For those brave enough to narrow their brand focus, the results have been astounding. For instance, when Helen Gurley Brown became editor of *Cosmopolitan* in 1965 she deliberately narrowed its audience from families to sexually liberated single women. In so doing, she created one of the biggest success stories in media history.

Toys 'R' Us, Subway and Nokia are the other successful streamliners who prove the 'narrow brand = big success' equation.

23 *Cosmopolitan*: the revolutionary brand

When *Cosmopolitan* was founded in New York in 1886 it was promoted as a 'magazine for the whole family'. It published fiction and journalism aimed at all ages, with a suitably wholesome feel.

Cosmopolitan's change of direction happened in 1965 when Helen Gurley Brown, author of the popular book *Sex and the Single Girl*, became chief editor. The circulation had been declining for years before her arrival, owing in part to its lack of a clearly targeted readership.

The new editor solved this problem by turning it into a magazine aimed at successful and open-minded women. The publishers gave her only a year to save the haemorrhaging publication, or she would have been relegated to *Good Housekeeping*.

Brown knew she had to come up with something unique. And she did. The very first magazine sold 90 per cent of its print order and soon became one of the top 10 US titles. It created a new type of magazine – which has now spawned a whole market of glossy titles aimed at women.

The brand kept on growing as feminism changed women's role in society. Brown herself has referred to *Cosmo* as a 'feminist' magazine, although its sex-based content was originally frowned upon by the feminist movement.

'We were inspiring,' she once said, commenting on the magazine's success. 'We tried to help you solve problems, realize dreams.'

According to Brown, *Cosmopolitan*'s success during her 20-year reign as editor was down to four factors: the glossy format, the inspirational message, good writing and telling the truth. Telling the truth meant breaking taboos on subjects such as the female orgasm, which no magazine had dared write about before.

This success has continued even after Brown has gone. *Cosmopolitan* now has around 50 international editions and although it has slipped from a position in the top five it is one of the 20 most popular magazines in the world. It has also launched a successful sister publication, *Cosmo Girl*.

Fact file

Website: www.cosmopolitan.com

Founded: 1886

Country of origin: USA

Brand fact 1: Cosmo women spend over US $1 billion a year on fashion.

Brand fact 2: Saatchi produced a 45-second TV commercial to launch the new brand.

Brand fact 3: The relaunched Cosmo's first print run of 350,000 was sold out by the end of publication day. A further 450,000 copies were printed, and sold out within two days.

The *Cosmopolitan* brand now extends beyond magazines into other product categories. Some of these extensions, such as Cosmopolitan Yoghurt, have flopped. Other more appropriate extensions, such as its brand of bed linen, have been a success.

The only danger is that the brand that so successfully tightened its focus in the 1960s may be losing the courage and direction it once had. After all, its success was due to sharpening, not broadening, its identity.

Secrets of success

- *Change. Cosmopolitan* radically changed direction in 1965, to pioneer a new type of magazine.
- *Mission.* Under Helen Gurley Brown, the magazine had a mission to empower women by tackling issues in a frank and open way. This mission sparked a revolution in magazine publishing.

24 Nokia: the streamlined brand

Today, the Nokia brand is solely associated with telecommunications and mobile technology.

However, the Nokia story began back in 1865, when the engineer Fredrik Idestam set up a wood-pulp mill in southern Finland and started to make paper. Throughout its long history, the company (which evolved into the Nokia Group in 1967) has concentrated on various different markets, including paper, chemicals, rubber, electronics and, of course, telecommunications (which the company started in the 1960s, with research into semiconductor technology).

By the late 1980s, it had become Europe's third-largest television manufacturer and the largest information technology provider.

However, having entered into so many diverse markets it lacked a coherent brand identity.

This became a major problem in the 1990s, when Finland entered a deep recession. In 1992, with the appointment of a new CEO, Jorma Ollila, the company decided to streamline its operations and to concentrate all its vast resources on the one market that looked the most promising for the future – telecommunications.

This was an incredibly brave decision, but the gamble paid off. Today, Nokia has over a third of the worldwide handset market, and a 50 per cent share of the European market. This is even more of an achievement when you consider that the wireless handset market is considered the world's largest consumer electronics industry, measured by units.

The company's pioneering research into multimedia messaging and 'next generation' phones, combined with its large production capacity (it produces well over half a million phones every day), means that the new, streamlined Nokia is likely to stay ahead of the market.

Fact file

Website: www.nokia.co.uk

Founded: 1865

Country of origin: Finland

Brand fact 1: Nokia produces over half a million phones every day.

Brand fact 2: Nokia is the world leader in mobile communications.

Brand fact 3: Nokia's ten largest markets are the Unites States, UK, Germany, China, UAE, India, Italy, France, Brazil and Spain, which represent 61 per cent of total sales.

Secrets of success

- *Size*. When Nokia streamlined in the 1990s it already had the advantage of size. As mobile manufacturers increasingly compete on price, Nokia's vast production volume is an obvious advantage.
- *Streamlining*. Nokia's decision to focus on only one market after years of diversity was a courageous one, but it has led to its current position as one of the top global brands. In 2002, Nokia was the highest-ranking non-US brand in Interbrand's list of the top 100 brands.

25 Toys 'R' Us: the contraction brand

Toys 'R' Us, the world's largest toy retailer, replicates the Wal-Mart model and applies it to toys. Like Wal-Mart, Toys 'R' Us builds giant warehouse-sized stores in suburban areas and stocks a lot of products. How many products? Roughly 10,000 per store, which is over triple the amount you would find in other large toy shops. As with Wal-Mart, this economy of scale means it can buy cheap. As Al and Laura Ries (1998) write, 'Toys 'R' Us makes its money buying toys, not selling toys.'

The thing that sets Toys 'R' Us apart from Wal-Mart is its narrow focus. Whereas Wal-Mart matches its big size with big variety, Toys 'R' Us only sells (you guessed it) toys. This gives it incredibly strong brand power.

Originally, it was called Children's Supermart and it sold furniture for children's bedrooms as well as toys. Children's Supermart's CEO Charles Lazarus then decided his brand needed a tighter focus, so instead of becoming a 'kiddie IKEA' it got rid of the furniture and changed its name to Toys 'R' Us.

This proved a wise move. The combination of massive stores selling only one type of product – a product explicitly indicated in the brand name itself – has turned Toys 'R' Us into the obvious stop for toy shopping.

Secrets of success

- *Size*. Toys 'R' Us buys in vast quantities because of its size. As a result it gets cheaper prices from toy manufacturers than smaller competitors.
- *Simplicity*. By concentrating on only one type of product, it has become intrinsically associated with toys in the consumer's mind.
- *Name*. This association is strengthened further by the mention of the word 'toys' in the brand name.

Fact file

Website: www.toysrusinc.com

Founded: 1948

Country of origin: USA

Brand fact 1: Toys 'R' Us is a US $13 billion business.

Brand fact 2: Toys 'R' Us has approximately 1,600 stores worldwide.

Brand fact 3: The Toys 'R' Us Times Square flagship store is one of New York City's top tourist destinations.

---

26 Subway: the focus brand

When Fred DeLuca created the Subway brand, he knew exactly what he was doing. Set up in the 1980s, when other fast-food chains were expanding their menus beyond all recognition, Subway was based around just one product, the sandwich. And, just in case that was too broad, he narrowed the focus to one type of sandwich – the submarine sandwich. Only the fillings were variable.

It is this narrow focus that is fast turning the brand into one of the fast-food giants. In Britain, McDonald's views Subway (who want to have 2,000 UK stores by 2010) as their number one threat.

The tight focus has helped the brand in several ways. It has certainly helped with the brand's perception. If a brand stands for one product, the consumer's perception of the brand is a lot clearer. People know exactly what is on offer when they enter Subway. The tight focus has also been helpful in naming the brand. Never underestimate the importance of a good brand name. Subway is a great name because it suggests the product, rather than spelling it out.

Another benefit of the tight focus is quality. McDonald's workers have to cope with up to 80 items on their menus, everything from salads to cheeseburgers. At Subway, staff only have to concentrate on making one product. It therefore doesn't take them as long to get good at making that one product.

Another advantage for Subway is that, unlike most other fast-food brands, it is not viewed as unhealthy, as its fillings are generally made of fresh ingredients. As the obesity crisis gains ever more urgency in the West, brands like McDonald's, Burger King and Kentucky Fried Chicken are inevitably going to be affected.

The advantage for Subway is that it offers the service benefits of fast food – speed and convenience – without the unhealthy connotations. If it keeps focused, Subway could therefore become one of the major brands of the 21st century.

Secrets of success

- *Focus*. At a time when most major fast-food companies have lost their focus, Subway's singular concentration on submarine sandwiches has turned it into one of the fastest-growing brands in the world.

- *Name*. Subway's tight focus is evident in the brand's name, which suggests the main product offering, rather than spelling it out. It is not a generic name, but works through subtle implication. Subway is also an easy name to remember, with relevant urban connotations.
- *Consistency*. Subway offers consistency of product and consistency of service, unlike some of its longer-established competitors.
- *Unhealthy rivals*. Although Subway has expressed fears of 'waking a sleeping giant' (McDonald's), the increasingly unhealthy image of the burger giant and other fast-food companies is helping Subway bite into their market share.

Fact file

Website: www.subway.com

Founded: 1965

Country of origin: USA

Brand fact 1: Subway has over 20,000 restaurants in 76 countries.

Brand fact 2: The Subway chain has been rated the number one franchise opportunity by *Entrepreneur* magazine for 12 of the past 16 years.

Brand fact 3: Many of Subway's sandwiches have 6 grams of fat or less.

CHAPTER 5

Muscle brands

In marketing, as in life, size matters.

The bigger brands become, the more marketing 'muscle' they wield and the more consumers gravitate towards them. Obviously, most of the brands in this book operate on a large scale. The brands singled out for this section are those that have become intrinsically associated with their size, as with IBM ('Big Blue'), or have consistently used their size to muscle their way into the marketplace.

As most of the cases illustrate, size can sometimes work against you. People will always warm to the underdog over the big bully. Indeed, it is no coincidence that some of the most widely unpopular brands – McDonald's, Microsoft, Nike, Starbucks and Wal-Mart – are included in this section.

Whether such mistrust is deserved is debatable. The giant brands themselves consistently deny that their bad reputation is deserved. But as the marketing law 'image is everything' is one that their brand strategies have always adhered to, they must understand how quickly perception can overtake reality.

Big brands have a problem. Size is their strength, but it can also slow them down or cast them as obvious villains.

In a world where globalization – which many choose to translate as 'Americanization' – is viewed in an increasingly negative, colonial light, many of the brand giants are suffering a serious image problem. Ultimately, no matter what the truth is about the associations of McDonald's with obesity or Nike with sweat-shops or Starbucks with 'clustering' or Microsoft with monopolistic practices, the perception is always enough to damage the brand.

However, size alone does not have to give you a bad name. As the example of IBM illustrates (the first case in this section), big brands can still generate equally huge respect.

27 IBM: the solution brand

Big brands are founded on big ambition, and IBM is no exception.

The ambition belonged to Thomas Watson, who became the General Manager of the Computing-Tabulating-Recording Company in 1914. The company made tabulating machines that processed information mechanically on punched cards. These machines had been invented in New York in 1890 to help the US Census Bureau accurately measure the population during the waves of immigration experienced during the Industrial Revolution. The company, in one form or another, had been around since 1896, but it took Watson only three years to double its revenue.

His ambition was also evident in his decision to rename the company International Business Machines, even though it still catered only for the US market. But Watson didn't want his business just to sound the part; he wanted it to look the part too, and he insisted that his salesmen were well groomed and wore smart black suits. He established the strong corporate culture that still sets IBM apart today.

Employee loyalty was created not only through generous sales incentives, but through a culture that involved employee sports teams, family outings and a company band. Watson stands alongside Henry Heinz and William Wrigley as one of the men who revolutionized the treatment of employees. IBM was one of the first companies to provide group life insurance, survivor benefits and paid vacations, all of which arrived in the mid-1930s.

As well as with its employees, IBM built strong, trusted relationships with its customers, the largest of which was the US government. During the Great Depression of the 1930s, IBM was able to expand in a tough economic climate due to a government contract to maintain employment records for 26 million people as part of the 1935 Social Security Act. Two years later, the Wages-Hour Act (requiring US companies to record wages and working hours) led to a large IBM contract. It also led to research into more advanced machines, with products such as the Selective Sequence Electronic Calculator (1947) providing the historical link between IBM the 'tabulating machine' company and IBM the computing giant.

By the time of Watson's death in 1956, IBM was already known for its size and smart-suited corporate culture (which included a company song). His son, Tom Watson Jr, who replaced his father as CEO, would stretch his father's ambition further, as very early on he realized computers were going to transform business.

In 1964, IBM introduced the System/360, the first mainframe computer. The System/360 was referred to as 'IBM's $5 billion gamble' by *Fortune* magazine. Famously, it cost more to develop than the atomic bomb. Unlike the computers that had gone before, the System/360 family of machines used interchangeable software and peripheral equipment.

The gamble paid off, and led to the 1969 decision to offer hardware, services and software individually, not just in all-in-one packages. This was another revolutionary decision, spawning as it did the software and services industries.

However, Watson Jr's emphasis was on corporate values, rather than what it made. The now massive IBM – 'Big Blue' as it was widely referred to (due to its scale and corporate colour) – remained tightly unified around a culture that valued each individual customer and each individual employee. Watson Jr understood that, for a technological company, where the products and services continually evolve, the values behind the brand name must remain consistent. These values led to IBM's trustworthy reputation – a reputation evident in the US maxim 'Nobody was ever fired for buying from IBM.'

The company fell out of Watson family hands in 1971, when Watson Jr stepped down as CEO. However, the organization kept on expanding as more and more businesses were adopting computer technology.

In 1981 IBM and the computer industry entered a new phase with the introduction of the IBM Personal Computer. This PC was the Ford Model T of computers, not advancing technology, but making that technology far more widely available than ever before. Apple's Apple 1 may have pre-dated the IBM PC by four years, but it was IBM that had the size and manufacturing power to take personal computing further into the mainstream.

However, the rise of the PC was a double-edged sword for IBM. Not only did more people now have computers, but these small computers ('clients') were linked to larger computers ('servers', which served data and applications to PCs). This completely democratized computing and also changed the way computers were bought and sold. Before, IBM was a big business dealing with other big businesses. Now, purchasing decisions were being made by individuals and departments that IBM had never dealt with before. Suddenly, IBM's main assets – its size, its long-standing customer relationships and its steadfast corporate culture – were working against the company. Younger, faster rivals were better positioned to adapt to this changing market structure.

It lost market share. But more significantly, it lost its credentials as the industry pacesetter. It also lost focus. Was it a computer company, a software company or a services company? What did IBM stand for? Many blamed the company's size for its lack of focus. Some shareholders called for the break-up of the company.

This didn't happen. Instead, in 1993, the notoriously inward-looking company made Louis Gerstner, a former chairman of RJR Nabisco, their new CEO. This was the first time a leader had arrived from outside IBM. It was Gerstner who managed to give the incredibly vast and broad organization a singular brand identity. In fact, he turned size back into an advantage, branding IBM as a 'solutions' provider. He realized that IBM, unlike many of its smaller rivals, had always been able to provide integrated computing solutions, rather than just individual components.

During the 1990s IBM started to move from a product-driven to a brand-driven culture. The determination to create a singular identity was evident in 1994, when IBM consolidated all of its advertising at one single agency, Ogilvy & Mather.

The next year, at a trade show in Las Vegas, Gerstner outlined IBM's new vision. The rise of the internet and the web had led him to believe that network computing would soon drive the industry and should therefore be central to IBM's strategy.

IBM hadn't made such a bold, industry-leading decision in years. Boldness paid off and by 1996, when companies were just starting to see the real value of intranets, extranets and network computing as a whole, the company's market value had risen to $50 billion.

IBM's sober image might have been at odds with the colourful brands of the internet 'gold rush' era, but following the dot-com crash in 2000 it was this sobriety that helped IBM regain its status as a voice of reason for the computer industry.

In recent years, expensive global advertising campaigns pushing the concept of 'e-business on demand' and boosting IBM's status as a 'solution' brand have paid off.

According to Interbrand, IBM is now the third-most-valuable brand in the world, behind only Coca-Cola and Microsoft.

Secrets of success

- *Message*. IBM has managed to unite one of the world's largest corporations behind a singular brand message formed around integrated business solutions.
- *Trust*. In a volatile industry where technology continually changes the market, the trust and confidence gained through

IBM's decades of experience are a major attribute. IBM's safe and sober connotations make 'blue' its perfect brand colour.

- *Brand focus*. IBM's switch from a focus on products to a focus on branding was the key turning-point in the 1990s. As a *Business Week* article ('The Best Global Brands', August 2001) put it, 'for technology marketers, IBM has become the model'.

Fact file

Website: www.ibm.com

Founded: 1896

Country of origin: USA

Brand fact 1: IBM is the world's largest information technology company.

Brand fact 2: In 2002, IBM Global Services signed US $53 billion in new contracts of which 42 contracts were each worth in excess of US $100 million, and five exceeded US $1 billion.

Brand fact 3: IBM has the greatest number of patents and inventions in the industry.

Brand fact 4: IBM retail solutions are installed in more than 60 of the world's top 100 retailers.

---

28 Wal-Mart: the scale brand

Wal-Mart, the US chain of discount stores, is a massively successful company enjoying a regular position at the top of *Fortune* magazine's top 500 corporations and annual revenues of around $250 billion.

In his book, *Made in America: My Story* (1992), Wal-Mart founder Sam Walton explained how he built the brand from its humble beginnings in 1945 in Arkansas (when Walton was only 27) and turned it into a brand giant. At the centre of his business philosophy was a determination to relate to customers. Number eight in his 'Rules for Building a Business' was: 'Let them [your customers] know you appreciate them.'

Wal-Mart has made sure it obeys this rule in a variety of ways. It has created a homely, all-American, neighbourly, personal image despite the giant size of the organization. It has deployed a variety of relationship marketing techniques, including a 'store greeter' whose job it is to welcome customers personally into the store and help them with a shopping cart.

This human element is also backed up by some serious technology. It was one of the first companies to use cash register scanners to monitor customer behaviour. Wal-Mart now deploys advanced data-mining software in all its stores in order to gauge patterns in customer spending. This information is then fed to Wal-Mart's suppliers and used by the company to make crucial decisions about what it should and should not be stocking.

However, the ultimate key to Wal-Mart's success is scale. It tries to personalize the experience with store greeters because the stores are intimidatingly vast. They are double and sometimes triple the size of its competitors' stores. This enables Wal-Mart to buy products in very great bulk, and therefore at cheaper prices per item. The big scale enables Wal-Mart's 'everyday low prices' to be lower than those of any other store.

And the scale is getting even bigger. Its new stores are built larger each year, and some of its superstores take up 200,000 square feet of floor space. However, charges of monopolistic practices have been growing since the 1990s, as smaller companies are suffocated out of the market, and this could ultimately lead to a full-scale Wal-Mart backlash.

There have been other problems too such as a sex discrimination class action against the company surrounding an allegation that

Wal-Mart systematically pays women less than men and passes them over for promotion. Regardless of the eventual outcome, such lengthy disputes inevitably damage the company's brand image.

However, there can be no denying that Wal-Mart's economy of scale strategy has, so far, paid off. Its acquisition of Britain's Asda supermarket chain in 1999 has, without doubt, strengthened its position internationally, and the investment it makes in technology and store greeters is nothing compared to the growth in sales it has made over the years. Wal-Mart is now, for better or worse, a full-time fixture on the suburban landscape, with almost 3,000 'big box' discount stores across the United States and eight other countries.

Secrets of success

- *Scale*. Big stores equal big discounts from suppliers equal low prices for customers.
- *Relationship marketing*. Despite its enormous size, Wal-Mart tries to add a human element to the store through store greeters and other tactics.

Fact file

Website: www.walmart.com

Founded: 1962

Country of origin: USA

Brand fact 1: Sam Walton's three basic beliefs which were established in 1962 are: Respect for the Individual; Service to Our Customers and Strive for Excellence.

Brand fact 2: In 2003 Wal-Mart was named by *Fortune* magazine as the most admired company in America.

Brand fact 3: More than 100 million customers per week visit Wal-Mart stores worldwide.

29 McDonald's: the service brand

McDonald's is, by most people's standards, a big brand. Indeed, for many, it is the ultimate epitome of a brand giant. Few brand identities are more instantly recognizable than that of McDonald's. In fact, more people now recognize the golden arches than the crucifix. And there are over 30,000 McDonald's restaurants in operation worldwide. Now that's big.

And yet, McDonald's is a brand in need of salvation. It is in trouble, and under fire from every angle. Everyone seems to have a gripe with the company: anti-globalization protestors; health authorities; lawyers; the food industry; parents. It is probably the most hated brand in the world. So how did this happen? Why such animosity? Well, before answering that question it's important to look at how McDonald's got so big in the first place.

In 1948, two brothers called Dick and Maurice McDonald opened up a hamburger restaurant in San Bernardino, California. They had a clear understanding of what their customers wanted: simple food, served fast. Hamburgers, malt drinks and fries were the staple offerings. The place was clean, and the foundations of McDonald's brand identity can be traced back to that restaurant (a golden 'M' shone out on to the road, and gleaming red and white tiles decked the interior).

The business expanded, and the McDonald brothers opened seven similar restaurants elsewhere in California. Then, in 1954, the small chain came to the attention of Ray Kroc. Kroc was a salesman, selling milkshake makers. He had enough money to buy the US franchise for McDonald's and he had total ownership of the firm by 1961.

To understand how McDonald's became a giant, you have to understand a little about Ray Kroc. Kroc was a man who loved money, and loved spending it. He would gloat at press conferences about his latest purchases: yachts; Arabian horses; a cattle ranch. He was ambitious, to say the least, and had an aggressive attitude towards the competition. 'If I saw a competitor drowning,' he once said, 'I'd put a live fire hose in his mouth.' Ah, how sweet.

But there was no questioning his business ability. Indeed, he has been referred to as the Henry Ford of the service industry. Kroc believed in QSC. No, not a home-shopping channel. It stood for 'Quality Service Cleanliness', a mantra he made sure all McDonald's employees were aware of.

From 1967, Kroc went international, opening restaurants around the world and snapping up the local competition. By 1990, McDonald's was part of the scenery in most countries. There was even a brand in Moscow (where the queues around the block provided the company with their best PR opportunity ever).

While the company expanded internationally, it was unstoppable. But when there were no new markets to conquer, the burger giant approached something equivalent to a mid-life crisis. With Kroc no longer at the helm, it had lost direction, and wondered what to do next.

The 90s were a troubling time for the McDonald's brand. Unable to expand geographically, they decided to keep on expanding their menu. The McDonald's menu had originally offered only 11 items. In the 90s the figure was sometimes 70. The service may still have been fast, but now the customers were taking 20 minutes just to read what was on offer.

Another problem was also starting to emerge. Just as the menu was growing, so too were the customers. In McDonald's home territory, the United States, a serious health problem was emerging, with the finger of responsibility being pointed towards the fast-food industry. Today, obesity has become a health crisis. According to the World Health Organization, 'Obesity is the dominant unmet global health issue, with Western countries topping the list.'

McDonald's, more than any other brand, has been brought into the centre of the obesity debate. It has been criticized for switching from vegetable oil to the highly saturated fat palm oil (or 'tree lard' as it has been called). It has been criticized for targeting children with potentially fattening foods, via Happy Meals, sponsoring education materials, offering Disney freebies, and various advertising initiatives aimed at young audiences.

Most of all though, McDonald's has been criticized for supersizing: that is to say, considerably increasing portion sizes. The idea originally belonged to David Wallerstein, one of the McDonald's directors. In the book *Fat Land* (2003), Greg Critser explains the logic behind super-sizing:

At McDonald's in the mid-1970s, Wallerstein faced a problem: With consumers watching their pennies, restaurant customers were coming to the Golden Arches less and less frequently. Worse, when they did, they were cherry-picking, buying only, say, a small Coke and a burger, or, worse, just a burger, which yielded razor-thin profit margins. How could he get people back to buying more fries?... Sell them a jumbo-size bag of the crisp treats.

Ironically, Ray Kroc had a bad feeling about the whole idea. According to John F Love's book *McDonald's: Behind the arches* (1985), there was a heated discussion between the two men. Kroc couldn't understand the idea: 'If people want more fries, they can buy two bags.'

Wallerstein was quick to respond. 'But Ray, they don't want to eat two bags – they don't want to look like a glutton.'

Kroc's bad feeling remained. In fact, it was only after Wallerstein conducted a survey of customer behaviour that he was finally swayed, and profits soon soared. Now, the legacy of that survey can be witnessed in the epic-sized, Alice in Wonderland portions handed over at the McDonald's counter.

However, while super-sizing has helped boost profits, there could be a law of diminishing returns at work here. The growing perception of McDonald's food as unhealthy is clearly making a dent in the company's profits.

Ray Kroc's belief that the 'US public are basically beef-eating people' may still be true. But in the United States, and the rest of the globe, diet patterns are beginning to alter as a new health consciousness emerges.

However, some experts believe the health debate is a side issue. The real problem isn't the obesity of McDonald's customers, but the obesity of the brand. Some say that McDonald's has grown too big and remained too centralized to stay ahead.

'McDonald's is teetering,' Professor David Upton of the Harvard Business School told the BBC's *Money Programme* in 2004. 'Maybe they've reached the limits of growth. They can't open McDonald's too close to each other.'

Then there's the issue of quality, which was always central to Kroc's philosophy.

'If they don't make the world's best burger, the core business is going to wobble,' reckons Rita Clifton, chairman of Interbrand. 'They've got to make the world's best burger, and they've got to move beyond the burger.'

Moving beyond the burger hasn't been easy. McDonald's has never really been an 'innovation' brand. Its attempts to move into healthier food ranges, such as salads, have received mixed results so far. Its efforts to upgrade the standard burger with the ill-fated Arch Deluxe was also a spectacular flop.

On top of all this, McDonald's has acquired something of an image problem. The negative PR caused by the McLibel Trial – where the company took out a libel suit against two British environmentalists who had handed out leaflets attacking the company – was widely considered to be an own goal. The company is one of the major villains in Naomi Klein's *No Logo*, and among the anti-globalization movement as a whole.

Then there's the problem of competition. For years, McDonald's main rival was Burger King, the perennial runner-up of the fast-food industry. Now, though, McDonald's faces a different type of competitor, with a different type of fast food.

'Even if McDonald's is improving, other people are improving faster,' says Professor David Upton. For 'other people', read Subway. Many experts, including Upton, consider the sandwich chain to be McDonald's main competitive threat. It certainly has the kind of aggressive expansion plan Kroc would have been proud of, especially in Europe. For example, the company has a target of 2,000 stores in the UK by 2010.

So what will happen? Will the competition, the health authorities and the activists get the better of the burger giant? The answer, of course, depends on McDonald's. For instance, if they fail to appease the health authorities by changing their menus or by providing warnings on their food, they could well face legal trouble in the future, just as cigarette companies such as Philip Morris have done. This would obviously help out the competition considerably. Most commentators agree that McDonald's needs to change in order to survive well into this century.

It is, like many other brands, the victim of its own successful growth. As Kroc himself once said: 'When you're green you grow, but when you're ripe you rot.' It remains to be seen whether these words come back to haunt the brand.

Fact file

Website: www.mcdonalds.com

Founded: 1954

Country of origin: USA

Brand fact 1: McDonald's is the world's leading food service retailer.

Brand fact 2: McDonald's has more than 30,000 restaurants in 119 countries.

Brand fact 3: McDonald's serves 47 million people a day.

Secrets of success

McDonald's may face difficulties, but its incredible early growth provides valuable lessons for any brand:

- *Familiarity*. Familiarity may breed contempt, but it also breeds comfort. McDonald's succeeded because people knew exactly what to expect: fast service and clean restaurants.
- *Pride*. Kroc had a pride and a love of what his business provided. As he once commented, 'it takes a certain kind of mind to see beauty in a hamburger bun'.
- *Persistence*. Kroc's ambition was unflinching. 'Persistence and determination alone are omnipotent,' he said.

30 Nike: the sports brand

Think of the world's top brands and it's not long before you think of Nike, formed in 1964 by track athlete Phil Knight and his University of Oregon coach Bill Bowerman. Knight, after leaving the University of Oregon, had studied for an MBA at Stanford Business School, and this was where he'd first had the idea of a running shoe company.

During its early years Nike's main selling point was price. The shoes, which were made using cheap Japanese labour, were a lot less expensive than those produced by Adidas, which at that time dominated the market. Nike did nothing new. It provided standard running shoes at low prices. But Nike wasn't going to follow the pack for too long. Soon it was going to lead it.

The breakthrough moment came when Bowerman experimented with a new type of running shoe, with a rubber outsole. Footwear would never be the same again. And neither would Nike. Like so many other brands mentioned in this book, innovation was the key to its success. When it had followed its competitors, Nike had done okay. But now it was leading the way, it was unstoppable.

And the company kept on innovating. For instance, in 1979 it introduced 'Nike Air' cushioning in the soles of trainers. Throughout the 1980s it marketed trainers in the way Audi and Fiat marketed cars, creating branded models with various features, such as the Pegasus (1988) and the Air Max (1987). Then came the Nike Air Jordan, and one of the most famous – not to mention expensive – celebrity endorsements of all time.

Michael Jordan – a superbrand in himself – remains one of Nike's key endorsers. He is now joined by Tiger Woods, whom Nike has helped turn into the highest-earning sportsperson of all time.

The company has also tried to create a strong association with the most global of sports – soccer – by sponsoring World Cup tournaments, and individual players such as Brazil's Ronaldo.

Most of Nike's multibillion-dollar marketing budget now goes on sponsoring individual athletes. Obviously, it makes sense for a sports brand to be associated with the leading sports figures in the world, but there are downsides.

Firstly, Michael Jordan, Tiger Woods and Ronaldo are brands in themselves. In some cases, the superstar endorsers have products of their own to sell. The question therefore arises: are the sports heroes working for Nike or is Nike working for the sports heroes?

The second, more damaging, downside is that the millions spent annually on each big name contrasts with the low wages paid to workers in its factories in Indonesia and Vietnam. Human rights organizations have highlighted the irony of an organization that has chosen factory locations on the basis of cheap labour, and that then chooses to spend most of its marketing budget on a handful of sportspeople. One such organization – the San Francisco-based Global Exchange – published an extensive report in September 1998 called 'Wages and Living Expenses for Nike Workers in Indonesia'. The report stated that Indonesian Nike workers were being paid the equivalent of 80 US cents a day, and asked the company to double the wages of its Indonesian workforce. This would have cost $20 million – the annual amount that was being paid to Michael Jordan to be an ambassador for the brand.

The report added fuel to the growing number of anti-Nike pro-testors who had already taken part in high-profile demonstrations, such as one outside the Nike Town store on Fifth Avenue in New York, where teenage customers told Fox News cameras: 'Nike, we made you. We can break you.'

Their anger may have been more to do with what they considered to be Nike's overpriced products than sweat-shops, but as the anger was stemming from the inner cities in the United States (arguably Nike's most important market) it couldn't be ignored. Indeed, this was at a time (the late 1990s) when kids were being beaten and attacked for their footwear. In one heavily reported case, a 14-year-old New York teenager from a housing project was repeatedly beaten for his Air Jordans and left unconscious on subway tracks to be hit by an oncoming train.

Such stories have all added to the portrayal of Nike as a corporate baddie. Even Phil Knight, who is now Chairman of the Board of Directors, has acknowledged the negative perception of Nike, saying that he has been depicted as 'the perfect corporate villain for these times'.

However, while the desire for such a villain is justified in a world saturated with marketing images yet dogged by poverty, a few words should be said in Nike's defence.

Firstly, Nike has responded to its critics through positive action. It joined the Apparel Industry Partnership, a group of manufacturers working towards a code of practice for overseas factories. Following the Global Exchange report, it did raise the wages of its Indonesian workforce. The company has also improved working conditions across Asia, and has promised not to hire anyone under 18 years old in its shoe factories.

In 2003, in a British documentary on Channel Four called *Why Globalisation Works*, Nike even invited cameras into its main Vietnamese factory, and the documentary makers discovered a clean and safe working environment full of satisfied employees, many of whom had previously been unemployed. Sure, they were hardly dream jobs, but then few factory jobs are. Obviously, it is hard to know whether this factory was representative of all Nike's manufacturing sites, but it certainly helped counterbalance the negative image of inhumane sweat-shops in second and third world countries.

Secondly, Nike cannot be blamed for inner-city 'sneaker crime', any more than fashion magazine editors can be blamed for anorexia or Britney Spears love songs can be blamed for teenage pregnancy. The argument that marketing is directly responsible for an individual's behaviour is a crude and simplistic one, to say the least. A pair of running shoes might be the object of a crime, but it's not the sole root cause. For that, we also have to look at the wider, more complex influence on young men growing up in deprived urban areas, often with very few positive role models. Indeed, there is an argument to be made that the Nike ad's hero worship of Tiger Woods and Michael Jordan helps to counteract the violent boasts and swagger of stars like 50 Cent and Eminem.

As for the issue of overpricing, well, on the face of it, Nike is guilty as charged. Their shoes cost only a few dollars to make and are sold for over a hundred dollars.

Nike gladly admits that brands are bigger than the products they represent. Scott Bedbury, the former vice-president of marketing at Nike (and the current vice-president of marketing at Starbucks) revealed in a February 2002 article in *Fast Company* ('Nine Ways to Fix a Broken Brand') that branding goes beyond the product. 'Offer more than the product,' he wrote. 'Create an experience around it and pay attention to the details.'

This 'experience' is what people are buying, just as much as the product they put on their feet. And that experience costs money. Billions of dollars, in fact. If Nike didn't spend a penny on marketing, and charged five dollars for each pair of running shoes, there would be no demand for the product. The marketing and the high prices turn products into aspirational items.

This is the catch-22 Nike faces. If it spends too much on marketing it gets accused of exploitation and overpricing by its customers. But it is exactly that marketing that has created those customers in the first place.

That is not to say that the brand is free from social responsibility. Of course it's not. Regardless of ethics, no brand in the information age can afford to ignore the concerns of its customers, employees or external activists. This is something Scott Bedbury recognizes, despite (or maybe because of) his tainted reputation among activists and *No Logo* readers. In the *Fast Company* article I quoted earlier, Bedbury talks about the way brands need to think responsibly about their markets, and not just about being cool. 'Contrary to what some people may think, Nike does not set out to be cool,' he writes. 'It knows that cool is defined by its customers. Be careful not to worship cool. It's a false god.'

Instead of cool worship, he recommends companies think about their 'karma':

> As a society, our concerns about the effects that globalisation has on cultures and the environment will only intensify, and the bar for corporate behaviour will rise. I expect that we'll look to our most trusted brands, big and small, to help reduce the enormous gap that exists between profits and benevolence.
>
> It's a new brand world out there. We are just starting to see the issues and opportunities associated with brand karma. However it evolves, I do know that strong karma will develop after years of doing the right thing.

And Nike does now seem to be taking on board the lessons of its former marketing man. The brand is certainly more transparent than it was in the last two decades of the 20th century. TV crews are inside its factories. Phil Knight has improved working conditions. And the company now appears to view corporate responsibility as more than a token PR gesture.

The Nike brand may still float high above the mundane reality of manufacturing, but it is no longer quite the target it once was. Maybe this is in part due to world events. After all, wars in Afghanistan and Iraq suddenly shifted the worries of liberal-minded people from sweat-shops and overpriced footwear to mass, state-approved violence and governmental hypocrisy.

But it is also because Nike, like many other members of brand royalty, is starting to wake up to the new era of marketing, an era in which brands cannot inflate their brand message too far, away from the reality of the product (from how that product is produced). It has been a tough lesson. In *No Logo*, Naomi Klein wrote that 'Nike was the most inflated of all the balloon brands, and the bigger it grew, the louder it popped.'

But Nike's brand value is still riding high. The Nike swoosh – along with Coca-Cola's swirly letters and McDonald's golden arches – remains one of the most visible logos on the planet. It has, so far at least, managed to weather the storm.

'Brands like Nike and Starbucks took lightning bolts early on because they were highly visible, global and influential,' reckons Scott Bedbury. 'These companies aren't perfect, but... they will help write a much-needed new chapter on brand management. They will prove that big doesn't have to be bad, that profits are only one measure of success and that great brands can use their unique superhuman powers for good.'

And indeed, Nike is likely to stay a superhuman brand, just so long as it also continues to listen to human concerns: those of activists, those of its workers and those of its customers.

Secrets of success

- *Inclusion.* When Scott Bedbury joined Nike in 1987, his aim was to help it become a more inclusive brand, and look beyond its core market of young, fit men. The 'Just Do It' slogan was the watershed. 'It established a broad communication platform from which we could talk to just about anyone,' wrote Bedbury.
- *Sub-branding.* Nike exemplifies the way sub-branding can work. Air Jordan and Air Max became strong brands in their own right, and their introduction added a freshness to the overall Nike image.

- *Aggression.* Nike's aggressive business and marketing strategies have often been compared to those of sports teams. 'Just Do It' is not just a slogan; it's a company motto.
- *Innovation.* Nike has produced innovative products since the 1970s. It has therefore become an initiator of trends rather than a follower.
- *Sponsorship.* The possibilities of sponsorship have been stretched to the limit with Nike. It sponsors the biggest sports events and the biggest sports stars. And these stars aren't simply smiling faces on TV ads; they are what the company calls 'brand ambassadors' who take a very active role. For example, Brazilian soccer hero Ronaldo designed the Mercurial soccer boot.
- *Plato.* The Greek philosopher might not be known for his marketing ability, but he inspired Nike's former marketing man Scott Bedbury. Plato's 'concept of essence' (the belief that deep within everything concrete is the idea of that thing) has been related to Nike's marketing strategy. 'Plato... was the first to articulate the importance of a brand's essence,' says Bedbury, without a shade of irony. 'Nike's essence... is authentic athletic performance.'

Fact file

Website: www.nike.com

Founded: 1964

Country of origin: USA

Brand fact 1: Nike is named after the Greek winged goddess of victory.

Brand fact 2: Niketowns have an average of 30,000 square feet of selling space. Currently, there are 13 US and four international Niketown stores.

Brand fact 3: In October 2001, Nike opened the first of two Nikegoddess stores, dedicated exclusively to active women.

31 Starbucks: the postmodern brand

In many ways, Starbucks is the archetypal brand. It has taken a physical, tangible business idea – the humble coffee store – and turned it into a big abstract concept.

Starbucks' vice-president of marketing, Scott Bedbury, once said that 'Consumers don't truly believe there's a huge difference between products.' It is therefore the purpose of Starbucks to forge 'emotional ties' with people through what Bedbury called 'the Starbucks Experience' in a 1997 article in the *New York Times*.

This view is supported by Starbucks' CEO Howard Schultz. 'The goal was to add value to a commodity typically purchased on supermarket aisles,' he told *Fortune* magazine in a 1998 interview. 'Starbucks is not a trend. We're a lifestyle.'

Howard Schultz, perhaps unsurprisingly, has a marketing background. Indeed, when he joined the Seattle-based company in 1982 – the first Starbucks store had been set up 11 years earlier by Gerald Baldwin, Gordon Bowker and Zer Siegl – Schultz's job was to help with marketing.

However, Schultz's early ambition for the company was thwarted by the management team. After a visit to Italy in 1986, he wanted his employers to expand by opening a chain of coffee bars in Seattle. They said no, and Schultz said goodbye. He went off and opened his own coffee stores, under the name Il Giornale, which made him enough money to buy out Starbucks for $4 million in 1987, with the aid of some local investors.

From then on, Starbucks gradually grew from a coffee store into a brand empire. At the start of 1988 Starbucks employed 100 people across 11 stores. Today, it has over 3,000 stores in non-US markets, and has around 40,000 employees.

Starbucks has managed to become what Schultz has referred to as 'the third place', that is, the place between home and work, where you go to meet friends or to have your 'alone time'.

In the book *Lessons from the Top* (Neff and Citrin, 1999), Schultz talks about the 'feeling' deliberately conjured by the brand:

> In the focus groups we've done people talk about how social Starbucks is. And then we say, 'How many people did you talk to while you were in the restaurant?'
> 'I didn't talk to anybody.'
> So we have learned that it's the experience – the music, the theatre, the romance of coffee and the break that we provide.

So Starbucks is about taking a bricks-and-mortar store that sells a physical product (a cup of coffee) and converting it into something that can yield a far greater emotional power.

This idea isn't just down to Schultz. It's also down to Bedbury, who had previously been one of the masterminds behind Nike's 'Just Do It' campaigns. In an August 1997 *Fast Company* article entitled 'What Great Brands Do', Tom Peters asked Bedbury to talk about the parallels between Nike and Starbucks.

'Nike... is leveraging the deep emotional connection that people have with sports and fitness,' Bedbury explained. 'With Starbucks, we see how coffee has woven itself into the fabric of people's lives, and that's our opportunity for emotional leverage.'

Starbucks is a postmodern brand. It simulates an experience of 'community' that may be as addictive as the caffeine in a cup of latte. It is about creating an environment that is, to borrow the title of a U2 song, 'Even Better than the Real Thing'.

This experience has not been created by the two-dimensional world of advertising (Starbucks spent less than \$10 million on advertising during the 1990s), but by the three-dimensional world of the stores themselves. The 'experience' is something you can walk into. It is multi-sensory: the sight of the friendly green logo, the smell and taste of the coffee, the warm cup in your hands, the background bustle and music. Every aspect is carefully thought out, and replicated in the thousands of Starbucks stores across the globe.

Instead of bombarding consumers with omnipresent advertising campaigns, the Starbucks strategy has been to focus on target areas and to create as many stores as possible within that area. This is the 'clustering' strategy that has been heavily criticized by anti-globalization campaigners such as Naomi Klein. In *No Logo*, she writes:

> The mechanics of Starbucks' dizzying expansion during the past thirteen years has more in common with Wal-Mart's plan for global domination than the brand managers at the folksy coffee chain like to admit. Rather than dropping an enormous big box on the edge of town, Starbucks' policy is to drop 'clusters' of outlets in urban areas already dotted with cafes and espresso bars. This strategy relies just as heavily on an economy of scale as Wal-Mart's does and the effect on competitors is much the same.

I would argue, though, that this policy of 'clustering' is not solely about killing off the competition – although that may be a part of it. For a brand like Starbucks, which wants to become 'the third place' or a default meeting point, it needs to be a part of the scenery.

Coca-Cola has managed to be everywhere through a combination of advertising and distribution. For a brand like Starbucks the stores *are* the distribution. They are also self-advertising: a concentration of stores in one area has the effect of a concentrated billboard campaign. It becomes a part of the scenery, and part of our collective subconscious. To become as well known as a Coca-Cola (which can be sold anywhere), the store had to be seen all over the place. Of course, this can be damaging for individual Starbucks stores as well as for competitors.

In an annual Starbucks report from the mid-90s, and quoted by Klein, the negative effects of clustering were briefly acknowledged: 'As part of its expansion strategy of clustering stores in existing markets, Starbucks has experienced a certain level of cannibalisation of existing stores by new stores as the store concentration has increased, but management believes such cannibalisation has been justified by the incremental sales and return on new store investment.'

So the strategy strengthened the brand and overall sales, despite weakening some individual stores. Schultz saw the bigger picture, and indeed continues to see the bigger picture, as Starbucks expands, location by location, across the globe. It is a controversial strategy, certainly, but it is also one that seems to be working.

Secrets of success

- *Emotion.* Starbucks' head of marketing Scott Bedbury believes that the brand seeks to 'align [itself] with one of the greatest movements towards finding a connection with your soul'. This sounds rather scary, but Starbucks' emphasis on building emotional ties is, without doubt, one of the reasons it is one of the leading brand globetrotters.
- *Replication.* Starbucks stores follow a similar formula. This not only helps customers to know what to expect, but it also helps to strengthen and tighten the brand's identity in the public's mind.

Fact file

Website: www.starbucks.com

Founded: 1971

Country of origin: USA

Brand fact 1: Starbucks has over 7,500 coffee shops in the United States.

Brand fact 2: Starbucks is the biggest coffee chain in the world.

Brand fact 3: Starbucks shops are in more than 30 countries.

- *Community.* The Starbucks brand signifies 'community'. This is what Starbucks sells, as much as physical cups of coffee. This concept defines the brand as much as the product does. As Bedbury himself says, 'consumers don't truly believe there's a huge difference between products'.

32 Microsoft: the dominance brand

In most surveys, Microsoft is now ranked as the world's number two brand, behind Coca-Cola. Its founder, college drop-out and self-confessed computer nerd Bill Gates, is now the richest man on the planet.

The remarkable thing about Microsoft, however, is that it is possibly the most widely despised and distrusted brand in history. The bewilderment at its success is evident all over the web. Take this extract from the Building Brands site (www.buildingbrands. com):

> The value of the Microsoft brand, according to an Interbrand study, is $65 billion. That's a lot of brand value for a company that no-one actually likes. And that's exactly our point. How can Microsoft's brand be worth so much? Aren't brands supposed to be about 'intangibles' and 'goodwill'? These may be old-fashioned terms when compared to the language of the latest brand gurus, but brands, after all, are about perceptions. Or are they?

Well, yes, they are. To an extent. And for many, the perception of Microsoft and Bill Gates is akin to that of a James Bond villain, plotting global domination through amoral and monopolistic means.

Bill Gates is no Blofeld, but the plot for global domination is not far off the mark. The original Microsoft mission was 'a computer on every desk in every home, running Microsoft software'. (The last three words were later knocked off the mission statement, but they were still implied.)

From the start, Microsoft didn't just want to lead the market; it wanted to dominate it. And it knew that it would need the help of big companies to get there. In 1981, when Microsoft was six years old, technology companies didn't come any bigger than IBM. So when Bill Gates's Seattle-based company was commissioned to provide the operating system for IBM's first-ever PC, he understood how big the opportunity was.

IBM, on the other hand, didn't realize the significance of this decision. After all, Microsoft was only supplying an intangible product – software. It wasn't like a computer, something physical that people could see. IBM hired Microsoft to save time and resources. Why waste your energies on creating software when someone else could do it for you? With hindsight, this may seem to have been a foolish frame of mind but this was a decade before the internet and 'Intel Inside'. In the 1980s, the big brands were about the technology *outside*. The hardware. The beige boxes. The stuff you could touch. If you had told the suits at IBM that this small Seattle software company was going to be the largest technology brand in the world within two decades they'd probably have fallen off their swivel chairs with laughter.

However, Microsoft has grown to become a brand that dominates the market in a way that even IBM never quite managed. By the end of the last century, IBM had only 10 per cent of the personal computer market, while Microsoft had 90 per cent of the market for desktop computer operating systems. What the IBM deal enabled Microsoft to do was to establish a common standard for software, an operating system Gates purchased from another company and renamed MS-DOS. In purely technological terms, experts tended to think that MS-DOS was not the best operating system. Many, for instance, thought Apple's system was far more user-friendly. But Apple's system was only for Apple computers, and Apple was small fry compared to IBM.

And so, in an irony of almost Shakespearean proportions, it was IBM that gave Microsoft its first leg-up on its path towards global domination. IBM was able to lend all its assets (large distribution, trust, dependability) to Microsoft's operating system. IBM's saturation of the PC market led automatically to Microsoft's saturation of the software market as every IBM PC ran MS-DOS.

Most importantly, although IBM was funding the development of Microsoft's operating system, the IBM–Microsoft contract stated that only Microsoft was entitled to license MS-DOS to other companies. So even as IBM'S PC started to struggle in an increasingly crowded market, Microsoft's operating system became more and more widely used as IBM's copycat competitors also adopted it for their own computers. MS-DOS soon became the industry standard.

People may have thought Apple's operating system was technologically superior but it was confined to Apple computers. Of all the bad press Bill Gates has received, the thing that is least justified is that he is a control freak. It was only through conceding total control – by licensing his software out to almost anyone who asked for it – that Microsoft has managed to become so big. By contrast, Apple was too insular, believing Apple's operating system served to sell Apple computers and therefore couldn't be licensed to third parties. Apple and IBM were walled brands. Microsoft broke down the walls and opened out its potential market further than any other technology brand in history. It knew that if it wanted to be everywhere it couldn't be too fussy about whom it worked with.

Microsoft used the base it had created and expanded even further as the computer revolution really got under way. From operating systems such as Windows to applications such as Excel and Word, in the 1990s it became *the* name in software. As most people's computers were running Microsoft operating systems and applications, brand loyalty was almost a given; if people were going to buy extra software or programming tools, it automatically made sense (psychologically, if not technologically) to buy Microsoft.

The company was also quick to recognize the significance of the internet, owning the largest e-mail application (Outlook Express) and one of the largest web brands (MSN).

Today, Microsoft dominates almost every aspect of home computing. It is so big that all the major issues affecting PC users are largely related to Microsoft. Of these issues, security is perhaps the largest. In 2002, Bill Gates declared security to be Microsoft's new top priority as computer viruses and 'worms' continued to target Windows and other Microsoft systems and applications. However, a year later Forrester Research found that 77 per cent of security experts said Microsoft products remained insecure.

Where others would see a threat, Microsoft saw an opportunity, and – in a typical Microsoft irony – its own branded security products were soon capitalizing on the growing market for security products.

Microsoft's domination of the software market is so heavy that security worries don't deter PC users. Or rather, they can't. After all, the decision to use Microsoft is not a carefully considered consumer choice. In fact, it's often not even a decision at all. Microsoft has dominated the market by practically *becoming* the market. After all, who needs popularity when customers use your brand without even thinking about it? The company that sells untouchable products has therefore become the ultimate untouchable brand.

Secrets of success

- *Luck*. There is no denying that Microsoft was lucky. If IBM had decided to choose another software company, or had been a bit tighter with its contract, the Microsoft story might have looked very different indeed.
- *Evolution*. Microsoft has evolved with the history of personal computing. When it started in 1975, it concentrated only on

developing programming languages. Today, it is a software company encompassing everything from operating systems to web applications.

- *Licensing.* By licensing its software to various companies it was able to broaden its base and establish its operating system as the industry standard.

Fact file

Website: www.microsoft.com

Founded: 1975

Country of origin: USA

Brand fact 1: The Microsoft corporate statement is 'Microsoft is the worldwide leader in software, services and solutions that help people and businesses realize their full potential'.

Brand fact 2: Bill Gates was a college drop-out. He is now worth over $40 billion.

Brand fact 3: In 1995, Microsoft Windows 1995 became one of the best-selling products of all time – helping the PC move into 250 million homes and businesses.

CHAPTER 6

Distinction brands

Some brands become successful by inventing a completely new type of product and service. They are the first in the category and dominate it from the start.

Other brands arrive a bit later in the game, but manage to succeed through distinction. These brands take an already established product – such as the wristwatch or household battery – and market it in a completely different way.

Typically, these brands work by contrasting themselves with the first in the category. Pepsi has created a brand identity that is almost the opposite of Coca-Cola's. Rolex was seen as a luxury wristwatch, so Timex became the affordable brand. When Hush Puppies arrived on the market, most shoe manufacturers produced formal, uncomfortable footwear. Hush Puppies therefore created a shoe designed around the concept of 'comfort'.

Distinction brands show how companies can enter established markets but still succeed, by defining themselves against (rather than following) the competition. They typically unite around a clear message or word such as 'purity' (Evian), 'export' (Heineken) or 'health' (Danone) and keep repeating that message over and over again to create a distinctive, singular identity.

Sometimes, as with the case of Evian and Duracell, a clear distinct identity turns the brand into a market leader. In other cases, such as Heineken or Pepsi, they stay in second or third place. However, by remaining distinct they always resist the attempts of their competitors to crowd them out of the market.

33 Pepsi: the differentiation brand

Pepsi is a successful brand. It is not as successful as Coca-Cola, but no brand on earth is as successful as Coca-Cola. Indeed, Coca-Cola's dominant position makes Pepsi's continued achievements all the more remarkable. It is certainly one of the best second-runners in the world, a lot closer to its chief competitor than, say, Burger King is to McDonald's.

The reason why Pepsi is one of the world's top 25 most valuable brands (according to Interbrand) is because it has defined itself against, rather than replicated, the market leader. As the first on the market Coca-Cola was always going to have the claim to words such as 'classic' and 'original', so Pepsi has gone in the other direction. Although it once marketed itself with the slogan 'The Original Pure Food Drink', it goes for a young and fresh identity even though it was actually founded in 1898.

Up until the 1950s Pepsi believed the best way to compete with Coca-Cola was on price. This led to its rather uncool status as 'the kitchen cola', which was considered a second-best alternative to 'the real thing'.

From 1958, however, Pepsi started to focus more on its brand identity. The 'Be Sociable. Have a Pepsi' slogan was the first to be aimed at the youth market. In 1961, the slogan became 'Now It's Pepsi, For Those Who Think Young' – the words 'now' and 'young' being defining attributes of the brand ever since. This slogan was also interesting in establishing the idea of youth as a state of mind rather than tied to actual age, a rather appropriate strategy for a brand that was already well into its sixties.

The key year for the Pepsi brand, however, was 1963. This was when it came up with the idea of the 'Pepsi Generation'. The Pepsi Generation campaign was influential because it showed how advertising could be based around attitudes rather than attributes (price, quality and so on).

In 1975 another breakthrough came with the Pepsi Challenge – a taste test that challenged not only consumers but also Coca-Cola, as it highlighted the preferable taste of Pepsi over Coca-Cola. Over the years the Pepsi Challenge message grew so strong that Coca-Cola was panicked into scrapping its original formula and coming up with New Coke. New Coke was a flop because it completely went against Coca-Cola's identity, borrowing values that belonged to Pepsi's taste and 'newness'.

As Coca-Cola wobbled, Pepsi embarked on what was quickly dubbed 'the most eagerly anticipated advertising of all time': the 'New Generation' campaign featuring Michael Jackson at the peak of his international fame.

Pepsi has since become one of the brands most associated with celebrity endorsement. The Pepsi celebrity roll-call has included such youth and music icons as Lionel Richie, Tina Turner and Michael J Fox in the 1980s; and Shaquille O'Neal, Cindy Crawford and the Spice Girls in the 1990s. On this side of the millennium, Britney Spears, Faith Hill, Robbie Williams, David Beckham, Beyoncé Knowles, Pink and Enrique Iglesias have all endorsed the brand.

Of course, a focus on celebrities can sometimes backfire. In one of Pepsi's more controversial endorsements the company tied itself to Madonna's *Like a Prayer* video in 1989, which featured the singer kissing Jesus and dancing through a field of burning crosses. Threatened with a consumer boycott and having been criticized by the Vatican, Pepsi withdrew the campaign. When *Like a Prayer* won the MTV Best Video Award, Madonna said: 'I'd like to thank Pepsi for causing so much controversy.'

However, Pepsi's celebrity focus has been a broad success and helped its identity as a 'now brand' for the MTV generation, which subtly contrasts with Coca-Cola's historical emphasis. (Where historical associations are used by Pepsi, as in its 2004 *Gladiator*-inspired ads starring Britney and Beyoncé, it uses them in a completely different way to Coca-Cola – as a source of postmodern playfulness and camp humour, not to emphasize its heritage.)

Another way in which Pepsi has distinguished itself from its rival is in its visual appearance. In 1941, in support of the United States' war effort, it adopted a patriotic red, white and blue colour scheme. In recent years it has shifted towards being a predominantly blue brand, which contrasts with Coca-Cola's signature red (Pepsi has even launched a new drink called Pepsi Blue). The word 'Pepsi' is now written in a futuristic typeface, which again couldn't be further away from the swirly handwriting of the Coca-Cola image.

As a result of this differentiation strategy – which is also applied to sub-brands such as Diet Pepsi and Pepsi Blue, as well as sister brands such as Mountain Dew – Pepsi continues to ride high. It seems that the further Pepsi's image gets away from Coca-Cola's, the narrower the distance between the two brands' value.

Secrets of success

- *Differentiation.* Coca-Cola is 'classic'. Pepsi is 'new'. Coca-Cola is red. Pepsi is blue. Coca-Cola's advertising is about timeless values. Pepsi's advertising is about celebrity and humour. Such different branding has helped distinguish two very similar products.

Fact file

Website: www.pepsi.com

Founded: 1898

Country of origin: USA

Brand fact 1: PepsiCo, Inc. was founded in 1965 through the merger of Pepsi-Cola and Frito-Lay.

Brand fact 2: Pepsi Cola is the world's number two soft drink.

Brand fact 3: During Nixon's presidency, Pepsi became the first foreign consumer product to be sold in the Soviet Union.

- *Lifestyle.* Pepsi was one of the first brands to shift from selling a product to selling an entire lifestyle, with the arrival of the 'Pepsi Generation'.

34 Hush Puppies: the casual brand

Like various other brands (see Vespa, for instance), Hush Puppies was started by post-Second World War government intervention. In the 1950s, the US government asked Wolverine (a leather-tanning company, not the X-Men character) to find a way to tan and use pig-skin leather.

Wolverine's chairman, Victor Krause, invented a process that created a new kind of material, suede. And shortly after, he created a new type of product for the US market – casual shoes.

Up until that time, American men didn't really have casual shoes in the way we have them today. There were running shoes, but they were worn by athletes. If men wanted to wash their cars or do some gardening, they simply wore a worn-out pair of formal shoes they had originally bought for work. As for women, they tended to wear heels or canvas plimsolls.

However, the 1950s was bringing with it a different type of lifestyle. The post-war baby boom saw a migration away from the metropolis to suburbs and the country. All of a sudden, the average home included a lawn and a driveway. Leisure time was becoming something to be valued as people entered the golden age of consumerism.

Victor Krause had realized that this new type of consumer needed a new type of footwear, and his new leather was perfect for the job. However, he still didn't have a name for the shoes he created. In fact, it was his sales manager, Jim Muir, who eventually came up with 'Hush Puppies'. Jim was travelling in Tennessee as part of the first major attempt to sell the unnamed suede shoes. He stayed the night at a friend's house, and was treated to fried catfish for his evening meal. On his plate, next to the catfish, were some fried cornmeal dough balls, which were a local Tennessee favourite. The dough balls were called 'hush-puppies', Jim's host explained, because farmers used them 'to quiet their barking dogs'. Jim Muir found this hilarious and nearly fell off his chair. In the United States in the 1950s, 'barking dogs' was also the phrase used for tired feet, as in 'these barking dogs are killing me'. Once Jim had stopped laughing he realized he had discovered the perfect name for a brand of comfortable shoes.

The quirky name was then matched by an equally quirky logo of a basset hound. This laid-back breed of dog has proven a fitting ambassador for the ultimate comfort brand.

Secrets of success

- *Invention*. The invention of suede leather helped create a distinctive footwear alternative.

Fact file

Website: www.hushpuppies.com

Founded: 1958

Country of origin: USA

Brand fact 1: Hush Puppies can be bought in 80 countries around the world.

Brand fact 2: Hush Puppies are marketed as the world's most comfortable shoe.

Brand fact 3: In 1963 sales of Hush Puppies shoes went sky high with one in ten American adults owning a pair.

- *Comfort.* Hush Puppies is the first brand you think of when you think of comfortable footwear, probably because it was literally the first proper brand of comfort shoes.
- *Style.* The risk of being a comfort brand is that you might be considered too safe to be stylish. However, Hush Puppies' quirky canine-inspired identity has assured the brand a laid-back sense of style. It remains an attractive brand by keeping the emphasis on quality, and by targeting key fashion influencers. For instance, Hush Puppies makes 'Tux Pups' for male film stars such as Nicolas Cage and Kevin Spacey, which are sent to be worn the day before the Oscar ceremony to help them relax.

35 Timex: the durability brand

What Ford was to cars, Timex was to the wristwatch. When the Timex wristwatch arrived in the 1950s, it echoed Henry Ford's achievement with the Model T 40 years earlier. Applying research and mass production together, it became the first completely accurate, durable wristwatch that could be afforded by almost everyone.

Rolex and other luxury brands had gone before, but these had been deliberately targeted to a limited and wealthy market. Before Timex, the working classes had to make do with pocket watches or unreliable wristwatches that broke easily.

Timex had been around in one form or another since the 1850s and had democratized timekeeping by making affordable timepieces such as Waterbury clocks and Mark Twain's favourite pocket watch, the Yankee.

The Timex wristwatch, however, was to be the most successful of all. The Timex slogan – 'It takes a licking and keeps on ticking' – was introduced right at the start, to emphasize the durability of the watches. This core brand asset was promoted further in adverts depicting Timex 'torture tests', where the watch survived through various ordeals such as being strapped to a baseball bat and hitting a ball, frozen in ice, stuck on to a lobster's claw, sucked into a vacuum cleaner and fastened to a turtle in a tank.

The ads were lent authority by the most famous 1950s US newsreader, John Cameron Swayze, who presented the commercials. The campaign became one of the word-of-mouth successes of the decade, and by 1960 one out of three US watches was a Timex. Fifteen years later, Timex increased its market share from a third to half of the market, having sold over 500 million watches.

Its position slipped slightly in the 1980s and 1990s, with rivals such as Swatch, Guess and Kenneth Cole taking over the younger end of the market. However, Timex is currently on a mission to win these customers back. It has also joined forces with brands such as Nokia, and abandoned the outdated 'It takes a licking' slogan and opted for the more contemporary 'Timex. Life is ticking'.

Fact file

Website: www.timex.com

Founded: 1854

Country of origin: USA

Brand fact 1: Timex is the United State's largest watch producer.

Brand fact 2: The brightness of Timex's indiglo watch helped a man lead people down 34 flights of stairs in the 1993 World Trade Centre bombing.

Brand fact 3: Timex is the third most popular of all women's accessory brands.

Secrets of success

- *Durability*. Timex successfully advertised its main strength through 'torture tests' and the slogan 'It takes a licking and keeps on ticking'.
- *Affordability*. Timex replicated Ford's high-volume, low-priced approach to create the first mass-market, affordable, long-lasting wristwatch.

36 Evian: the purity brand

Evian has grown from its humble 19th-century origins – when it was drunk solely for medicinal purposes – to become a global brand leader. This success is remarkable because it is competing with a free product, tap water, which is perfectly drinkable in many of the 120 countries where it is sold.

And Evian is not particularly cheap. It costs more than Budweiser, Coca-Cola and most soft drinks. It's even more expensive than most brands of bottled water.

So cheap prices aren't the secret behind Evian's success. And neither is product differentiation. After all, there are hundreds of brands of still water out there, with marginal taste differences. Indeed, many people think that a really good bottled water should taste of nothing.

I visited Evian-les-Bains once. It is a nice town: clean air, clean streets, open spaces. The whole place has a wealthy, if slightly sterile, feel to it, like something out of a JG Ballard novel. Personally, I preferred its neighbour, Thonon-les-Bains, a characterful, bustling little town that also produces its own bottled mineral water, called simply Thonon-les-Bains. To me it tasted absolutely indistinguishable from Evian, and it was cheaper too. But the market for Thonon-les-Bains started and finished with Thonon-les-Bains.

So if we are trying to explain the success of Evian we should try to forget about price and product. The secret of Evian's success is due to branding, specifically, the purity of its branding.

Firstly, the water is marketed as pure. Every Evian label tells us that the water spends at least 15 years slowly filtering down through a vast protected aquifer deep within the mountains. Its Alpine origins are emphasized further through the mountain imagery on the label, and even moulded into some of the bottles. 'Untouched by Man. Perfect by Nature' is one of the brand's trademarks.

Evian is pure in a marketing sense, also. It is itself, and nothing else. Evian is Evian. You can't get lemon-flavoured Evian or fizzy Evian or sulphate-free Evian. It may come in different sizes but there are no brand extensions or spin-offs to dilute the brand. It has remained singular, and consequently it has remained strong. Just as the drink is bottled at one source (Cachat Spring in Evian-les-Bains in Western France), so does the brand signify one product.

Of course, Evian has benefited from health advice that tells us to drink eight glasses or two litres of water a day. It has become increasingly associated with a healthy lifestyle and has even included the word 'detox' on some of its bottles.

Whereas other drinks brands are suffering from an increased awareness of health issues such as obesity and alcohol-related diseases, Evian's market share continues to expand.

It is not the only successful brand of still mineral water. There are others: Volvic, for instance, which like Evian is now owned by Danone. Both brands, to an extent, are associated with purity, but Evian still has the edge over its stable-mate. Part of this is due to the identity of each brand. Think of Evian and you think of snow-capped mountains and ice-filtered water. Think of Volvic and you think of a volcano. As most people prefer their mineral water chilled, the snowy Alps are a better association than molten rock. Also, Volvic's identity is slightly weaker due to its brand extensions such as Volvic Touch of Fruit.

Evian has all the right associations, and none of the wrong ones. If brands are religions, then Evian is one that promises to purify us. Like other brand-religions it places itself above humans and remains 'Untouched by Man'.

It may not offer a miracle as great as that of turning water into wine but, in an Evian bottle, water does metamorphose into something else, something that could cleanse and cure us and make us feel better about ourselves.

The Evian religion is growing. There may not be pilgrims flocking to Evian-les-Bains (although there are a few), but 5 million litres of Evian are bottled each day. Over a billion litres are consumed each year, making it the world's premium water of choice.

Secrets of success

- *Purity*. In 1789, the time of the French Revolution, the French nobleman Marquis de Lessert discovered the Cachat Spring in Evian-les-Bains. He believed that the purity of the spring water cured his many ailments. Today, millions of people are equally attracted to the purity of the product, and the brand.
- *Singularity*. Evian has stayed true to itself. There aren't flavoured or fizzy versions of the brand.

Fact file

Website: www.evian.com

Founded: 1789

Country of origin: France

Brand fact 1: Five million litres of Evian Spring Water are bottled every day.

Brand fact 2: Evian is available in more than 120 countries.

Brand fact 3: The Evian bottle is recyclable and is designed to be easily compacted.

- *Association.* The Alpine associations are emphasized on the label and by the mountain-peak sculpted bottle, which was introduced in 1995.
- *Health.* In 1826, when the Duke of Savoie granted the first official authorization to bottle Evian, it was intended as a medicinal drink. Indeed, until 1960, it was sold only in chemists. Today, it is still viewed as a healthy detox brand.

37 Duracell: the longer-lasting brand

Duracell is the bestselling brand of batteries because it is the one with the clearest and most singular identity. Everyone knows what Duracell has told us time and again through memorable advertising, deploying clever gimmicks such as the Duracell bunny, outhopping rabbits powered by other batteries.

The durability of Duracell was, and remains, a result of intensive research. Its predecessor company, PR Mallory, had used research to introduce the first-ever mercury battery, in 1944, which helped lead to today's alkaline battery.

Fact file

Website: www.duracell.com

Founded: 1964

Country of origin: USA

Brand fact 1: Duracell is the world's leading manufacturer of high-performance alkaline batteries.

Brand fact 2: Duracell batteries had to be rationed in the 1970s as supply caught up with demand.

The emphasis on research is still evident today through the Massachusetts-based Duracell Worldwide Technology Center. The researchers have, in recent years, provided a more environmentally friendly battery (mercury-free) and an even longer-lasting one (Duracell Ultra).

This research emphasis is combined with, and helps sustain, one of the clearest identities in brand history. Providing no rival arrives with a battery that lasts even longer, Duracell is likely to remain one of the 100 most valuable brands.

Secrets of success

- *Single message*. Duracell is a classic example of a brand built around a single value proposition. It is the longest-lasting battery in the market.
- *Visual identity*. Duracell has matched a clear value proposition with a clear visual identity. The trademarked Copper Top battery was introduced in 1971, seven years after the Duracell name was adopted.
- *Value-added features*. Duracell adds value through innovative features such as the Copper Top Tester (the first on-pack battery tester, introduced in 1990) and Power Check (enabling consumers to monitor how much power is left in the battery, introduced in 1996).
- *Research*. The Duracell Worldwide Technology Center keeps the brand's focus firmly on research, and has created even longer-lasting batteries.

38 Danone: the health brand

Barcelona, 1919. Thousands of children are suffering from intestinal disorders. Isaac Carasso wants to help them and looks into Nobel

Prize-winning research conducted a decade earlier into yoghurt lactic acid bacteria. He buys some lactic cultures from the Pasteur Institute in Paris and launches the first Danone yoghurt through pharmacists.

Like other brands that were first prescribed by pharmacists – such as Evian (which is now owned by the Danone Group) or Coca-Cola – Danone has broadened out into the mass market. The brand is now the world leader in the fresh dairy products sector.

However, it is still a brand firmly associated with health. The Danone Vitapole research centre ensures that the health claims made by the brand are scientifically backed up. One of its most recent successes was Danone Actimel – a probiotic dairy drink that has educated consumers about the concept of 'friendly bacteria'.

The taste and health benefits of Danone products are often promoted simultaneously. For instance, one of Danone's slogans in the United States (where the brand is given the phonetic spelling 'Dannon') is: 'How can something that is so good for you taste so good?' Such simple messages tackle the main consumer deterrents of health food (taste worries) and tasty food (health worries) both together.

Fact file

Website: www.danonegroup.com

Founded: 1919

Country of origin: France

Brand fact 1: The name of Danone was chosen because it was diminutive of the name of Isaac Carasso's son, Daniel.

Brand fact 2: Nearly 31 per cent of Danone's sales are from emerging markets.

Brand fact 3: Danone is the leading brand worldwide for fresh dairy products.

Danone's equal appeal to pleasure and conscience is a winning formula among increasingly health-conscious, but no less self-indulgent, consumers. It is a formula that has turned it into one of the top five food brands in the world.

Secrets of success

- *Differentiation*. Danone products often invent a new market rather than eat into an old one. This point of difference is often exaggerated through packaging – such as the unique bottle shape and 'dose' size of Danone Actimel.
- *Education*. Danone is the expert at translating complicated science into a simple consumer message.
- *Health*. The health associations are enforced through various Danone Institutes and also by the Danone International Prize for Nutrition.

39 Heineken: the export brand

There are hundreds of things you could say about the Dutch brand of beer that began life in 1863 and has risen to become one of the world's most popular beers.

There's the emphasis on quality, initiated by the brand's founder, Gerard Adriaan Heineken himself, who travelled Europe in search of the best raw material. There was the early decision to sell the brand in supermarkets, thus widening its distribution network considerably.

There's the increasing use of sports and music sponsorship, through events such as the US Open, the Heineken Classic Golf Tournament, the Rugby World Cup and various jazz festivals.

Most fundamental to the brand though is the energetic pursuit of exports, which began in the 19th century, and which established Heineken as the first truly global beer brand. The export strategy was based on clever opportunism, which saw Heineken enter the US market only three days after the end of prohibition in 1933, triggering massive growth.

Exporting was only the first stage, however. Licensing contracts and participations with local breweries have helped to consolidate its early entry into foreign markets.

Heineken's marketing strategy now firmly concentrates on its export identity. Indeed, one of its sub-brands is even called Heineken Export. It emphasizes its identity as an export product in the same way Coca-Cola promotes its authenticity as 'the real thing'.

Of course, this may seem a foolish strategy in the age of globalization, as all major brands are exported to some extent. However, Heineken has a broader reach than most and, according to *Business Week* magazine, 'is the closest thing there is to a global beer brand'. It was also one of the first brands to realize the significance of cross-border deals.

Unlike Coca-Cola, which acts as though it belongs everywhere, Heineken has built a reputation (outside Holland, at least) as a brand that always belongs to 'somewhere else'. Subconsciously, its export status gives it a slightly illicit, exotic identity, as if preserving the appeal it would have had in the United States post-prohibition. In a world where we believe the grass is always greener somewhere else, we are willing to believe that the drink inside those immediately recognizable green bottles is going to be better than any taste of home.

Secrets of success

- *Exporting.* Around the 1950s, exporting switched from being solely a distribution strategy and became Heineken's core brand identity. The Heineken brand is now a passport to somewhere else.

- *Recognition*. Heineken's global reach means it ranked second only to Budweiser in a global brand survey jointly undertaken by *Business Week* and Interbrand. Indeed, in tests, Heineken is the only beer brand people can recognize from the bottle alone, after it has been stripped of its label.

Fact file

Website: www.heineken.com

Founded: 1863

Country of origin: Holland

Brand fact 1: In 2002, Heineken sold 22.9 million hectolitres of Heineken.

Brand fact 2: The main ingredients in Heineken are water, barley malt and hops.

Brand fact 3: Heineken can be found in more than 170 countries.

CHAPTER 7

Status brands

Every time a friend succeeds, a small part of me dies.

(Gore Vidal)

Human beings are insecure creatures. We get jealous of other people's success, because we want that success for ourselves. We crave attention and admiration from fellow members of our species, and certain brands can help satisfy this craving.

These are the brands that seek to separate their customers from the crowd, by signifying wealth and status. Never mind 'you are what you eat'; in our materialistic society that has been replaced by 'you are what you buy'. If people buy a BMW or wear Louis Vuitton or check the time using a Rolex, they are clearly trying to distinguish themselves from the Ford-driving, Gap-clad, Timex-wearing masses.

Of course, status brands cannot use the word 'status'. After all, people do not want to advertise their own ego. No one wants to admit to status anxiety, or the desire to feel above their social circle. So brands use words like 'luxury', 'performance' or 'engineering', to make people feel a bit more comfortable about their buying decisions.

Prestige brands therefore work in subtle ways to overcome our status anxiety. They do not compete on cost or convenience, but something more abstract. They are deliberately superfluous. After all, a BMW gets you to the same place as a Volkswagen, and in roughly the same time, even if it costs three times as much. High-fashion brands are the archetypal status providers because they are almost never bought for their practical use.

In his magnificent book on human nature, *The Blank Slate* (2002), psychologist Steven Pinker links human status symbols with those of other animals, such as peacocks:

> Status symbols are typically objects made by arduous and specialized labour out of rare materials, or else signs that the person is not bound to a life of manual toil, such as delicate and restrictive clothing or expensive and time-consuming hobbies... The same principle [explains] the evolution of outlandish ornamentation in animals, such as the tail of the peacock. Only the healthiest peacocks can afford to divert nutrients to expensive and cumbersome plumage. The peahen sizes up males by the splendour of their tails, and evolution selects for her males who muster the best ones.

Humans don't have fancy feathers to set them apart. They have brands. And the status brands that are most successful are those that most appeal to our inner peacock. The more superfluous, the better.

40 Rolex: the superior brand

In 1914, just before the shooting of Archduke Ferdinand would throw the world into bloody conflict, the Bavarian Hans Wilsdorf was paying little attention to world events. Having established his London-based watch company Rolex in 1908, he had decided to test the accuracy of his products by sending them off to a Swiss observatory. It was a decision worth taking, as Rolex was rewarded with the world's first timing certificate for a wristwatch. And just in time. Accurate wristwatches were needed by soldiers in the First World War, as they were easier to use than pocket watches in the trenches.

Wilsdorf realized accuracy was his key brand asset and publicized it wherever he could. When Mercedes Gleitze decided to become the first woman to swim the English Channel in 1926, Wilsdorf offered her his newest model, the Rolex Oyster, so she could record her time, creating valuable publicity for the growing brand.

If accuracy is one key behind the brand's success, another is innovation. In 1931, Rolex patented the perpetual winding mechanism, which meant the manual winder on the side of the watch was no longer needed. In 1945, it became the first watch to have a date window. Later innovations included the first diving watch and the first dual time zone watch.

Given such inventions and developments it is easy to see why the history of Rolex is considered to be the history of the wristwatch industry. The Rolex Oyster was judged by a panel of leading watch industry figures to be 'The Watch of the Century'.

It is not just the combination of quality and innovation that has helped; marketing has also been a factor. For a brand to be truly desired, demand must always outweigh supply.

There are retailers around the world who sell Rolex watches, but over the years the company has reduced the number of these retailers. Unlike most companies who would want their distribution network to get wider and wider, Rolex has gone the other way. As a result, most watch retailers do not sell Rolexes. Consequently, demand has rocketed and the brand's symbolic status has intensified.

People don't wear a Rolex for its accuracy. They wear it to make a statement about who they are and how big their bank balance is. It is a wearable Porsche, and signifies the same qualities.

A Rolex is an investment. Its longevity and desirability ensure that it is the easiest watch in the world to sell second-hand.

Ironically, for a brand that can tell you exactly when it is with split-second accuracy, Rolex has a timeless identity. Because of its close associations with the history of the watch, the brand could very well stay around until we no longer want to tell the time by looking at our wrist.

Secrets of success

- *Quality*. Rolex concentrated on quality from its very first wristwatch in 1908. It confirmed its quality by sending its watches to be tested by a Swiss observatory a few years later.
- *Distribution*. The brand stimulates demand by limiting distribution. Only certain retailers are allowed to sell Rolex watches.
- *Historical association*. Rolex did not single-handedly invent the wristwatch, but it was the first brand to popularize them. The company is also responsible for some of the biggest developments in wristwatch history, such as the perpetual winding mechanism.

Fact file

Website: www.rolex.com

Founded: 1908

Country of origin: UK

Brand fact 1: The name Rolex was used because it was easy to pronounce in any European language and short enough to fit on the dial of a watch.

Brand fact 2: In 1945 the Oyster Datejust was invented and it was the first watch to display the time automatically.

Brand fact 3: The company still makes most of its products by hand to control quality.

41 Courvoisier: the mystery brand

Great status brands depend on great mystery, and one of the most mysterious brands (not to mention the classiest) is Courvoisier cognac. Part of this mystery has to do with cognac itself, as the exact process behind the production of the golden spirit is a well-guarded secret. Added to this mystery is the legend of Courvoisier itself.

The brand stretches back to the early 19th century, when the spirit merchant Felix Courvoisier came up with the drink and distributed it through one of the largest wholesalers in France, the Gallois family. As the Gallois family were the chief wine and spirit suppliers to Napoleon's Imperial Court, they were paid a visit by the man himself in 1811 before he boarded his ship to St Helena. He was there to sample the wines and see which ones should be taken on his journey. After sampling a cognac, he bought several barrels to take with him. The sailors on board were delighted, and quickly dubbed the drink 'The Brandy of Napoleon'.

Today, the Napoleon connection is still emphasized on the bottle with the words 'Le Cognac de Napoleon' printed in elegant writing underneath the brand name, along with Napoleon's silhouette in the logo and the sensuous bottle shape suitably named 'Josephine'.

Courvoisier has now become synonymous with cognac in the 142 countries where it is sold. Over 14 million bottles are drunk every year by people who appreciate the quality of the award-winning spirit (it is the only cognac to have ever won the Prestige de la France award, the highest honour for any French wine or spirit).

However, it is not the quality of the drink that qualifies it for inclusion in this book, but the quality of the brand, because as a brand it has faced and overcome a dilemma. Courvoisier, the brand, has always stood for luxury and tradition. The trouble is that luxury brands operate in a different world to the one they inhabited 100 or

50 or even 10 years ago. Luxury today is no longer about class or privilege. It is something that anyone can buy their way into, if they have a fat enough wallet. Luxury is now about high-fashion brands such as Gucci and Louis Vuitton, and the aspirational imagery of rock and hip-hop videos.

In 2000, Courvoisier embarked on a US marketing campaign portraying the brand as a fashion label, with 'the House of Courvoisier' branded across images of sexy leather boots. The stuffy image of Courvoisier was radically transformed while the luxuriousness of the brand remained intact. Now people are as happy to drink it in trendy Manhattan or Paris VIP bars as they are in stuffy members' clubs.

That this image change worked is evidenced by its appeal among the hip-hop community, where it has overtaken Crystal as the ultimate status drink. The Busta Rhymes/P Diddy 2003 track 'Pass the Courvoisier' has managed to do for cognac what the Run DMC hit 'My Adidas' did for three-stripe trainers back in 1986.

This kind of endorsement is something brands like Nike or Tommy Hilfiger would pay millions for, but it didn't cost Courvoisier anything. Instead, it has spent its money on building its associations with fashion, sponsoring the New York Fashion Week and linking with hip British lingerie brand Agent Provocateur to design sexy underwear with a 'Napoleonic' flavour.

'Courvoisier is now a glamour accessory,' says Marcel Knobil, the editor of *Cool Brand Leaders* (2003). 'Courvoisier's authenticity… has ensured that the drink has remained the cognac of choice amongst those in the know.'

Napoleon, staggering around that wine cellar in the sky, must be looking down with drunken pride.

Secrets of success

- *Sophistication*. Courvoisier is a sophisticated product matched by a sophisticated, self-confident brand.

- *Adaptation*. Courvoisier has succeeded where so many traditional brands have failed. It has adapted itself to the modern market without selling out its core values.
- *Fashion*. By rubbing shoulders with high-fashion names, Courvoisier has itself become a designer label.

Fact file

Website: www.courvoisier.com

Founded: 1811

Country of origin: France

Brand fact 1: Courvoisier cognac is owned by Allied Domecq.

Brand fact 2: Courvoisier is still aged in hand-crafted oak barrels. Courvoisier exclusively uses French limousin oak, preferred by spirit makers worldwide.

Brand fact 3: Courvoisier is acknowledged by many experts to be the world's finest cognac. Courvoisier exclusively uses Ugni Blanc grapes, from the four finest crus of the Cognac region: Grande Champagne, Petite Champagne, Borderies and Fins Bois.

---

42 Louis Vuitton: the desirable brand

Louis Vuitton is the ultimate status brand. It manages to combine mass production with a highly aspirational image. It is the world's largest luxury label, with 13 production workshops, an international logistics centre, over 300 exclusive shops in 50 countries and approximately 10,000 employees. Its brand value far exceeds that of Gucci and is over double that of Prada. The chairman of LVMH (Louis Vuitton Moët Hennessy – the French conglomerate that owns Louis Vuitton), Bernard Arnault, is the richest man in the fashion industry. If that wasn't enough to convince you, Louis Vuitton regularly ranks higher than MTV, Adidas, Chanel, Pizza Hut, Amazon, Apple and numerous other global names in Interbrand's annual survey of the top 100 brands.

So, it's successful. But why? What advantages does it have over other status brands?

Well, firstly, it has been around a long time. Over 150 years in fact. Louis Vuitton, a carpenter's son, founded the company in 1854. Louis made his name famous by creating luggage, bags and accessories associated with travel. This was at a time when only the very wealthiest members of society could afford to go on holiday. Travel is the ultimate association for a luxury brand, as it signifies the wealth and freedom enjoyed by the jet set. In the 19th century, when 'tourism' was a completely new concept, its significance was even greater. As Yves Carcelle, CEO of Louis Vuitton, has put it: 'The birth of Vuitton also marked the start of modern life. It is not by chance that it was born in the mid-19th century, when the nature of travel was revolutionized.'

However, the rise of international terrorism and lower fares have inevitably taken some of the glamour out of travel. It is therefore very wise that Louis Vuitton has now broadened into a wide-ranging fashion brand. Under the direction of Marc Jacobs, a hip US fashion designer, its ranges now include clothing, shoes, watches and jewellery.

Rather than dilute the brand, as is often the case with extensions, they have strengthened it. Products bearing the famous 'Damier' LV logo are now desired everywhere from the boulevards of Paris and the streets of London and New York, to markets such as India and China, where Louis Vuitton is a recognized pioneer.

Part of this desire is due to celebrity endorsement. In Louis Vuitton's own lifetime, Empress Eugénie was perhaps his most famous customer. His son Georges catered for various movie stars and maharajas in the first half of the 20th century. Later Audrey Hepburn was often snapped carrying Louis Vuitton luggage during the height of her fame. And in recent times, Jennifer Lopez is perhaps the brand's most famous endorser, baring all for a global print media and billboard campaign that began in 2003.

But Louis Vuitton's real secret is control. The brand does everything itself, from design to distribution. This not only means ensured quality, but also high operating margins of around 45 per cent, far higher than those of its closest competitors.

This control has enabled Louis Vuitton to pull off the ultimate high-wire act. It has managed to balance prestige with populism, retaining the connotations of a luxury brand with a mass-marketing mentality.

The brand, like Coca-Cola and other mass-marketers, has overtaken the product. The luxury signified by the Louis Vuitton logo has become all that matters. It has become a social signifier, commanding our attention simply because we know it commands other people's attention.

Fact file

Website: ww.louisvuitton.com

Founded: 1854

Country of origin: France

Brand fact 1: Moet Hennessy Louis Vuitton is the world's largest luxury goods group.

Brand fact 2: The Louis Vuitton brand is embodied by the Monogram canvas.

Brand fact 3: Louis Vuitton employs nearly 10,000 people throughout the world, 60 per cent of whom are based outside France.

When it comes to Louis Vuitton, there appears to be no law of diminishing returns at work. The greater the awareness of the brand, the greater the desire for the products. Louis Vuitton is now the instant cure for status anxiety, as it is guaranteed to be recognized by everyone around you.

The brand's symbolic power now even baffles some of Louis Vuitton's management team. In February 2004, one anonymous executive reportedly told the *International Herald Tribune* that the success of the brand he works for represents 'the biggest sleight of hand since snake oil'. He added: 'Can you imagine that this is all based on canvas toile with a plastic coating and a bit of leather trim?'

Secrets of success

- *Mass marketing.* Louis Vuitton deploys mass-marketing techniques such as celebrity endorsement and sports sponsorship (its name is attached to the America's Cup yacht race).
- *Control.* 'We do everything ourselves,' boasts CEO Yves Carcelle, 'from creativity through manufacture and design.'
- *Status.* Louis Vuitton has managed to gain higher sales while retaining its high status. The high status has been enforced through carefully targeted advertising in high-end publications and selective distribution.
- *Travel.* The roots of the brand are in travel. And even today the connotations of exoticism and escape associated with travel are evident within the Louis Vuitton identity.

43 Moët & Chandon: the vintage brand

Think champagne and it is not too long before you think Moët & Chandon. It is a brand icon, which retains a relevant image despite being over 260 years old. The House of Moët & Chandon was established in 1743, and quickly became associated with high society. Louis XIV was an early customer. Queen Victoria was a later fan, and awarded the brand the royal warrant in 1893.

It has been considered a drink to be seen drinking, which is important for any champagne brand. In the 1930s 'mini Moëts' (a miniature version of the bottle) were an instant hit in Paris cafés among the fashion conscious, and added new life to the brand.

Moët & Chandon has held on to its fashionable credentials into the present, with carefully considered sponsorships of events such as London, Paris and New York fashion weeks. In 1998, the Moët & Chandon Fashion Tribute Award was launched, which helped confirm its high-fashion status. In 2003, the London-held award ceremony managed to generate an estimated £2.5 million in terms of media coverage with high-profile guests such as Naomi Campbell and Alexander McQueen. There is now even a Moët & Chandon bar in London's leading department store, Selfridges, and other Moët bars are now opening in Europe.

However, the brand isn't just successful because of its continued association with fashion and high society. It is also the most innovative champagne brand, having been the first to produce a vintage champagne (back in 1842) and the first to produce a 'mini' version.

It has even published its own magazine, *Vintage*, which conveys the three core values of the brand, quality, fashion and heritage, values that look likely to secure one of the oldest brands in the world a healthy future.

Secrets of success

- *High-society associations*. For luxury brands it helps to have a few high-society endorsements. And society didn't get much higher than Queen Victoria and Louis XIV.
- *Relevance*. The brand has stayed relevant by associating itself with the right events, such as those in the fashion industry.

Fact file

Website: www.moet.com

Founded: 1743

Country of origin: France

Brand fact 1: Moët & Chandon is leader in the export market, the house sells over 80 per cent of its production to foreign markets.

Brand fact 2: A Moët & Chandon cork pops somewhere on Earth every single second.

Brand fact 3: Moët & Chandon's vineyards span a total of 771 hectares making it by far the greatest in the region.

44 Burberry: the heritage brand

Burberry is the archetypal heritage brand. It started in 1856, when Thomas Burberry opened a small clothing shop in Basingstoke, England. It built its reputation as a clothing manufacturer after Burberry's invention of a tough new fabric called 'gabardine', which was endorsed by the British royal family and military. It has held 'royal warrants of appointment' for nearly a century, and Burberry's weatherproof outerwear – including the 'trench coat' – was worn by the British army in the First World War.

The weatherproof quality of Burberry was confirmed when the Norwegian explorer Captain Roald Amundsen chose Burberry clothing for his 1911 expedition, when he became the first person to reach the South Pole.

In 1955, when Burberry was acquired by Great Universal Stores (GUS), Burberry already had a long heritage, and the unique Burberry fabric was being sold internationally. GUS continued its international expansion as the decades rolled by, but did little to update Burberry's increasingly old-fashioned image.

By 1997, GUS was being advised to sell Burberry for $300 million or less. The 'heritage' tag was becoming a burden that was sending the Burberry name into slow, terminal decline. Yes, it was still a quality, British brand, but it was also seen as stuffy and boring.

A new CEO, Rose Marie Bravo, changed all this and turned Burberry's fortunes completely around. Rather than ignore Burberry's heritage, she exploited it and used it as a route into the high-fashion luxury goods sector, helping the brand stand alongside the likes of Prada and Louis Vuitton. Carefully targeted advertising campaigns in the fashion media, combined with updated designs using the traditional Burberry tartan, gave the brand instant appeal among the fashion crowd and British celebrities such as Victoria Beckham and Kate Moss.

Burberry became a brand associated with the catwalk and the *Sex and the City* lifestyle, while retaining its long British heritage. Having successfully made the move upmarket to become a lusted-after luxury, it was valued at $1.5 billion in 2002.

Of course, fashion brands need to work hard to keep their aspirational status. Burberry's association with British football hooligans, as highlighted in the BBC's Hooligans TV series, may end up damaging its high fashion status in its native land. However, Burberry's popularity on the football terraces has not yet done anything to put off the fashionistas. It seems that, in the short term at least, the brand can successfully straddle two worlds.

Today, the Burberry checked print, which was introduced in the 1920s, is recognized everywhere from Brazil to Japan, and provides an instantly recognizable brand signifier. Just as a tartan provided a way of uniting a Scottish clan, so the familiar Burberry pattern provides a useful way for the brand to unify its identity, and for the tribal-minded fashion-conscious to display their allegiance to the hippest of heritage brands, whether on the football terraces or their yacht on the Riviera.

Secrets of success

- *Quality.* Thomas Burberry's innovative new fabric provided high-quality and durable outerwear.
- *Endorsement.* Burberry's brand was built on the endorsement of the British royal family, explorers and the army. Today its favour among models, celebrities and fashion stylists has successfully helped revive the brand.
- *British identity.* Burberry is one of the few brands that has managed to channel the diverse image of Britain (an image that encompasses everything from punk rock to royalty) into a successful and focused brand attribute.

Fact file

Website: www.burberry.com

Founded: 1856

Country of origin: UK

Brand fact 1: The 1960s saw the Burberry check being used on umbrellas, luggage and scarves. Before then it had been mainly used as a coat lining.

Brand fact 2: Burberry operates 60 stores and 10 concessions.

Brand fact 3: Humphrey Bogart wore a Burberry mac in Casablanca (1942).

45 BMW: the defining brand

Status brands don't just define products. They define ourselves.

Take BMW. BMW is a 'corporate brand'. In other words, the name of the company and the name of the brand are one and the same. Unlike other car manufacturers – such as Ford or Volkswagen or Toyota – it doesn't spend money on creating sub-brands. BMW does not have an equivalent of a Mondeo or a Beetle or a Lexus. It simply has BMW. This leads to a stronger ability to define its customers, at least potentially.

The challenge for any corporate brand is in keeping a uniform identity. After all, any new direction risks diluting the BMW image.

This hasn't happened, because BMW has kept the focus firmly on one attribute: motoring performance. When the company started in Munich in 1916 it made aircraft engines (the blue and white BMW logo is meant to represent the sky as seen through a moving propeller). It switched to motorcycles and trucks in 1923 and, from 1928, started making automobiles. The emphasis on motoring performance, however, remained consistent. Indeed, it is even reflected in the no-nonsense BMW name itself, which stood for Bayerische Motoren Werke (Bavarian Motor Factory).

BMW is, of course, a luxury and elitist brand. Not everybody can afford one. BMW appeals to people who won't accept second-best, through its main organizing brand principle, 'the ultimate driving machine'. Of course, 'ultimate' is a purely subjective term, and not something that can be legally tested, but it *sounds* like a bold statement – and that, in branding terms, is the main thing.

As a result of this tight focus – which has stayed in place for 30 years, through three separate advertising agencies – the BMW has become the perfect personality statement. After all, if brands help us define who we are, no brand does that better than a BMW.

Secrets of success

- *Definition.* A BMW defines its owner. It says the owner is likely to be wealthy, adrenalin-seeking, competitive, driven and looking for an 'ultimate' experience.
- *Focus.* Although BMW has made the odd mistake of moving too far up- or downmarket, it has generally kept the kind of tight focus necessary for any corporate brand.

Fact file

Website: www.bmw.com

Founded: 1916

Country of origin: Germany

Brand fact 1: The BMW Group currently has 23 production and assembly plants in seven countries.

Brand fact 2: The BMW Group received the Best Innovator Award in 2004 as judged by the publication *Wirtschaftswoche* and management consultants A.T. Kearney.

Brand fact 3: In 2002, the BMW Group was the first European company to receive the Outstanding Corporate Innovator (OCI) Award in the United States.

---

46 Gucci: the exclusive brand

Every brand has to be sensitive to changing trends, but when you are a fashion brand you are even more vulnerable.

Founded by Guccio Gucci in 1920, Gucci was originally a saddlery. Over the decades it broadened into a wider-ranging luxury brand, and in the 1960s it found favour with the emerging international jet set. In particular, Gucci handbags with bamboo handles became a must-have accessory.

However, by the 1980s Gucci was looking old and tired. Furthermore, the Italian family behind the House of Gucci was suffering from infighting and embroiled in scandal and even a murder charge.

Although this resulted in lots of negative press, the real problem in terms of branding was that the company had diversified too far. By 1990 the once-exclusive brand was now licensed to more than 22,000 products. The Gucci name had been spread so thin it had little meaning.

However, 1990 was also the year the Texan designer Tom Ford joined the company as the womenswear designer. Four years later Domenico De Sole became the Gucci Group's chief operating officer. These two appointments were responsible for the brand's revival during the 1990s. Ford completely redefined the Gucci image, designing sexier, navel-baring clothes worn with ultra-high heels, and transforming dark and old-fashioned Gucci stores into light and airy modernist environments with chrome decor. Meanwhile, De Sole was re-establishing Gucci's exclusivity by limiting distribution to Gucci Stores and very carefully selected high-fashion department stores. Together, Ford and De Sole focused the brand on its core leather products and gave the Gucci name an edge through provocative, sexually charged advertising campaigns.

Today, thanks to the renewed exclusivity and focus, Gucci's brand value has soared into the billions, and the Gucci Group has risen to become one of the largest luxury companies in the world.

Secrets of success

- *Limited distribution.* Like Rolex and Harley-Davidson, Gucci has limited its distribution to increase its value.

- *Edge*. Gucci has regained its fashion edge by revamping its stores, by designing sexier and more courageously glamorous clothes and by creating provocative advertising campaigns.
- *Focus*. Gucci's previously ever-expanding range of goods has been streamlined to give the brand new focus.

Fact file

Website: www.gucci.com

Founded: 1920

Country of origin: Italy

Brand fact 1: Gucci is one of the world's leading purveyors of personal luxury goods.

Brand fact 2: In 2003, Gucci generated 1.5 billion euros in revenue.

Brand fact 3: The company manufactures and sources all products in Italy.

---

47 Tiffany & Co: the sparkling brand

The New York luxury goods purveyor Tiffany & Co is one of the world's most distinctive brands. To understand how it has become such an iconic brand we should look at the various things signified by the brand, namely:

- *New York*. Tiffany & Co has been based in New York since it first opened in 1837. Although there are now over 100 Tiffany

& Co stores and boutiques around the world, it is still firmly associated with its home city.

- *Tiffany Blue.* The Tiffany Blue Box is a design classic. The brand's signature blue was introduced by Tiffany's founders, Charles Tiffany and John Young, in its very first year. Dark blue is a colour signifying luxury, because it used to be the hardest and most expensive colour for painters in the Italian Renaissance to find and make (it was therefore reserved for depictions of the Virgin Mary). Tiffany's have never used any other colour as their signature.

- *Breakfast at Tiffany's.* The brand was immortalized in the 1961 film, starring Audrey Hepburn as Holly Golightly, a character who adored strolling the aisles of the store.

- *Jewels.* In 1878, Charles Tiffany acquired one of the world's largest and finest fancy yellow diamonds, uncovered from the Kimberley diamond mines in South Africa, weighing over 287 carats. The 'Tiffany Diamond' was worn by Audrey Hepburn in photographs to promote *Breakfast at Tiffany's*, and today can be found on the first floor of the Fifth Avenue store in New York. In 1887, Tiffany's even acquired the French crown jewels. It sells numerous items of diamond and other jewellery, working with high-profile jewellers such as Jean Schlumberger.

- *Celebrity.* Audrey Hepburn may be the most iconic face associated with the brand, but it has been associated with lots of high-profile figures. In 1861, Abraham Lincoln commissioned the company to create a pitcher for his presidential inauguration and, while he was at it, bought a Tiffany seed-pearl jewellery set for his wife. The company has also worked with high-profile designers such as Paloma Picasso and Coco Chanel.

- *Silver.* Tiffany's has long been associated with silverware and even supplied swords for soldiers in the American Civil War. Charles Tiffany's silver designs were recognized by the Paris Exposition Universelle in 1867, which awarded him with the Award of Merit – making him the first American to receive such an honour.

- *Gold.* Tiffany also has a reputation for gold, and in 1930 designed the gold America's Cup, the most prized yachting trophy.

Alongside these associations, which Charles Tiffany and his numerous successors have successfully strengthened in people's minds, the Tiffany's brand has also succeeded through inclusivity.

It is a luxury brand, for sure, but anyone can enter a Tiffany store. Although many of the products are out of the budget range of most people's pockets, there are always cheaper items that anyone could afford, and they are packed in the same tantalizing blue box tied with a silk ribbon.

Even the cheaper products have the same hallmark of quality and attention to detail as the brand's diamond-encrusted jewellery, so the brand's high-class status is not watered down through some low prices. Indeed, if you look at many luxury brands, they make a large part of their income through their lower-priced products. For instance, people buy a Gucci aftershave to find an access point into a brand they may otherwise not be able to afford. Likewise, when people buy a small piece of china or some understated earrings from Tiffany's they are entering into the same brand that owns one of the largest diamonds in the world. They leave the store happy to share something in common with Audrey Hepburn.

Innovation is another factor behind Tiffany's success. Almost all of the brands in this book are innovators, and Tiffany's is no exception.

When it opened in New York in 1837 its prices were non-negotiable. At the time, this was a policy unique enough to make front-page news. In 1845, the Tiffany Blue Book became the first retail catalogue in the United States. Another newsworthy innovation came when Tiffany was asked to redesign the 'Great Seal of the United States of America' in 1885. Its revised design is still used on every US one-dollar bill.

Now, although still a trailblazer in terms of many of its designer goods and accessories, Tiffany's is a brand about consolidation. It is well aware of what it stands for and seeks to confirm and consolidate that identity as it continues to expand. Following successful Tiffany boutiques in Tokyo and London, there are now stores in major cities around the world.

The brand remains as bold and strong as the blue of its boxes, and is in no risk of fading yet.

Secrets of success

- *Visual identity*. Charles Tiffany was a branding genius long before the term 'branding genius' would have made any sense. His 1837 decision to tie the brand with one colour – what is now called Tiffany Blue – is still applauded by brand experts today.
- *Innovation*. Tiffany's set prices and retail catalogues changed the way people shopped.
- *Luxury*. The Tiffany brand retains the same luxurious connotations it created in the 19th century. These have been sustained by working with some of the leading jewellery and accessory designers in the world.

Fact file

Website: www.tiffany.com

Founded: 1837

Country of origin: USA

Brand fact 1: Tiffany & Co's first day receipts totalled US $4.98.

Brand fact 2: Jewellery represents approximately 82 per cent of Tiffany's net sales.

Brand fact 3: The United States represents approximately 60 per cent of Tiffany's sales, while Japan represents 25 per cent.

- *Mythology.* Like the best brands, Tiffany has a rich mythology. Its associations with Abraham Lincoln, the American Civil War, the America's Cup, Audrey Hepburn and Charles Tiffany himself have helped ensure that the brand remains more than just the sum of its well-designed parts.

CHAPTER 8

People brands

I am not an artist. I am a brand.

(Damien Hirst)

If, as advertising guru David Ogilvy suggests, brands should seek to become personalities, we must also expect personalities to seek to become brands.

Indeed, the branded personality has been around for quite a while now. There have been global sports-star brands – Tiger Woods, Michael Jordan, David Beckham. There have been global pop-star brands – Jennifer Lopez, Michael Jackson (a brand in decline), P Diddy, Britney, Madonna, even Elvis. There have been global author brands – Stephen King, JK Rowling, John Grisham. There have even been business-leader brands – Bill Gates, Richard Branson, David Ogilvy himself.

In fact, we all, to an extent, have to build a brand identity for ourselves, that is to say a simplified version of ourselves designed to create a good impression. We brand ourselves on application forms. We brand ourselves on first dates. We brand ourselves to our bank manager.

The identities we create for ourselves never capture the fundamental, contradicting mass of human thoughts and emotions. They are designed simply to capture a side of us we hope will be attractive for a particular person or audience.

Some people, however, are better at this process than others, building and then capitalizing on their celebrity to become walking, breathing, multimillion-dollar industries.

48 Oprah Winfrey: the saviour brand

Oprah Winfrey's first major taste of fame was as an actress in Stephen Spielberg's 1985 adaptation of Alice Walker's novel, *The Colour Purple*, for which she earned an Oscar nomination. From then on, she has carefully built the reputation of Oprah Winfrey into one of the most successful brands in the world.

Her talk show, *The Oprah Winfrey Show*, which began in the mid-1980s, has been the key driver of brand Oprah. This was the perfect platform for Oprah's personality, enabling her to interact with her studio guests (celebrities, authors, psychologists, people with personal problems to resolve during the course of the show) and the audience in her Chicago studio.

Like all successful brands – from Coca-Cola to Budweiser – the Oprah Winfrey brand had a claim to authenticity. Before the phrase 'reality TV' even existed, Oprah wasn't afraid to let people into her own reality. Viewers knew what her house looked like. They'd been introduced to her husband, her chef and her nutritionist. They knew all about her yo-yo dieting, as entire shows had been devoted to it.

She fast became the voice of middle-brow America, as her annual income inched towards the billion mark. The show itself has received a total of 38 Daytime Emmy awards.

The Oprah brand, as well as being based on her charisma, was built on sound business sense. As producer of her own show she made sure it never dumbed down or over-sentimentalized, even when the arrival of other talk shows such as Jerry Springer and Ricki Lake moved the genre further downmarket.

In fact, her TV show enabled her to affect US law and highlight serious issues. In 1991, she called for a US National Child Protection Act, to establish a national database of convicted child abusers. Two years later President Clinton signed what became known as 'Oprah's Law'.

However, it is her business sense that really sets her apart. She has established a massive business empire under the name Harpo ('Oprah' spelt backwards), which not only produces her TV work but also has divisions in film (involving a partnership with Disney) and print media. Indeed, she has always been determined never to be tied to one media form. She has succeeded not only in cinema and television, but also in magazines with the launch of *O: The Oprah Magazine* (published by Harpo Print).

Oprah is a brand that translates well internationally, as her TV show has been syndicated to over 100 different channels worldwide, and her magazine is also sold in many markets.

Another indication of Oprah's brand strength is her Midas touch, adding value to almost everything she touches. Her domestic chef has published her own successful cookbooks. Her TV show's resident psychiatrist Dr Phil now has his own successful talk show. And when she launched Oprah's Book Club she managed to turn novels into bestsellers almost single-handedly, and gave various US publishers a significant boost.

As her media ventures continue to grow, the Oprah brand remains in good shape. She is unlike other US stars who appealed to similar markets – such as Martha Stewart and Rosie O'Donnell – in that her life has remained relatively scandal free.

In 2003, at the age of 49, she became the first African-American woman to make the annual *Forbes* magazine rich list, with a fortune of about $1 billion.

Secrets of success

- *Control.* Oprah runs a tight ship. Despite having various media interests, she keeps close control over all of them. This control has been most evident in her TV show. 'Nothing gets booked if I don't want it,' she once said.

- *Drive.* Oprah works hard, and survives on only five hours' sleep a night.
- *Human approach.* 'I am a human being first trying to speak to that human connection that is in all of us,' she says.
- *Inclusivity.* The Oprah brand may be primarily aimed at women, but at no one specific type. At a press launch for her magazine she said it was aimed at 'women who are interested in living their best lives, all races, all colours'.
- *Holistic approach.* Brand expert Hermann Behrens once said in an interview with the BBC that Oprah is a personification of a brand that has been built holistically. 'Every aspect of a brand affects its image and reputation, not just what it looks like on the outside. Consistency and being true to the brand promise is key to building a powerful brand, and Oprah has recognized that.'
- *Saviour.* If brands are religions, people brands are the prophets we hope will save us. Stephen Spielberg once said that every day on her TV show Oprah tried to 'save the entire world'. Oprah,

---

Fact file

Website: www.oprah.com

Date born: 1954

Lives: USA

Brand fact 1: In 1984 Oprah moved on to be the host of AM Chicago, which became The Oprah Winfrey Show.

Brand fact 2: In 1986, The Oprah Winfrey Show went national and Oprah was Oscar nominated for The Color Purple.

Brand fact 3: In 1996 Oprah launched her now famous book club.

never shy of big claims, agrees: 'That's really what I try to do in my life – try to reach out and save other people.'

- *Suffering*. As with their religious equivalents, we like to know our branded saviours have suffered. Oprah's weight problems are one source of suffering many women can identify with.

49 Jennifer Lopez: the superstar brand

According to Michael Levine, author of *A Branded World* (2003), Jennifer Lopez is 'the greatest brander in the entertainment industry'.

Since her first album, 'On the 6', was released in 2000 she has grown from what Levine refers to as a 'hottie singer-actress' to become a household name through 'a very carefully orchestrated branding campaign'.

She has used the two highest celebrity platforms – movies and music – to launch a mini-empire based around her name. She has set up the clothes company Sweetface Fashion Company, which manufacturers the J-Lo brand of clothes, and she has launched her own perfume ranges, the first of which was J-Lo Glow, which hit stores in 2002.

Although she has made some disastrous choices in her love life and movie career (choices that combined with her role in 2003's box-office flop *Gigli* alongside Ben Affleck), her gift for marketing never slips. For instance, just as *Gigli* was gaining bad reviews in the international press, she was appearing on billboards around the world as the new face of Louis Vuitton. By associating herself with the world's most popular luxury brand, she boosted the aspirational qualities of her own brand identity.

Aspiration is certainly the key to understanding J-Lo's brand power. Ever since her appearance at the Grammy awards in a much-discussed green, navel-baring Versace dress, she has become one of the most glamorous and publicity-friendly icons of the red carpet.

However, the power of Jennifer Lopez is not simply that she is glamorous, but that she offers a route into glamour. She has been very successful at using her music and film career to highlight her journey from her tough childhood growing up in the Bronx to the shiny celebrity bubble she now inhabits. The title of her first album, 'On the 6', referred to the number 6 bus she used to take to get out of the Bronx. A single from a later album established her as 'Jenny from the Block', where she told fans 'I know where I'm coming from.' Her fairy-tale role in the Cinderella-inspired box-office hit *Maid in Manhattan* also echoed her own life, as she played a poor working woman from the Bronx who ended up finding love and a lot of money.

Like the most successful brands she has created a story around her own name. Because of her troubled relationships with celebrities such as Ben Affleck and P Diddy (a phenomenal brand in his own right), the story is ongoing and remains interesting.

Brands such as Coca-Cola and McDonald's continually have to strive for emotional appeal and media interest. With a 'person brand' such as Lopez that is already built in.

Like Coca-Cola, she also has universal appeal. This is because she seems continually to straddle two worlds. She is always, in brand terms, somewhere between the streets of the Bronx and the red carpets of Hollywood. The first truly global superstar, she is the hyphen in Latin-American, the link between two cultures.

Because she has never been pinned down – as a singer, an actress, a dancer, a fashion designer or a businesswoman – she retains a certain mystery despite her massive media exposure. She has branded the Jennifer Lopez 'story' – which is in fact the old American Dream story of self-belief and aspiration – and in so doing blurred the line between her real-life and her superstar persona. As such, her fans always know a lot about her, but they can never know enough.

As a role model for young women she is a phenomenally powerful brand, as people who buy J-Lo jeans or wear her perfume are also buying into the Jennifer Lopez story itself. They may never be able to become superstars themselves, but by buying her products they can feel like they share a small piece of her success even as they fuel it.

Secrets of success

- *Message.* Jennifer Lopez has a clear brand message of inspiration and aspiration, which appeals to young women, minorities and anyone who dreams of superstardom.
- *Aspiration.* Jennifer Lopez has kept her brand aspirational through her associations with luxury brands such as Louis Vuitton.
- *The 'in-between' factor.* Because Jennifer Lopez has an identity that floats between singer and actress, the Bronx and Hollywood, celebrity and reality, she cannot be pinned down. This means people can project their own aspirations on to her, aspirations they can channel by buying into the Jennifer Lopez brand itself.

Fact file

Website: www.jenniferlopez.com

Date born: 1970

Lives: USA

Brand fact 1: In 2001, Lopez's fragrance and apparel line became an overnight sensation, bringing in US $130 million during its second year.

Brand fact 2: In 1997 J-Lo's profile was raised when *People* magazine named her as one of the 'Fifty Most Beautiful People'.

---

50 David Beckham: the icon brand

David Beckham is an excellent footballer, but his brand power is about much more than the soccer prowess he has displayed for Manchester United and Real Madrid.

Beckham, a man of famously few words, is also a brand that speaks to many people. He is a footballer, a fashion icon, a father, a sex symbol, half of a celebrity power couple. He is, in short, an all-purpose branded celebrity – a blank canvas on which people can project their ideals.

His appeal crosses gender lines, partly because he is one of the few sportsmen who openly embraces his feminine side. After all, Beckham loves jewellery, manicures his nails, dyes his hair and isn't afraid to wear a sarong.

The Beckham brand also travels well internationally. He is a hero in England and Spain, and his camera-friendly looks, ever-evolving hairstyles, ostentatious fashion sense and eye for a PR opportunity have also made him hugely popular elsewhere, particularly in Asia.

He has the knack of choosing the right sponsorship deals, which accentuate a different aspect of the Beckham brand. For instance, he has endorsed sports brands such as Adidas, youth brands such as Pepsi, fashion brands such as Police sunglasses and British brands such as Marks & Spencer.

Whether his brand value remains high after he has hung up his football boots remains to be seen, but at the moment he remains one of the most iconic, and certainly the most multifunctional, of branded sports stars. The allegations of an extra-marital affair with Rebeca Loos, and a below-par performance in Euro 2004 may have lowered his God-like status, but his brand power is still far above mere mortals like the rest of us. A 2004 survey conducted by the BBC found that 37 per cent of the British population believed that David Beckham was more influential than God.

Secrets of success

- *Broad appeal.* David Beckham appeals to a broad section of society. He is a gay icon who is also the face of Marks & Spencer's schoolwear. Like the most successful brands he is able to cross gender and cultural lines with apparent ease.
- *Brand association.* Beckham's brand value has been enhanced through his associations with other global brands, such as Adidas and Pepsi.

Fact file

Website: www.davidbeckham.com

Born: 1975

Lives: UK and Spain

Brand fact 1: David Robert Joseph Beckham has an OBE.

Brand fact 2: Beckham first signed a trainees contract with Manchester United in 1991.

Brand fact 3: In 2003 Beckham signed a four-year contract with Real Madrid potentially worth £25 million.

CHAPTER 9

Responsibility brands

With great power there comes great responsibility.

(Strapline for *Spiderman*)

No brand exists in a vacuum. It is always connected to wider society in some way. There is the connection to customers, the connection to employees, the connection to suppliers and distributors, and the connection to other brands.

There are sometimes wider connections too. Some brands impact on the environment or a nation's economy or, in the case of food and drink companies, a nation's physical health. These connections mean that brands have a responsibility. They are not simply money-making machines working in some kind of pure, soulless economy. They have an influence on real issues and real people.

Of course, not every brand acknowledges this influence. For most companies, 'corporate responsibility' is a token gesture that takes up less than 1 per cent of their annual spend.

For others though, responsibility is not a side issue but something that is fundamental to the brand. For these brands, acting responsibly isn't something that eats into profits but actually helps to generate them.

After all, in branding, perception is reality. The whole process of creating a brand is about creating a positive perception. Traditionally, that used to be about what a brand makes. Now it's also about how a brand *acts*.

Those brands that treat consumers and the wider world with visible respect earn the respect, and the custom, of a growing number of consumers. In a world where brands are blamed for everything from obesity to child labour, it pays to be good.

51 Johnson & Johnson: the crisis management brand

Johnson & Johnson was a major pioneer when it emerged in the 1880s, as the ready-to-use surgical dressings it offered were the first of their kind. The soft absorbent cotton and gauze antiseptic dressing was the first to put the theory of antiseptic wound treatment into practice. The products were designed to combat what the British surgeon Joseph Lister had identified as 'invisible assassins' – airborne germs that could infect wounds in operating theatres.

Before Johnson & Johnson had come up with their mass-produced solution, surgeons had used dirty cotton, gathered from sweepings on the floors of textile mills, for surgical dressings.

The Johnson & Johnson brand built on this pioneering start, launching other significant products such as Band-Aid plasters and Johnson's baby cream in the 1920s.

But the company's innovative approach didn't stop with the products. It also extended to the way business was conducted.

The company was one of the first to acknowledge its corporate responsibility. In 1935, almost 50 years after he decided to revolutionize surgical procedure, Robert Wood Johnson decided to revolutionize business with 'a new industrial philosophy' he set out in a pamphlet called 'Try Reality'. In the pamphlet, Johnson expressed the need for business to act responsibly to customers, employees and the community.

A few years later, in 1943, an elderly Robert Johnson published the 'Johnson & Johnson Credo', outlining exactly how these responsibilities should be applied to his business, and his management team embraced it wholeheartedly. The Credo – which suggested putting customers first and stockholders last – received massive attention from businesses and the public. In 1943, this was a truly revolutionary approach to business.

Over the years, Johnson & Johnson has stayed very much influenced by its founder's guidelines. Indeed, they were exemplified in two of the most significant incidents in the company's history, now referred to as the 'Tylenol crises'.

Tylenol was the company's own brand of painkiller. In 1982 seven people in Chicago died after taking the tablets. It turned out that the tablets had been contaminated with cyanide.

Johnson & Johnson's handling of the incident is probably the best, and certainly the most referenced, example of crisis management in corporate history. Rather than hide from the media or deny the responsibility, it recalled 31 million Tylenol bottles and enabled customers to swap tablets for capsules for free. It then introduced the tamper-proof, sealed packaging that is now used by pharmaceutical companies everywhere.

Although Tylenol's market share plummeted from 35 per cent to under 7 per cent straight after the crisis, within nine months it was back up to 35 per cent. A repeat incident happened again in 1986, and Johnson & Johnson acted equally effectively, remembering the Credo of responsibility, and the Tylenol brand has been preserved.

Today, the company conducts surveys to evaluate how successfully it has carried out its Credo responsibilities, and any failings are corrected. It's an approach that works, as Johnson & Johnson is now the world's largest manufacturer of health and care products.

Secrets of success

- *Responsibility.* The emphasis on responsibility is not just a way of dealing with conscience. It also makes sound business sense, as the success of the Johnson & Johnson brand – along with sub-brands such as Tylenol, Band-Aid, Neutrogena and Reach toothbrushes – testifies.
- *Philosophy.* Johnson & Johnson has one of the strongest brand philosophies, which was originally set out by Robert Wood Johnson (one of the original Johnson brothers) in 1943.
- *Customer-centric focus.* At the heart of this philosophy is a customer-led approach, which has helped the organization gain and keep trust in all its brands.
- *Crisis management.* Following its handling of the two Tylenol crises in the 1980s, Johnson & Johnson is now widely regarded as one of the best crisis managers on the planet, owing to its responsible approach.

Fact file

Website: www.jnj.com

Founded: 1886

Country of origin: USA

Brand fact 1: Johnson & Johnson has 110,600 employees in more than 200 operating companies in 57 countries around the world, selling products in more than 175 countries.

Brand fact 2: Johnson & Johnson is one of the biggest healthcare companies in the world.

Brand fact 3: The Red Cross let Johnson & Johnson use its symbol even though it discouraged others from doing so.

52 Ben & Jerry's: the caring brand

If brands were superheroes, Ben & Jerry's would be Spiderman. Indeed, the *Spiderman* motto – 'with great power there comes great responsibility' – could have been invented for the ice-cream company.

According to the company's ex-hippy founders, Ben Cohen and Jerry Greenfield, business is the most powerful force in society, and it should therefore have a responsibility for the welfare of society as a whole.

However, such grand beliefs weren't evident at the start, when Ben and Jerry opened their Ben & Jerry's Homemade Ice Cream Scoop Shop in a renovated gas station in 1978. They'd started the shop with a $12,000 investment, of which a third was borrowed, after they'd taken a $5 correspondence course in ice-cream making.

Ben and Jerry wanted to make a bit of money and have some fun in the process. They became known for staging events such as a free summer movie festival (projecting movies on the outside wall of the gas station) and Free Cone Days (free scoops of ice-cream all day long).

In 1980, they started packing their ice-cream in pint-sized containers and distributing them to grocery stores around Burlington, Vermont, the town where the shop is based. The following year, the first franchise store opened and they moved their pint-packing operations from a spool-and-bobbin mill to a larger location as demand increased.

The following year, though, Ben Cohen was starting to worry about being part of the business world, and he and Jerry decided to sell the company and move on to something else. Ben expressed his concerns to his close friend, Maurice Purpora, an eccentric artist.

'Business exploits the community; it exploits employees; it exploits the environment,' Ben said.

Maurice was quick with his response. 'Ben, you own the company,' he said. 'If there's something you don't like about the way business is done, why don't you do something different?'

This was the pivotal moment. Maurice's words sank in, and Ben told Jerry they weren't going to sell the company, and that they should pursue 'caring capitalism' (a term he still loves using today).

From then on the company was to be associated not only with tasty ice-cream and quirky activities but also with its social conscience. Here are just some examples of Ben & Jerry's 'caring capitalism' in action:

- *The Ben & Jerry's Foundation.* In the mid-1980s they set up the Ben & Jerry's Foundation to fund community projects. And this was no half-hearted, token gesture. The company poured in 7.5 per cent of its annual pre-tax profits. This meant that, from the start, the foundation was given at least $2 million a year (and the amount grew considerably).
- *1 Percent for Peace.* A few years later they established a new non-profit initiative known as '1 percent for Peace', with the goal of redirecting 1 per cent of the US defence budget to fund peace-promoting projects and activities. This has evolved into the organization known as Business for Social Responsibility, with national offices in New York and San Francisco.
- *Seabrook.* In 1990, Ben & Jerry's protested against a proposed nuclear power plant at Seabrook in New Hampshire with a billboard declaring, 'Stop Seabrook. Keep our customers alive and kicking.'
- *Festivals.* As well as rescuing the legendary Newport Folk Festival by becoming its sponsor, Ben & Jerry's held its own One World, One Heart Festivals across the United States, which highlight music, arts and social action.

In addition, Ben & Jerry's has subsidized its dairy farmers, has joined the American Children's Defense Fund, has campaigned against the use of bio-engineered growth hormones in food products and has partnered with Metro Community Investment, a non-profit organization dedicated to reducing poverty by providing economic development. Ben and Jerry have even produced a book (*Ben & Jerry's Double-Dip*, 1997) outlining their belief in social responsibility.

Ben & Jerry's product line has also been affected and influenced by its ethical stance. It has produced products such as Peace Pops and Rainforest Crunch to promote good causes. In the 1980s the company stopped making its Oreo Mint flavour because it couldn't stand doing business with tobacco giant RJR Nabisco, the Oreo supplier. In 1995, the company turned down the offer of a Japanese company to help distribute Ben & Jerry's to the Japanese market on the basis that the corporation had never supported social goals. Three years later it introduced the 'eco-pint' carton, the ice-cream industry's first pint container made from unbleached paperboard, reducing the use of a chemical process that leads to toxic water pollution.

Ben & Jerry's is also famous for its treatment of employees. The company regularly conducts Employee Work Life Surveys to gauge workers' opinions on pay and benefits, and general employee treatment. The results are then acted upon by the management to help provide an even better working environment.

Alongside a wide variety of benefits, which include daily free tubs of ice-cream, paid family leave and a stock purchase programme, there is also something called the Joy Gang. The Joy Gang is arguably the most eccentric feature of the most eccentric of global brands. It is given $20,000 a year and its official aim, according to the company, is 'to keep work from becoming a grind through a combination of organized events, special purchases and even guerrilla tactics of sorts – like an impromptu assault with a hidden squirt gun'. The Joy Gang is made up of volunteers from the company and meets during lunch-breaks to plan activities and events such as a massage and pizza day, National Clash Dressing Day (where employees won awards for the worst outfits) and even a Barry Manilow Appreciation Day. There are also 'Joy Grants' to fund purchases such as a hot cocoa machine.

The belief in employees is linked to Ben & Jerry's belief in social care, and many workers are attracted to the company on those grounds.

Not only does Ben & Jerry's value the opinion of its employees, it also trusts its customers enough to let them decide its products. Indeed, many of its most popular flavours, such as Cherry Garcia (named after Grateful Dead guitarist Jerry Garcia) and Chunky Monkey (banana ice-cream with walnuts and chocolate chunks), were suggested by customers.

The incredible thing about Ben & Jerry's isn't that it started off as a small, quirky company. After all, many major brands *started* that way. No, what's incredible is that Ben & Jerry's has retained its eccentric appeal and ethical principles even as it has grown.

Even when it advertises for a new boss, the company does it in style – with a 'Yo! I'm Your CEO!' contest, inviting 100-word applications from anyone interested in the job (first prize) or in a lifetime supply of ice-cream (second prize). The 1995 winner was former McKinsey & Co partner Robert Holland, who submitted a poem (even their job applications are worthy of media attention).

The founders have moved into a more backseat role as new CEOs have come and gone, and the company was acquired by Unilever in 2000, but the core values of Ben & Jerry's remain undented. Indeed, in 2002, the company partnered with the Dave Matthews Band and SaveOurEnvironment.org in a campaign to fight global warming.

Indeed, Unilever seems to understand that to deprive Ben & Jerry's of its 'caring capitalism' image would be to strip the brand of its core identities. 'Ben & Jerry's is an incredibly strong brand name with a unique consumer message,' said Unilever, when the $326 million takeover deal was announced. 'We are determined to nurture its commitment to community values.'

Although the brand may have lost some of its hippy connotations by becoming part of a massive conglomerate, most of its employees and customers remain happy. Ben & Jerry's has shown that big doesn't have to be bad and that 'corporate responsibility' is more than just a buzz-term to stick in your company brochure.

Secrets of success

- *Personality.* Ben & Jerry's has a hippy personality. It might be ageing a lot better than a lot of hippies, and it's certainly a hell of a lot richer, but it has shown that well-meant values of peace and love can be turned into practice through business.
- *Thinking beyond products.* With a Nike or a Coca-Cola or a Benetton, thinking beyond products means spending the equivalent of the gross domestic product of a small country and ploughing it into advertising. With Ben & Jerry's, it means allowing consumers to become ambassadors for social values simply by buying ice-cream.
- *Principles.* Ben Cohen and Jerry Greenfield had principles that extended beyond economic law. In fact, they often made decisions that went against economic principles for the sake of preserving the ethics of the brand.
- *Employees.* Part of the company's mission states that, as well as making profits, Ben & Jerry's must also create 'career opportunities and financial rewards for our employees'. This focus on employee care has earned it lots of awards and recognition from the media. It has made *Fortune*'s Best Companies for Minorities List, and was one of *Working Mother* magazine's Best Companies for Working Mothers.
- *Philanthropy.* The company gives 7.5 per cent of its pre-tax profits to charitable organizations, compared to 1 per cent by the average US corporation. This is shared between The Ben & Jerry's Foundation, Corporate Giving (where the company matches

each dollar given by employees to a charity) and Community Action Teams (made up of employees organizing community service work for the local community, and contributing to groups such as US Fish and Wildlife).

- *Fun.* Ben & Jerry's is a fun brand, from the Joy Gang to ice-cream flavours such as Phish Food, Chubby Hubby, The Full Vermonty and KaBerry KaBOOM!
- *Tough action.* Like Spiderman, Ben & Jerry's are responsible citizens, but they aren't scared of a fight. When Häagen-Dazs tried to limit distribution of Ben & Jerry's, the company filed a suit against Häagen-Dazs's parent company, Pillsbury, in its now famous 'What's the Doughboy Afraid Of?' campaign.

Fact file

Website: www.benjerry.com

Founded: 1978

Country of origin: USA

Brand fact 1: Ben and Jerry started off in the bagel delivery business, in a company they called UBS (United Bagel Service).

Brand fact 2: Ben and Jerry met in 7th grade gym class in New York.

Brand fact 3: Ben & Jerry's generated over 390 million media spots in 1999.

53 Seeds of Change: the goodness brand

Seeds of Change is good. Just take a look at its mission statement:

> To protect the planet's biodiversity and promote organic agricultural practices by offering a diverse range of open pollinated 100 percent organic seeds and products. To promote the benefits of organic farming and food. To help people and future generations improve their lives and enjoy wholesome, natural, pure, chemical free foods.

The word 'goodness' even features in the brand's slogan – 'goodness from the ground up'. This sums up the brand just as much as it sums up the products it sells (seeds and organic convenience food).

When the seed business began in 1989 it really did have to be built 'from the ground up', as the company had to build a growers' network from scratch. This meant finding farmers who were interested in growing seeds and then educating them about how to save the seeds they grew.

Such nurturing took time, but it paid off. The company is now the largest organic seed company in the world, with over 2,800 varieties of seed including fruit, vegetables, medicinal and culinary herbs and flowers. Seeds of Change has grown in accordance with worries about the quality of the food we eat. As more and more people demand organic food, many farmers are having to use organic seeds – and Seeds of Change is the only seed catalogue in the world that is 100 per cent organic.

Howard Shapiro, the vice-president of the company, is one of the leading experts on organic farming, and it was therefore a surprise to many people when the company was acquired by Mars, the confectionery company, in 1997. After all, when you think of wholesome, natural, chemical-free foods, you don't automatically conjure up mental images of chocolate bars.

To understand how this unlikely marriage happened we have to go back to 1992, when a young man called Stephen Badger turned up at Howard's Seeds of Change farm offering his services. Howard and his wife Nancy were impressed by Stephen's knowledge of food and his enthusiastic attitude to work, so they put him to work with the rest of the team.

Once Stephen was working there he revealed that he was, in fact, a member of the family behind Mars. Although Mars had never produced organic food, it had been looking for a way to enter the organic market.

Howard and Nancy were simultaneously looking for a way to reach a wider audience with their organic mission, and Mars provided the perfect opportunity. What is more, they didn't have to sacrifice any of their founding principles as Mars wanted them to remain 100 per cent organic.

However, Mars was thinking a bit bigger than seeds. Typically, it wanted to get the brand on supermarket shelves. So in 1997, soon after Mars had bought the company, a range of quality organic convenience foods were launched in key target markets (the UK, Scandinavia, USA, Australia and Ireland).

Over the past few years, Seeds of Change has become a trusted favourite in health-conscious households. Howard is still firmly in the picture, helping direct the Seeds of Change brand, and acting as the research manager of plant science for Mars as a whole.

The brand is now synonymous with the 'goodness' of organic food. As Seeds of Change says on its website, 'organic... [is] good for us, it's good for the planet, and it's good for our future'. And so buying Seeds of Change is, by implication, good for our conscience.

Secrets of success

- *Mission*. It's always easier to get inspired by a mission than a product. And Seeds of Change has a clear mission to spread the word about organic food.
- *No compromise*. Seeds of Change has grown 'from the ground up' into a well-known brand, without having to compromise its simple '100 percent organic' values.
- *Right time*. Seeds of Change arrived on our shelves just as the organic message was starting to be received. This is an age when we are very wary about what our food contains and where it comes from, but as the brand's website claims 'With Seeds of Change, you always know what you are eating.'

Fact file

Website: www.seedsofchange.com

Founded: 1989

Country of origin: USA

Brand fact 1: The company sells over 2,800 varieties of seeds.

Brand fact 2: All of the companies seeds are 100 per cent organic.

Brand fact 3: Seeds of Change won the Organic Food Award 2003 for its 'Fresh Cherry Tomato with Basil and Parmesan Pasta Sauce'.

54 Cafédirect: the fair-trade brand

Brands used to be shields. They used to protect companies from the truth about their products. For instance, in the 19th century they hid the facts about industrialization and mass production behind the smiling faces of Uncle Ben and Aunt Jemima.

In the 20th century, the trend continued. The brand identity distracted us from the realities of production. We didn't have to think too hard about the 'Made in Indonesia' label on our running shoes as we watched Michael Jordan telling us to 'Just Do It'. And we didn't have to worry too much about what our French fries were cooked in, while we had a red-and-white, curly-wigged clown skipping over our TV screens with a line of children following behind, as if he was the pied piper.

Consumers are wiser now. They check the label. They read the ingredients. They have made the connection that the money spent on advertising comes directly from their pockets.

They want brands they can trust. Of course they always wanted this. But now 'trust' isn't just about something that tastes nice or is good value or that won't give them food poisoning. For many, trust also means ethics. They want to know how the product was made, and that no one was exploited in the process.

To gain this kind of trust brands can no longer be shields. They have to be open and transparent, and shown to care.

One such brand is Cafédirect coffee. It was founded in 1991 by Oxfam, Traidcraft, Equal Exchange and Twin Trading in response to the collapse of the International Coffee Agreement two years before. This collapse sent coffee farmers into crisis, as coffee prices reached a 30-year low. Cafédirect therefore established a guarantee always to pay more than the market price for coffee, and to support the growers through a major producer support and development programme.

The result is significant. For a standard non-fair-trade jar of instant coffee, farmers receive only 5 per cent of the price consumers pay in shops. With Cafédirect the farmers receive 20 per cent of the purchase price.

On the face of it, this seems to run against good business sense. In a market as competitive as coffee, the economic impulse would be to cut overheads wherever possible. Those who still adhere to Adam Smith's principles of economics would argue that 'free trade' should lead to a kind of economic Darwinism. If the coffee farmers are in crisis, that's the coffee farmers' problem and not the responsibility of the manufacturer. Businesses should adopt a 'survival of the fittest' mentality and cut costs rather than raise them. Right?

You would think so. Or at least, you would think so if we lived in a world where rigid principles of economics always equated with reality, where perfect competition existed and where people could always be sliced into 'demographic sectors' in neat little pie-charts.

But the fact is, business doesn't work like that. As much as many economics lecturers would love to pretend that business is a numbers game where human emotions don't count, in reality it isn't like that.

This is a branded age. People buy products for not only their price or their contents but also what they stand for. Brands, whether they like it or not, are becoming politicized. This turns the act of shopping into an electoral process. Instead of placing a cross on a ballot paper, consumers are voting with their wallets, boycotting the likes of Nescafé and opting for conscience brands such as Cafédirect.

Obviously, conscience brands do better in some locations than others. In the UK, they are doing particularly well, as other brands suffer from bad reputations. According to the Co-operative Bank's Ethical Purchasing Index, UK consumers who boycott big brands for ethical reasons cost firms £2.6 billion in 2003. Between 2000 and 2002 fair-trade products rose by 90 per cent, according to figures from the Fairtrade Foundation.

In this new environment, relatively small brands such as Cafédirect can take on established category leaders without the aid of massive marketing budgets. Indeed, as soon as a brand embraces its political identity it is guaranteed a lot of PR coverage.

Indeed, Cafédirect has received a disproportionate amount of media attention because of its status as a champion of fair trade. A BBC documentary even followed the company's managing director, Penny Newman, on her journey to the coffee growers of the Cafédirect Machu Picchu Mountain Special, in Peru.

Such PR is priceless, but it wouldn't work if PR was the main objective. With a company such as Cafédirect the ethical aims are always at least as important as the financial or marketing ones. In fact, they go hand in hand.

Unsurprisingly then, consumers are valued not only as a source of income, but also as participants in the cause. There are even Cafédirect Campaigner Packs to help customers spread the word by giving talks about fair trade and Cafédirect.

And it all seems to be working. Cafédirect may still be only the sixth-largest coffee brand in the UK, but it is rising fast. Its sister brand, Teadirect, is now the fastest-growing British brand of tea. Cafédirect was also voted favourite coffee by the UK's leading consumer magazine, *Which?*

It is able to make such inroads into what many saw as a closed market by offering something completely different. This difference is not about taste or price or aspiration, but about empowerment.

The brand not only empowers South American coffee farmers by paying a fair price and introducing development projects, but it also empowers European consumers. In an age when people feel increasingly shut out of the political and corporate worlds, a brand like Cafédirect enables people to have an influence over both. And all they have to do is buy a jar of coffee.

Secrets of success

- *Integrity.* Cafédirect doesn't simply support good causes, but is actually a good cause in itself. And a profitable one.
- *Issue.* Cafédirect is a brand about an issue. And not just any issue, but one of the most important business and geopolitical issues there is, namely fair trade.
- *PR.* As a brand so inextricably tied to one issue the PR opportunities are automatic.
- *Empowerment.* The brand empowers farmers by helping them make a profit, and empowers consumers by enabling them to contribute to the cause and even to spread the word.
- *The new economics.* Cafédirect is one of the emerging brands that acknowledges the new principles of economics. In other words, it places business in the context of a world where people want to understand not only how much they are spending but also where their money is going.

Fact file

Website: www.cafedirect.co.uk

Founded: 1991

Country of origin: UK

Brand fact 1: Cafedirect is the UK's largest Fairtrade hot drinks company.

Brand fact 2: Cafedirect buys from 33 producer organizations in 11 countries which means 250,000 coffee growers are guaranteed a decent income.

Brand fact 3: Cafedirect puts 8 per cent of its gross profit back into the producer partners' organizations.

55 MAC: the cause brand

MAC (Make-up Art Cosmetics) is the leading brand of professional cosmetics. Since it was founded in 1985, it has grown through word-of-mouth endorsement from models and make-up artists and other fashion and beauty professionals.

Indeed, MAC is a brand almost single-handedly built on word of mouth. It originally shunned advertising, still resists gimmicky promotions and continues to put its products in minimalist packaging.

Its brand ethos is equally straightforward: 'all races, all sexes, all ages'. Within the fashion industry it has forged a reputation for quality products, and a commitment to society. It is against animal testing (and makes sure its ingredient suppliers are too). It promotes recycling. It does a lot of work for AIDS via the MAC AIDS Fund, which was set up in 1994. The Fund generates money directly from MAC products.

The brand's caring credentials and fashionable status give it obvious appeal for celebrities, and it has been endorsed by celebrities such as Mary J Blige, Lil' Kim, Shirley Manson and Elton John.

Now a part of Estée Lauder, MAC has increasing appeal among general consumers as well as those inside the fashion industry. Because of its association with models, make-up artists and fashion photographers, it has had something of a head start with its word-of-mouth marketing.

In his book, *Unleashing the Ideavirus* (2000), US marketing guru Seth Godin reveals that the secret of word-of-mouth or viral marketing is to target 'chief sneezers'. This doesn't mean running around to the chemist's and handing out flyers to cold sufferers. Godin says 'chief sneezers' are the people most likely to spread an 'ideavirus', which can be translated as a brand message.

If you are selling make-up, your chief sneezers are going to be models and make-up artists. As MAC started as a brand for professionals, these are its original and core market. It has therefore been relatively easy for the MAC brand to make inroads into the mass market, as there has been an automatic 'trickle-down' effect in the 46 countries where it now operates.

It would have certainly been a lot harder, if not impossible, if MAC had started as a brand for the general consumer and then tried to gain acceptance among the fashion and beauty elite.

Secrets of success

- *Low-key approach.* In a market saturated with glossy advertising, MAC built its name via word of mouth and, initially, a low-key approach to marketing.
- *High-fashion associations.* As the leading professional cosmetics brand, its high-fashion associations have been automatic. These associations have been reinforced as the company expanded into the consumer market – for instance, in 2002 celebrity fashion photographer David LaChapelle was responsible for the campaign advertising the Viva Glam make-up range.
- *Expertise.* MAC stores don't just have shop assistants. They have 'Retail Artists' who are, according to MAC, 'extensively trained to advise consumers on the latest trends, formulas and application techniques'. Additional services they offer are brow shaping, bridal sessions and false lash application.
- *Media.* MAC has always been popular among beauty journalists, who have given the brand a lot of valuable free PR.
- *Celebrities.* MAC deliberately targets celebrities who are – to borrow the terminology of Seth Godin – the ultimate 'chief sneezers' for any viral marketing campaign. As well as having high-profile endorsers such as Elton John and Mary J Blige, they also target VIP events such as the Sundance Film Festival, offering the high-profile visitors a variety of freebies.
- *The 'trickle-down' effect.* When celebrities and fashion industry professionals use and wear MAC products there is an obvious

'trickle-down' effect, creating desire for the make-up ranges among normal members of the public (or 'civilians', as Hugh Grant likes to say). The MAC website encourages this, by highlighting which celebrities are using their products. So visitors are told, for example, that celebrity socialites Paris Hilton and Nicole Richie (the daughter of Lionel Richie) love the latest MAC lip-gloss. Hold the front page!

● *Feel-good factor.* MAC not only makes consumers feel good about their looks, but also helps appease their conscience as MAC is a conscience brand against animal testing and funding AIDS projects through the fund it set up in 1994.

Fact file

Website: www.maccosmetics.com

Founded: 1985

Country of origin: Canada

Brand fact 1: The MAC AIDS Fund has raised over US $14 million dollars through the sales of VIVA GLAM, VIVA GLAM II and Kids Helping Kids greeting cards.

Brand fact 2: MAC is the leading brand of professional cosmetics.

Brand fact 3: MAC is now sold in over 30 countries worldwide.

Brand fact 4: Singer k. d. lang was the face of VIVA GLAM II, and the shade was an instant hit, selling over US $650,000 worth in the first seven weeks of its launch.

56 Hewlett-Packard: the employees' brand

Hewlett-Packard is known for a lot of things. Its printers and its computers are what make it world famous among consumers, but in the business world it is probably most known for its revolutionary approach to management. The open management or 'HP Way' now associated with the company started with founders Bill Hewlett and Dave Packard. However, it was more by accident than design.

Indeed, when the Stanford University classmates founded the company in 1939 – building audio 'oscillators' (electronic test instruments used by sound engineers) from a garage in California – creating a global enterprise was the last thing on their minds. As Dave later said: 'We thought we would have a job for ourselves. That's all we thought… We hadn't the slightest idea of building a big company.' They had no long-term business plan. In fact, they were laid back about the whole corporate side of things. They chose the name by tossing a coin (if it had landed on the garage floor facing the other way we would have the name 'Packard-Hewlett' on our laser-jet printers). They took on jobs as it suited them, without paying too much attention to researching the market. The technology itself was always the motivating factor.

Dave developed a new management technique – which he gave the sophisticated name 'management by walking around'. Every employee was treated as equally significant and an 'open-door' policy was established. This wasn't just a metaphor either: all the executive offices had no doors, and all the other staff worked in open cubicles. And this was decades before open-plan offices became fashionable. Staff could discuss any problems with the management team without the risk of reprisal. Hewlett-Packard was, without doubt, a great place to work. There were regular parties and picnics. Everyone called each other by their first names. Each member of staff had medical insurance and a healthy Christmas bonus.

This open, caring and sharing style did not lead to a lack of discipline or focus. The opposite, in fact. Everything and everyone was geared to one task: the creation of technologically advanced products.

At a time when most businesses were talking about 'market share' and 'corporate strategy', Hewlett-Packard was focusing on a broader picture. Take this 1961 memo from Dave to all HP employees: 'Our main task is to design, develop and manufacture the finest products for the advancement of science and the welfare of humanity. We intend to devote ourselves to that task.'

The company has almost single-handedly changed management thinking. Once criticized (by Richard Pascale, business consultant and author) for its 'terminal niceness', it has proven that being kind and caring to employees leads to a stronger company and ultimately a stronger brand.

As Mary Furlong, founder and CEO of Third Age Media, wrote in a February 1999 *Fast Company* article ('Fast Pack 1999'):

Companies need to be able to outlive their leaders. One of the great examples of this is the HP Way: People who come to work at Hewlett-Packard know what the HP Way is. They may not be able to name the current CEO... but HP has made the transition from being the inspiration of its founders to creating an enduring brand that has its own values and its own vision.

Since its successful merger with Compaq in 2002, Hewlett-Packard now has 150,000 employees in over 160 countries. It has a brand value of $20 billion. This is not simply a result of clever marketing. Of course, this has been a factor. Its recent hip advertising campaigns have succeeded in targeting a younger consumer market – essential for a brand capitalizing on digital technology.

However, it is also a result of the culture within Hewlett-Packard, as HP CEO Carly Fiorina told a management forum in Tokyo in October 2000: 'Ultimately, strong branding is not just a promise to our customers, to our partners, to our shareowners and to our communities. It is also a promise to ourselves... to show a positive, inspiring face to our employees around the world.'

Secrets of success

- *Technology.* HP's technology focus makes it a strong bet for the future. 'When you think of the categories that are growing, digital imaging and digital entertainment, we bring things to the party that no one else can,' says Carly Fiorina.
- *Open management.* The 'HP Way' is perhaps the most referenced of all company cultures. Its focus is on looking after and listening to employees through open management.

Fact file

Website: www.hp.com

Founded: 1939

Country of origin: USA

Brand fact 1: One of HP's first customers was Walt Disney Studios, which purchased eight oscillators to develop and test an innovative sound system for the movie *Fantasia*.

Brand fact 2: HP dedicates US $4 billion annually to its research and development of products and new technologies.

Brand fact 3: HP serves more than one billion customers in more than 160 countries on five continents.

CHAPTER 10

Broad brands

To become a successful brand, you need to narrow your focus. 'One product, one brand' is the mantra among marketing academics and theorists.

However, there are a number of brands that unite numerous different types of products and services under one name. These brands remain resistant to the relatively new orthodoxy. Such untamed brands apparently do whatever they please, entering into completely new product categories while keeping the same old name.

Yamaha sells motorbikes and electronic keyboards. Virgin sells pensions and rock music. Caterpillar sells bulldozers and walking boots. Much to the annoyance of brand purists all three of these companies enjoy huge success, despite being associated with different and often contradictory products in the customer's mind.

However, these apparently broad brands still understand the need for a clear identity. By focusing on specific attributes rather than fixed categories, they highlight the way brands can remain unified even as they sell widely different products.

57 Yamaha: the ignored brand

Pick up almost any book on branding and you won't find a mention of Yamaha. The reason is not because Yamaha is a failure. Far from it. Indeed, it is the world's largest manufacturer of musical instruments and the second-largest manufacturer of motorcycles.

The reason Yamaha is often neglected and ignored by brand experts and theorists is because its success is at odds with almost every established idea of how branding works.

Branding is supposed to be about focus, about concentrating on one type of product, about being the first in a category and dominating that category. If you want to extend the brand you should provide a variation of your product (as Coca-Cola did with Diet Coke) or launch a complementary product (as Gillette did with its shave foams) or contract your brand (as Toys 'R' Us did when it stopped selling children's furniture).

If a company really can't resist expanding into unrelated categories it normally conjures up new brand names, following the example of Procter & Gamble and Johnson & Johnson.

Yamaha, however, doesn't follow any of these rules. As well as motorcycles and musical instruments it also produces audio-visual products, semiconductors, computer products, sporting goods, golf carts, furniture, outboard engines, water vehicles, home appliances, industrial robots, speciality metals, machine tools and snow-mobiles – all of which are given the Yamaha brand name.

It is perhaps unsurprising that Richard Branson, the ultimate business rule breaker, is a fan of the Yamaha brand. After all, the Virgin brand is now applied to everything from airlines to pension schemes. Unlike Virgin, however, there is no high-profile celebrity entrepreneur to unite the brand's activity, and nor does it position itself as a champion of consumer causes entering into troubled markets.

Yamaha's success is a testimony to the quality and performance of its products, rather than through advertising or listening to brand consultants. It is this high-quality performance that manages to unite even the most diverse of products.

Secret of success

- *Performance*. At a time when many brands are concentrating on marketing at the expense of production, the case of Yamaha provides a useful counterbalance, illustrating that quality, high-performing products, not glossy advertising campaigns, keep customers coming back.

Fact file

Website: www.global.yamaha.com

Founded: 1887

Country of origin: Japan

Brand fact 1: Yamaha is the world's largest maker of musical instruments.

Brand fact 2: Yamaha motorcycles are number two behind Honda.

Brand fact 3: The Yamaha company also runs music schools worldwide.

58 Caterpillar: the rugged brand

Caterpillar was started in 1925 by two men – Daniel Best and Benjamin Holt – who had dedicated their entire lives to creating and manufacturing a better form of tractor. (They had improved on 19th-century steam tractors by pioneering track-type tractors and diesel-powered engines.)

The company expanded throughout the last century and has grown to become the world's leading manufacturer of construction and mining equipment, diesel and natural engines and industrial gas turbines. It is a name associated with yellow bulldozers and building sites.

Yet in recent years the brand has also become associated with something else – clothing. On the face of it, Caterpillar jeans and walking boots couldn't be further away from the company's original purpose. They initially seem to disobey every rule of brand extensions as they bear no tangible relation to construction machinery or any of Caterpillar's other heavy-industrial equipment.

But the move into clothing has been one of the brand's recent successes and has helped the brand break the $20 billion barrier in 2001. For the consumer, the extension made sense. Although it was an unrelated category, Caterpillar transferred the rugged, hard-wearing qualities associated with its machinery over to its clothing ranges. As a result, the Caterpillar brand has successfully maintained a singular identity while its products have moved into very different consumer and business markets.

Secrets of success

- *Value association.* By thinking in terms of value rather than function, a brand can maintain coherence while making very different products.

- *Business-to-consumer crossover.* Caterpillar, like IBM and Hewlett-Packard, is one of the many brands featured in this book to have built a name in the business-to-business market before targeting consumers. It is much harder to do it the other way around.

Fact file

Website: www.cat.com

Founded: 1925

Country of origin: USA

Brand fact 1: Caterpillar is the world's leading manufacturer of construction and mining equipment, diesel and natural gas engines and industrial gas turbines.

Brand fact 2: Caterpillar invested nearly US $670 million in research and technology in 2003.

Brand fact 3: Caterpillar employees earned more than 3700 patents since 1997.

---

59 Virgin: the elastic brand

Virgin began with Virgin Records in the 1960s. Originally it was a mail-order company designed to compete against record stores. It grew during the 1970s into one of the most credible record labels, becoming home to a variety of groundbreaking acts including The Sex Pistols.

Then, in 1984, Richard Branson's brand launched an airline, Virgin Atlantic. People were sceptical that an avant-garde music label associated with 'Anarchy in the UK' could apply its name successfully to transatlantic air travel. The scepticism quickly evaporated, however, as Virgin Atlantic became one of the brand success stories of the decade.

Over the next two decades the Virgin brand stretched into other areas: Virgin Megastores, Virgin Cola, Virgin Radio, Virgin mobile phones, Virgin Books, Virgin financial services, Virgin Vodka, Virgin condoms and Virgin bridalwear (under the obvious name, Virgin Brides).

Branson, the self-proclaimed 'people's capitalist', has created a brand not around a specific product category, but around a specific set of values. He has built a brand with a Robin Hood identity, taking on greedy corporate giants in widely different markets.

Not every venture has been a complete success. Virgin Cola and Virgin Brides were two instances where the brand didn't get it right. But the successes have been many, and often attributable to Branson himself. He is famous for putting everything into the promotion of his brand, and never misses a photo opportunity. Once, he even turned up to a media launch in a tank.

I met him in 1999. I was at a press launch for a company that had just joined forces with Virgin Sun holidays. The company was offering clubbing holidays to Ibiza and was there with Virgin Sun to announce the joint venture in the Virgin Megastore on London's Oxford Street. To conjure up the authentic Ibiza spirit on a cold February morning, there was an array of colourful performers, such as transvestite stilt walkers. One of them bent down and whispered something in his ear. Branson gave his famous grin and agreed to the unheard request. The next thing we knew, the stilt walkers had picked him up by his armpits and tipped him over so he was dangling upside down high in the air. The Branson grin remained heroically undented even as the blood pressure made his face turn scarlet.

I can remember thinking that there probably aren't that many CEOs of global companies who would be found upside down between a pair of 10-foot transvestites with a beaming smile on their face. Well, not in public anyway.

The next day the photo made its way into Britain's most popular newspaper, the *Sun*, along with a good deal of information about the joint venture. This was the perfect place for it to appear, as many *Sun* readers would be likely to go on a clubbing holiday to Ibiza. And without the photo, there would have been no story.

As Virgin Mobile's marketing director Jean Oelwang has pointed out, Branson 'lives and breathes the brand's values'. He will do anything to promote his company because, in a sense, he *is* the company. Branson and Virgin have become almost indistinguishable.

Of course, the Virgin brand is not just Branson's. Indeed, many of the Virgin companies, such as Virgin Radio, have been sold. Others have been franchises where Branson has agreed to lend the Virgin name to other business people. It is Branson however who has the talent for opportunism. Whether it is a photo opportunity or a market opportunity, he rarely misses it. He may not be as rebellious as the punk acts he used to distribute, but he has staged a brand revolution of sorts. After all, Virgin showed that a brand name does not need to be fastened down to one category. There has to be a unifying factor, but that factor can be about service levels, supporting consumers and adding fresh life to stagnant markets.

The Virgin model has now been replicated by other companies, such as the Easy Group, where a unifying concept ('low costs', in the case of Easy) holds the brand together even as it spills into different markets.

In *Brand Failures* I covered many brands – such as Xerox, Gerber, Bic, Harley-Davidson and Heinz – that have been unsuccessful in stretching their brands beyond their normal product ranges into other categories (such as Bic underwear and Heinz cleaning products). Virgin also features in that book, with its unsuccessful assault on Coca-Cola and Pepsi. Generally though, Virgin has proven to be a very elastic brand. By initially focusing on consumer-led markets such as records and airlines, and then revolutionizing them, it managed to build a strong reputation as a brand of the people.

Branson himself was another unifying factor. By being such a public face for the brand he became inextricably associated with the Virgin name. If people liked Branson, they liked Virgin by default.

One problem Virgin will face in the future is what the company will do after its charismatic leader departs. After all no brand, and no Branson, can live for ever.

Secrets of success

- *Elasticity*. Virgin has proved the most elastic of brands because it has shifted the focus away from product towards less specific notions of a rule-breaking, dynamic, consumers' brand.
- *Leadership*. Through his opportunistic eye for PR and marketing, Richard Branson has become a globally recognized brand in his own right. Having such a clearly visible leader has helped the brand's image remain cohesive even as the company has diversified.

Fact file

Website: www.virgin.com

Founded: 1968

Country of origin: UK

Brand fact 1: Virgin have created over 200 companies world-wide.

Brand fact 2: Virgin employs over 25,000 people.

Brand fact 3: Virgin's total revenues around the world in 2002 exceeded £4 billion.

Brand fact 4: Virgin has minimal management layers, no bureaucracy, a tiny board and no massive global HQ.

- *Market choice.* Generally, Virgin has entered markets where there is a considerable amount of customer dissatisfaction. The brand can therefore portray itself as a 'white knight' fighting for the consumers' interests.
- *Reverse thinking.* Ultimately, Virgin is always likely to be significant to the rest of the business community because it has reversed mainstream marketing thinking. It has reversed the idea of 'one category, one brand', and it has also switched the concept of 'first mover advantage' on its head. In a way, it follows a principle of 'last mover advantage', where it can learn from the mistakes made by established companies within a market, then coming in and doing it right.

CHAPTER 11

Emotion brands

Branding is an emotional process. It is about inspiring trust, comfort, desire, even love.

Emotions don't stem from facts. They aren't conjured up by selling a product on the basis of its price or function. No. Emotions are intangible, and are hard to pin down. It is hardly surprising that the brands that inspire the strongest emotions are equally intangible and difficult to reduce to a list of facts and figures.

Harley-Davidson. Jack Daniel's. Apple. Guinness. Zippo. Chrysler. These aren't simply companies. They represent something beyond business – something that strikes a strong emotional chord with consumers. They are brands built around myths, legends and individual philosophies as much as the mundane number-crunching of economics. The strong emotions they create are based on the attitudes they stand for as much as the products they represent.

These are the true brand alchemists, transforming a humble object such as a computer or a cigarette lighter into something worthy of devotion.

60 Apple: the cult brand

Computer owners fall broadly into two camps. There is the large camp, filled with people who want a cheap, functional PC and don't care too much who makes it. Then there is the smaller camp, filled with people who are passionate about the computers they use. They want a computer that reflects their personality, which provides a stylish and human face to technology. This is the Apple camp.

Apple is a technology brand like no other. Its computers, such as the legendary iMac, are design icons. It has taken the fear factor out of technology by giving it a personality.

It is literally a touchy-feely brand. You see an iMac computer or an iPod audio player and you want to touch it, or maybe even more. As Apple founder and CEO Steve Jobs once said of his curvaceous candy-coloured range of iMacs, 'they make you want to lick them'. You can bet Michael Dell never said that about his computers.

Apple is one of the few brands that genuinely inspire love. This love is a result of revolutionizing the way we view the technology sitting on our desks at work or at home.

Computers are crucial to 21st-century living. They are a source of information, entertainment and communication. They are now a fundamental part of most people's lives.

What Apple did from the start was match function with form. In its hands the beige and boxy PC has been turned, Cinderella-style, into something beautiful. It appeals to people because, in beautifying technology, it is simplifying it. Instead of having to consider modem speeds and random access memory, people can choose their computers on the basis of aesthetics. With the iMac, the choice was reduced to: what's my favourite colour? Should I go for pink or blue or graphite?

You see, unlike the owners of computer companies, the average computer buyer is not a technology geek. Apple was the first company truly to acknowledge this fact. Its products have therefore been designed from the outside in, with the consumer's perspective firmly in mind. The words 'megabyte' and 'hard drive' are not turn-ons for most people.

Apple, with its edible name and lickable computers, has understood that people choose brands based on emotional responses. A PC might be a machine, but it is not sold to robots.

Human beings are visual creatures. We like things that look nice around the house or office, even when we are not using them. In fact, *especially* when we are not using them. Because when you are not using a computer it is simply another item of furniture, so it might as well be pleasing on the eye.

Apple is often considered a 'cult brand'. According to Matt Ragas, co-author of *The Power of Cult Branding* (Ragas and Bueno, 2002), a cult brand is one that dares to be different and take risks. 'In cult branding, the management and marketers behind it are willing to take big risks and they understand the potential pay-off,' says Ragas.

This certainly applies to Apple, a company that has taken a risk on practically every product it has made. Some inevitably haven't paid off. For instance, the Apple Newton 'personal digital assistant' failed because – remarkably for an Apple product – it confused consumers. (Even Apple seemed confused about the function of the product and ran adverts with the strapline 'What is it?')

The risks that have paid off, such as the iMac and iPod, have more than compensated for such failures. And as a result Apple has some of the most loyal customers there are. In fact, the word 'customers' doesn't do them justice. Apple inspires fans and followers more akin to a rock group than a computer company. They discuss the brand in great detail on internet message boards. On the Kevin Roberts website (www.saatchikevin.com) one anonymous Apple user leaves the following post on the message board, while voting for Apple as his favourite brand:

An Apple computer is the first thing I switch on every morning and the last thing to be turned off every night. Apple's computers enhance my life, and make what I do possible in a way similar products by other makers never do. I am amazed at what Apple comes up with every time they release a product... Apple's story, their myth, their mystery is unassailable. I never cease to be fascinated. I wish them well even when they do things that exasperate me.

Exasperation is not unusual among Apple customers, according to Apple's senior vice-president for worldwide product marketing, Phil Schiller. 'There are strange people out there,' he says. 'And they seem to have a personality that has a strong affinity to attach to things like cults.'

Schiller receives around 300 e-mails a day and admits that some of the customers are swearing and angry. 'You have to deal with their rage and accept it and be proud that the reason you're getting this hate-mail with screaming and swearing is because they love your product, they love your brand.'

Apple products inspire strong emotions because the brand defines the identity of its customers. Just as owning a Harley-Davidson motorcycle says something about you, so does owning an iMac. It offers, like all cult brands, a collective individuality. People want to be different, but they want to belong. Cult brands such as Apple manage to satisfy both impulses simultaneously.

Fact file

Website: www.apple.com

Founded: 1976

Country of origin: USA

Brand fact 1: The late 1980s brought trouble for Apple when it refused to license its Macintosh operating system to would-be cloners.

Brand fact 2: Apple's iPods are the number one digital music player in the world.

Brand fact 3: In its first year, iTunes sold more than 70 million songs.

Secrets of success

- *Revolutionary products.* Apple didn't invent the computer, but it has revolutionized our perception of it, through user-friendly and attractive technology.
- *Anti-conformity.* The Apple ethos was summed up in a 1984 advert for the first-ever Apple Macintosh. Directed by Ridley Scott (the man behind cult movies such as *Alien* and *Blade Runner*), the Orwell-inspired ad depicted the IBM world being destroyed by the new machine.
- *Good looks.* Apple products are design icons and cause people to react and respond just by looking at them.
- *Emotion.* Brands are built around emotion. Products are built around function. Apple's computers combine both together.

61 Harley-Davidson: the masculine brand

Harley-Davidson does not produce the best-performing motorcycles in the world. It certainly doesn't produce the fastest. Or the cleanest. Or the most environmentally friendly. Or the cheapest. Furthermore, Harley-Davidson has made more than its fair share of mistakes. In *Brand Failures* I wrote about one of them – Harley-Davidson perfume, a brand extension that contradicted the masculine, rugged values associated with the Harley-Davidson name.

But, for all its shortcomings and failures, Harley-Davidson is a brand legend. Its logo is probably tattooed on to more human beings than any other. It has gone beyond a trademark into what advertising guru Kevin Roberts has called a 'lovemark'. People love the brand because of its associations: the Hell's Angels; Marlon Brando in *The Wild One*; Jack Nicholson in *Easy Rider*; the cult book *Zen and the Art of Motorcycle Maintenance*.

It is a brand of mystery and legend, which inspires a quasi-religious devotion among its customers. The throaty growl of the engine, the low leather seats, the high handlebars. None of these things improve the quality of the bike, but they give it character – a character that generates deep devotion among biker types around the world.

Personally, I don't like Harley-Davidson. It is not a brand that appeals to me. In fact, it doesn't appeal to a lot of people. Most brands with a strong identity are likely to alienate more people than they attract. In a way, that's the point. By choosing one brand over another, people are making a statement about who they are – and who they are not. The stronger the brand, the stronger the statement.

Brands are membership clubs. When people buy Prada clothes they are joining a designer, high-fashion club of Prada wearers, which distinguishes them from the saggy jean brigade they walk past on the street.

Likewise, Harley-Davidson riders may pass a Volvo on the same road, but the brands place their owners in separate worlds.

Secrets of success

- *Belonging.* People want to feel like they belong. By owning a Harley-Davidson, they can make a clear statement about who they are and associate themselves with other like-minded people.
- *Masculinity.* Harley-Davidson is the most masculine of brands, possibly because it is loved by members of the Hell's Angels. Sonny Barger, the founder of the Hell's Angels, says he loves riding his Harley because it 'gurgles down in your groin and gives you the feeling of power'. (Insert your own Freudian analysis.)
- *Mythology.* Harley-Davidson is a legend with its own mythology. It is therefore a brand where facts and statistics become irrelevant. Nobody buys a Harley for its zero-to-sixty speed. They buy it to become a part of the Harley myth itself.

- *Cult status*. If brands are religions, Harley-Davidson is a cult. It inspires extreme devotion, specific body adornment, bizarre biker rituals, a certain dress code and communal worship (Harley owners often ride in packs). It offers itself as part of a counter-cultural lifestyle designed to exclude as many as it includes. It is, in short, a legend.

Fact file

Website: www.harley-davidson.com

Founded: 1903

Country of origin: USA

Brand fact 1: The Japanese motorcycle industry was founded in 1935, as a result of Harley-Davidson licensing blueprints, tools, dyes and machinery to the Sankyo Company of Japan. The result was the Rikuo motorcycle.

Brand fact 2: In 1933 an art-deco eagle design is painted on all Harley Davidson gas tanks. This decision was made to stimulate the low sales numbers caused by the Great Depression.

Brand fact 3: The first Harley-Davidson dealer came in 1903. Now there's a network of more than 1,300 dealers.

---

62 Zippo: the longevity brand

Like Apple and Harley-Davidson, the Zippo lighter is a brand that attracts a cultish loyalty from its customers. Indeed, Zippos are collected by thousands of people around the world, and there is even a national Zippo Day in the United States when over 7,000 collectors get together for a Zippo convention.

How does a cigarette lighter become a cult? One answer, and the answer provided by Saatchi and Saatchi US chief Kevin Roberts in a September 2000 *Fast Company* article ('Trust in the Future') on 'trustmarks', is sensual design. 'You want to hold it, open and shut its lid, handle it,' he said. As with the original Coca-Cola bottle – another handheld product – the touchability factor should not be underestimated.

However, there is another key aspect: longevity. This longevity is emphasized through the lifetime guarantee that comes with every lighter and that is stated in its trademarked slogan, 'It works or we fix it free.'

The product is enduring in another way, as it has hardly changed since 1932, the year George G Blaisdell decided to design a windproof lighter that would look good and be easy to use. Over the years, the Zippo lighter has remained almost exactly the same, with only marginal adjustments such as an improved flint wheel.

This continuity means the Zippo is instantly recognizable, as every single one of the 330 million Zippo lighters that have been produced follow the same design principles.

Zippo, like most cult brands, has not needed to pay millions on marketing or celebrity endorsement to build its name. It has done something far cleverer. It has stepped outside of time.

Secrets of success

- *Longevity.* In an age of constant reinvention, Zippo stays stubbornly similar. Its classic design doesn't belong to any one period, and its lifetime guarantee promises the product will work as long as you need it.
- *Timelessness.* A sense of timelessness is going to be attractive to Zippo's main customers, smokers. After all, they are reminded of their own mortality on every cigarette packet. A brand that

stands for longevity and timelessness is destined to appeal. The illusory, subconscious hope is that the immortality of the brand might just rub off on the user of the product.

Fact file

Website: www.zippo.com

Founded: 1932

Country of origin: USA

Brand fact 1: Zippo has produced over 325 million windproof lighters since its founding in 1932.

Brand fact 2: Zippo took its first step toward diversification with the introduction of a six-foot flexible steel pocket tape measure in 1962.

Brand fact 3: The company produces the Zippo Lighter Collectors' Guide. Clubs for lighter collectors have been organized in Italy, Switzerland, Germany, Japan and the United States.

---

63 Jack Daniel's: the personality brand

In the book *Ogilvy on Advertising* (1983), David Ogilvy argues that brands are 'personalities'. The stronger the personality, the stronger the brand. He provides the example of Jack Daniel's as a strong personality brand and argues that personality sets the whiskey apart.

If you were looking to list the qualities of the Jack Daniel's personality you would probably include some of the following key words:

- tradition;
- Tennessee;
- quality;
- homespun;
- masculine;
- old-fashioned;
- unpretentious;
- confidence;
- genuineness;
- honesty.

The last four words in the list are not mine. They have been used by Sue Chapman, who plans Jack Daniel's advertising campaigns, to sum up the values promoted through the brand's marketing. In an article called 'Translating Brand Essence', published in *Promo Magazine* (July 2002), Chapman talks about 'an overall strategy... to build a lifelong friendship with the drinker'.

As part of this 'friendship' strategy, the Jack Daniel's people travel the world conducting focus groups and asking opinions. This involves showing photos of different people and asking 'Who are the Jack Daniel's drinkers?' Chapman says that, whichever country she is in, the response is the same: 'People everywhere pick the "rough, free guy," the Harley rider, Mr Cool.' That people identify the same Jack Daniel's drinker should not be a surprise. The brand has similar, although not identical, values around the world.

Global brands are built on what Chapman calls 'universal truths', which form the 'brand essence' – and this is where she uses her key words: 'for Jack, that means staying true to its unpretentious confidence, genuineness, and honesty'.

However, the interesting thing about Jack Daniel's is that the 'universal truths' are received in different ways in different countries.

The brand's market researchers have found that Germans value the quality of the product most of all, while Australians are attracted to its manliness, and in Japan the brand is an icon of cool.

Jack Daniel's is therefore a fully developed personality, with a variety of traits appealing to different people. The personal aspect of the brand is enhanced further by being intrinsically linked to a real individual, the original Jack Daniel, who first developed the charcoal mellowing process that sets the taste of the whiskey apart.

Jack Daniel's provides a lot of information on its eponymous founder. For example, we are told that Jack Daniel once lost his temper and kicked the old safe in his office. Initially, he suffered only a mild limp, but it got worse as gangrene set in. The leg became increasingly painful and infected until, six years after he kicked the safe, he died.

The Jack Daniel's brand, nearly 100 years after his death, remains in a much healthier state.

Fact file

Website: www.jackdaniels.com

Founded: 1866

Country of origin: USA

Brand fact 1: The Jack Daniels smoothness is created by a special charcoal mellowing process.

Brand fact 2: In 1895, a salesman with Illinois Alton Glass Company showed Jack Daniel a unique, new, untested bottle design – a square bottle with a fluted neck. The square bottle remains a symbol for Jack Daniel's quality.

Brand fact 3: Jack Daniel was the first to register his distillery with the government in 1866 which makes it the oldest registered distillery in the United States.

Secrets of success

- *Personality*. Jack Daniel's has a well-rounded personality that appeals to different people for different reasons.
- *Name*. Brands named after their founders have an obvious head start when it comes to adding personality. The company strengthens the association with its founder through various advertising and marketing materials. The result is that Jack Daniel the man and Jack Daniel's the brand merge into one identity.
- *Warmth*. People often say that the whiskey has a warm taste, attributable to the process of 'charcoal mellowing' that Daniel developed. This warmth is matched by advertising campaigns shot in warm, natural colours and accentuating the brand's Deep South 'good old boy' heritage.

64 Chrysler: the romance brand

According to Jeff Bell, Chrysler's vice-president of marketing, 'romance and expressiveness' are the core values of the Chrysler vehicles.

Chrysler cars, which began in the 1920s, still have something of 'jazz era' America about them. They conjure up nostalgic images of old Americana: F Scott Fitzgerald, Bonnie and Clyde, Clark Gable, gangsters and molls, guys and dolls.

When people define Chrysler cars they use adjectives like 'graceful', 'thoughtful', 'elegant', even 'dreamlike'. Unlike other car brands that constantly seek to redefine themselves and set new trends with every car they produce, every Chrysler car from the classic PT Cruiser to the sporty Chrysler Crossfire stays true to its original brand DNA, concealing advanced technology within classic design. As the corporate website boasts: 'the influence of the Chrysler brand's past upon its future manifests itself in every new product'.

Secrets of success

- *Emotion*. Romance evokes emotion, which leads to customers who are passionate about the Chrysler brand.
- *Technology*. Chrysler uses the most sophisticated technology, such as Mercedes-Benz engines, within its classic-looking vehicles.
- *Distinction*. Chrysler's unconventional old-American identity has helped, rather than hindered, its international expansion, as it helps the vehicles stand out in an increasingly standardized car market. It has successfully expanded into new international markets such as Europe, where it now sells over 100,000 cars a year.

Fact file

Website: www.chrysler.com

Founded: 1924

Country of origin: Canada

Brand fact 1: Chrysler was the largest tank factory in the United States and produced 25,000 tanks during World War II.

Brand fact 2: Chrysler says the PT cruiser defies categorization.

Brand fact 3: Beginning in July 2002, all Chrysler vehicles gained a new 7-year/70,000-mile warranty, which is transferable to subsequent owners.

65 Guinness: the timeless brand

Guinness is the leading brand of stout beer. It was founded in Dublin in 1759, and the heavy, dark-coloured drink is now interwoven into the fabric of Irish life and culture.

Originally, the key to its success was the use of high-quality ingredients, which not only gave the drink its flavour, but also helped it to keep a long time. The drink was distinctive, in terms of taste and looks, and this distinction helped the Guinness brewery to become the largest in the world by the end of the 19th century, having expanded its market as far as America, Australasia and Africa.

In terms of branding, it always had one natural advantage. There was nothing quite like it. Even as other stouts rose to be successful, the taste of Guinness remained unique.

It also adapted well to the age of advertising. In 1928, it ran a furious campaign in Britain (one of its largest markets) with the slogan 'Guinness is good for you'. The simple message was successful. For many years, a large proportion of the British public – even those who hardly drank alcohol – took Guinness for medicinal purposes. My grandmother was among them, and believed Guinness was a panacea that could be used to cure almost any ailment. When I was eight years old she recommended to my mother that I should have a glass of the 'black stuff' to cure a stomach ache. 'It will sort him out in no time,' she advised sagely. My mother was sceptical, and tutted disapprovingly. This was the 1980s, and Guinness was no longer marketed for its potential health benefits.

The direct message of 'Guinness is good for you' had evolved into the abstract 'Pure Genius' campaign, fronted by movie star Rutger Hauer. (In between, during the 1960s, Guinness had initiated the trend for surrealist adverts with its 'talking toucan' brand mascot.) Hauer, with his light-coloured hair and black suit, provided a visual echo of the product itself – black, with a white head. Another echo could be found in the slogan, where the word 'Genius' offers a loose association with 'Guinness'.

Such abstracted connections became the hallmark of what became one of the most significant campaigns in advertising history, ushering in a new, postmodern approach to marketing. As sociologist Dominic Strinati writes in his chapter on postmodernism in *An Introduction to Theories of Popular Culture* (1995):

> Once Guinness was supposed to be good for us. Now all we see is an actor, in some obscure setting, drinking a glass of Guinness without any positive suggestion being made as to why we should follow suit. Postmodern adverts are more concerned with the cultural representations of the advert than any qualities the product advertised may have in the outside world, a trend in keeping with the supposed collapse of 'reality' into popular culture.

The choice of Rutger Hauer was therefore appropriate, not only because of his looks and his dark, gravel-voiced performance, but also because he was most famous for his role in Ridley Scott's cult sci-fi film *Blade Runner* (1982). The movie, which showed a futuristic city filled with android 'replicants' and saturated with neon-lit advertising, is considered to be a postmodern masterpiece. One reason why it is referred to as 'postmodern' is its timelessness. Ancient temples, present-day skyscrapers and futuristic flying vehicles all inhabit the same place. Postmodern advertising also works by creating a space outside time.

Guinness advertising since the late 1980s has kept this sense of timelessness. You never know quite where (or when) you are in a Guinness ad. In one award-winning campaign, shot in black and white, galloping horses emerge from giant ocean waves rising high above surfers' heads. It is an incredible sequence of images, set to a pulsating soundtrack from dance music group Leftfield. The black-and-white filming and the classic look of the surfers collide with state-of-the-art special effects and a futuristic soundtrack.

Of course, none of this has anything directly to do with the product, but it has everything to do with branding. The timelessness of the ad rubs off on the brand. The message seems to be that Guinness isn't a product to be sold, but something that will always be there. Guinness is as eternal as the waves, and as powerful.

Such campaigns have widened the Guinness market and helped it reach younger drinkers while retaining its traditional customers. In the late 1980s, the average Guinness drinker was 47. A decade later the average age had fallen to under 35.

Today, Guinness adverts remain dark and mysterious and masculine, and continue to create archetypal and timeless images fitting a 245-year-old brand.

Fact file

Website: www.guinness.com

Founded: 1759

Country of origin: Ireland

Brand fact 1: Formed by the 1997 merger of alcoholic beverage Guinness with food and spirits company Grand Metropolitan, Diageo is the world's largest producer of alcoholic drinks.

Brand fact 2: Arthur Guinness started brewing the famous stout in Dublin having purchased a dormant brewery with £100 left in his godfather's will.

Brand fact 3: Guinness is not actually black but rather dark ruby because of the way the ingredients are prepared. Some malted barley is roasted, in a similar way to coffee beans, which is what gives Guinness its distinctive colour.

Brand fact 4: 10 million glasses of Guinness are enjoyed every single day around the world, and 1,883,200,000 pints are sold every year.

Secrets of success

- *Innovative advertising*. From 'Guinness is good for you' and 'Pure genius' to the art-house ads it uses today, Guinness has always advertised successfully.
- *Timelessness*. The Guinness product has hardly changed since the start of the 19th century. Its advertising builds on this longevity by creating literally timeless images. It has managed to avoid the trap of traditional, historical brands through careful marketing that places the brand outside of time altogether. Like Coca-Cola, Guinness is not a 'then brand' or a 'now brand' but an 'always brand'.
- *Distribution*. Advertising creates a brand identity. Distribution supports it. Indeed, before advertising in the United States, the company waited five years to make sure its distribution network was fully prepared.

CHAPTER 12

Design brands

It is no coincidence that many of the most successful brands are associated with great design. After all, branding is a sensual activity. The way a product looks and feels is important, because it is this that – more than any other factor – leads to the emotional attachment people have towards a particular brand. It is certainly not by chance that the world's most successful brand was built with the help of one of the most sensual designs in the history of marketing – the Coca-Cola bottle.

The brands that are included in this section are not the ones that necessarily use the most cutting-edge or innovative design. They are simply those that use design more than any other factor in the creation of their identity. Think of Volkswagen and you soon think of the radical shape of its most famous car – the Beetle. Think of Converse and you think of the iconic design of its unchanging basketball shoe. In these cases design doesn't just distinguish the brand identity, but actually constitutes that identity.

Design shifts from being a useful way to identify a product into an organizing principle for the whole brand. And in the first case in this section, IKEA, design extends even further – into a philosophy aimed at changing the way people live and into a mission that keeps the whole company driving forward.

Incidentally, many of the brands that fitted in the last section could have easily fitted in here. After all, design is a way of charging products with emotion. Apple, for one, is both equally an 'emotion brand' and a 'design brand' because the feelings inspired by the brand stem from design.

66 IKEA: the democratic brand

IKEA, like most successful brands, is about one simple idea. The idea, which has been detailed in Bertil Torekull's comprehensive book, *Leading by Design: The Ikea Story* (1999) is that of 'democratic design'. This basically means good-looking, highly functional and inexpensive furniture.

To understand the ethos of the brand, it is important to appreciate its history. IKEA began in the 1930s, as the idea of a dyslexic farmboy called Ingvar Kamprad (the 'I' and the 'K' in the brand name). IKEA grew by word of mouth in Sweden, where customers would often spend a day travelling to their nearest store. The appeal may have been partly due to low prices, but it was also about something else. The company's central principle of democratic design grew out of the context of depression-era Sweden, where Kamprad would use cheap materials to make simple and functional items of furniture.

As Kamprad always said, IKEA is a 'concept company'. In 1976 he even produced a manifesto or, as he called it, 'a furniture dealer's testament'. At the heart of this testament was a reiteration of the 'IKEA spirit', which consisted of enthusiasm, thrift, responsibility, humbleness and simplicity. This was more than just airy waffle. IKEA practises what it preaches, not only in its creation of good-value products, but also in its working practices. For example, IKEA is not big on hierarchy. The usual 'us and them' mentality is not allowed within the company's management culture, where all employees are referred to as 'co-workers'.

Although it had been a success in Sweden for decades, it was in the 1990s that IKEA became an international phenomenon. It has even been estimated that 1 in 10 Europeans born in that decade were conceived in an IKEA bed.

Furthermore, IKEA has managed to become big without sacrificing any of its founding principles. Consider, for example, this recent mission statement: 'To contribute to a better everyday working life for the majority of people, by offering a wide range of home furnishing items of good design and function, at prices so low that the majority of people can afford to buy them.'

Low prices are obviously one of the essential ingredients in IKEA's brand philosophy, yet remarkably it has never crippled itself by underpricing. Part of the reason is because of the sheer volume of sales for each IKEA store. Another is the sourcing of low-cost materials – evidencing the thriftiness IKEA has always been proud of.

IKEA's 'democratic' values extend beyond price, however. IKEA believes that customers should have as much information as possible about the products they are buying, as any IKEA catalogue testifies. Go to any IKEA in-store restaurant and you will find comprehensive information on placards, explaining how they source and prepare their ingredients.

As a keen believer in corporate social responsibility, IKEA uses many recycled products. It even requests its customers to return their product packaging so the company can re-recycle it.

This fits with the new emphasis on truth and conscience in branding, which is now viewed as a major key to success. According to an article on the website of leading brand consultancy Wolf Olins (www.wolfolins.com), brands that succeed are prepared to open up and tell the truth:

Truth means recognising that consumers' interest in your product may well extend beyond what's in the pack and how it got there and what the environmental costs of that journey have been. It means making that information available right where the product is served. It means internalising the demand for corporate social responsibility and delivering against it at every brand touch-point.

It is perhaps no surprise who Wolf Olins single out to be the ultimate truth brand. As they put it: 'a global consumer brand that has consistently played by these rules over decades is IKEA'.

However, while IKEA believes in the truth, it probably wishes some facts could be successfully buried. For example, newspaper journalists have unearthed quite a few facts about IKEA's beloved founder, including his former Nazi sympathies and drinking problem.

Such revelations have done little to dent sales. Indeed, IKEA is now stronger than it has ever been, and has a presence in over 30 countries. Like the early days, when people travelled all day to get to the store, going to IKEA is still treated as a 'day out' by many. Crèche facilities and in-store restaurants certainly make it easier for people who want to take a lot of time over their furniture shopping.

One of the reasons why IKEA has remained true to its founding principles is because it has stayed privately owned, and it has always been able to finance its expansion plans (rather than having to be part-funded by third parties). The brand has managed to resist being watered down or compromised. This is, of course, a good thing. It means that most people know what IKEA stands for.

The only risk is that, if trends in interiors radically change, IKEA could come unstuck. After all, at least part of its international success during the 1990s was due to being in tune with the zeitgeist. This was the era when people reacted against the over-the-top maximalism of the 1980s, in favour of a more sober and minimalist style. IKEA helped to bring the 'loft living' look to the masses with its range of simple, clean Swedish furniture. In other words, the world had caught up with IKEA. The worry now must surely be: what if the world overtakes IKEA? After all, once a brand identity has become so strong in people's minds, it becomes hard to adjust it radically.

Already, many design experts are predicting a return to more ostentatious design styles. The return of William Morris-inspired wallpaper patterns and opulent, Napoleonesque furniture in the background of arty adverts and rock videos must surely fill the company with dread. Trends in furniture may not disappear quite as quickly as those on the fashion catwalk, but they do eventually move on. Whether IKEA can stay attractive to all and not just those on a budget remains to be seen.

Secrets of success

- *Cost.* IKEA is one of the few brands that manages to be both cheap and respectable.

Fact file

Website: www.ikea.com

Founded: 1943

Country of origin: Sweden

Brand fact 1: When Ikea started Ingvar Kamprad used to distribute his products via the county milk van.

Brand fact 2: Last year a total of 286 million people visited the IKEA Group's stores around the world.

Brand fact 3: The IKEA catalogue printed 118 million copies in 45 editions (23 languages) in 2003.

- *Continuity.* The core brand value of 'democratic design' has remained the same over the decades.
- *Information.* IKEA tries to be as transparent as possible, giving customers detailed information about its products and business practices.
- *Difference.* IKEA has always stood out from the crowd. This difference has been there from the start and is attributable to what IKEA founder Ingvar Kamprad once referred to as 'the underdog's obsession with always doing the opposite of what others are doing'.
- *Concept.* 'We are a concept company,' said Kamprad. This concept was outlined in 1976 when Kamprad outlined what he called the 'IKEA spirit' – a rather sober cocktail of 'enthusiasm, thrift, responsibility, humbleness and simplicity'. The same 1976 document also said that IKEA is about 'asking why we are doing this or that... [and] refusing to accept a pattern simply because it is well established'.

67 Audi: the advancement brand

The person who established the Audi car company was a man called August Horch. Horch already had a reputation for being an innovative engineer when he created his first automobile in 1901. The next year he had his eureka moment when he realized the car would operate better if he used lightweight alloys to reduce mass.

In 1909, Horch decided to set up the Audi company ('audi' means 'listen' in Latin; 'horch' means 'listen' in German). To boost awareness of the Audi brand, Horch entered his cars into various motor-racing competitions, and won many of them. This tradition continues to this day, with a string of wins over the past few decades at events such as Le Mans 24-hour race.

In the 1980s it came up with one of the most effective slogans of all time, 'Vorsprung durch Technik' (which literally means 'advancement through technology').

Audi cars have always had a reputation for sleek, understated technology, and new models such as the Audi TT (launched in 1999) and the Audi A8 (2003) became instant design classics. The engineers and designers who worked on the TT apparently listened to old Jimi Hendrix albums while they sketched down ideas.

Like Sony, Audi has always understood the way to give technological products an emotional appeal, with an emphasis on intelligent aesthetic values as well as technological quality.

Ultimately, the Audi brand is about design, and the company has capitalized on this identity by establishing the Audi Design Foundation. The foundation provides grants and awards to innovative and underfunded young designers from all fields, to help their designs become a reality.

Fact file

Website: www.audi.com

Founded: 1909

Country of origin: Germany

Brand fact 1: Since 1932 the Audi emblem has been the 'four rings', which stand for its amalgamation with DKW, Horch and Wanderer to form Auto Union AG.

Brand fact 2: Impressive successes in the International Austrian Alpine Rallies from 1912 to 1914 confirmed the high performance of the brand.

Secrets of success

- *Innovation.* Innovative design, innovative technology and innovative marketing have combined to keep Audi at the cutting edge.
- *Performance.* Audi was the first to break the 400 kilometres per hour land speed record and the first to introduce a permanent four-wheel-drive rally car.
- *Safety.* Trust is important for any type of brand, but even more so for those within the automobile industry. Audi, along with Volvo, led the way in car safety, and was the first company to perform systematic crash tests.

68 Bang & Olufsen: the improvement brand

Not all successful brands are inventors. Some are improvers. The Danish brand Bang & Olufsen did not invent the radio. They just made it better. The first Bang & Olufsen radio in 1925 looked and sounded a lot sharper than it had before. In the 1950s and 1960s, the brand moved beyond radios to all types of audio equipment, transforming the market by improving both form and function.

Today, its name is still associated with advanced style and technology. The company has never had to compromise its standards because it has remained independent. It can therefore spend as much time as necessary to develop its state-of-the-art products, such as its BeoSystem hi-fis and BeoLab speakers, some of which were over two decades in development.

The objective is simple: the very best sound quality, from aesthetically pleasing designs. This emphasis on elegant design has even been recognized by the Museum of Modern Art in New York, which has 21 Bang & Olufsen products in its design collection.

A classic art deco logo (which dates back to 1932) and subtle, understated advertising match the sophisticated identity of the brand, helping it sustain a reputation among design lovers the world over.

Secrets of success

- *Improvement.* Bang & Olufsen does not want to introduce new types of products. It just wants to improve old ones through its marriage of acoustic and aesthetic excellence.
- *Independence.* By staying independent, Bang & Olufsen has managed to move at its own pace, without being pressured by anxious third parties into releasing products too early. The approach not only creates better hi-fi systems, but it also earns the company an annual income of $1 billion.

Fact file

Website: www.bang-olufsen.com

Founded: 1925

Country of origin: Denmark

Brand fact 1: Bang & Olufsen has approximately 1,770 stores in more than 40 countries.

Brand fact 2: The UK and Denmark are the brand's largest markets.

Brand fact 3: Nearly all of the companies products are made in Denmark.

69 Muji: the minimal brand

Throughout most of marketing history, the main principle behind creating a brand has been to stand out from the crowd. The idea of most brands is therefore to take a product – or a range of products – and to exaggerate or overemphasize the values of that product through the brand message, a message communicated via advertising, shiny packaging and look-at-me-style publicity.

Yet, somewhere towards the end of the last century, branding hit a point of crisis. With an ever-wider range of companies and products to choose from, the consumer became overloaded with look-at-me messages. As a result, many became tired and cynical of the bloated claims and promises that were made about relatively standard products. A woollen sweater, despite what some advertisers would have us believe, does not equate with a vision of racial harmony. Neither will drinking a fizzy drink make for a happier society. Brands seemed to believe that the only way to stand out was to amplify their message to such an extent that the advertising and the product started to bear little relation to each other.

However, not all brands have turned up the volume. Some have realized that inflated brand messages ultimately frustrate the increasingly disillusioned consumer. These brands have turned the attention back towards the product itself, and have opted for understatement rather than exaggerated or abstract adverts about people joining hands or singing in the street or making the world a better place by drinking a flavoured carbonated water or by wearing a scarf.

The archetypal, understated brand hails from Japan. It is Muji, the retail store that sells a wide range of inexpensive, minimalist products including stationery, face and body products, furniture, clothes and kitchen equipment.

The clue behind the brand's identity lies in its name. 'Muji' is an abbreviation of 'Mujirushi Ryohin' (its original name), which means 'no-label quality goods'. In other words, it's the anti-brand, a brand that reverses the logic of marketing. It doesn't scream out 'bigger' or 'best' from the shelves. In fact, it doesn't scream anything. Products are often packaged in brown cardboard containers with the uniform Muji label stuck on to let you know the price.

In a world where most brands, metaphorically speaking, are communicating through a loud-hailer, Muji whispers its message to customers. And that message is kept firmly focused on the products themselves. Indeed, Muji goods are inspected thoroughly throughout the production process to ensure their quality. After all, a company that doesn't blow money on excessive, overblown marketing campaigns can devote a greater portion of its budget to production costs.

This simple, stripped-down formula has stayed with the brand from its conception in 1980. In 1989, the Ryohin Keikaku Company was set up to market the concept internationally (this was when the 'Muji' abbreviation first arrived). In 1991, the brand stepped – or should that be tiptoed? – into the European market, with the opening of a London store. The British style magazine *The Face* compared the brand to 'a kind of funky Marks & Spencer'.

The brand has now spread across Europe and Asia, and has opened a 3,000-square-metre flagship store in its home town, Tokyo. Internationally, Muji is a success, but in Japan it is a phenomenon, with nearly 300 stores. The success has been largely a result of word of mouth, with customers impressed by the products and the simple shopping experience of the Muji stores.

One of the reasons why the products retain their appeal has to do with Muji's advisory board. The official brand advisers include a wide range of high-profile Japanese designers, such as leading fashion designer Yohji Yamamoto, who help to oversee the brand's direction.

As Muji is a brand that has never attempted to patronize its customers through grandiose marketing tactics, it is fitting that it now also allows customers to have a say in the product design process. Whereas most commercial websites are tools for marketing, Muji has converted its Japanese website, MujiNet, into a tool for design and production. The site has enabled customers to be included in the consultation process for a variety of recent products.

Secrets of success

- *Style*. Muji is, undoubtedly, a stylish brand (its clothes have even been exhibited at London and Milan's fashion weeks), but it is a style that stems from the product, rather than trendy marketing.
- *Simplicity*. As the design journalist Stephen Bayley wrote in an article for the British newspaper *The Times*, 'Muji is the ordinary thing, done extraordinarily well'.
- *Value*. Without spending most of its money on advertising, Muji can keep prices low while still ensuring quality products.
- *Uniformity*. Muji may be the anti-brand in terms of marketing, but it does adhere to one key principle of all strong brands – uniformity. Its identity is consistent, and this consistency

---

Fact file

Website: www.muji.com

Founded: 1979

Country of origin: Japan

Brand fact 1: Muji's range offers over 5,000 products.

Brand fact 2: Muji's catalogue represents nearly all of its marketing expenditure.

Brand fact 3: One of the most successful recent projects was Naoto Fukasawa's CD player. The product sold 50,000 units in the first eight months, taking 0.6 per cent of the Japanese CD player market.

encompasses the design and packaging of its products, the layout of its stores and its simple brown paper bags branded with the Muji logo.

70 Vespa: the beautiful brand

From William Hoover to Bill Gates, the people behind leading brands are those with the foresight and confidence to break with convention: which leads us to Vespa, and an Italian aeronautical engineer called Corradino D'Ascanio. D'Ascanio was one of the great engineers of the 20th century, and the man responsible for fulfilling Leonardo da Vinci's vision of air travel centuries earlier, with the construction of the first modern helicopter.

A man of well-recognized genius, D'Ascanio was considered to be the only person who might be able to solve his country's transport problem in the aftermath of the Second World War. Italians wanted a cheap form of transport that could be driven by anyone anywhere, even on the many old and narrow streets that could be found in some of its towns and cities. The Vespa scooter was D'Ascanio's solution. Compared to the car and the motorcycle, the mechanics of the scooter were very simple. This simplicity was also evident in the straightforward design that enabled drivers to step on and off very easily.

Typical of Italian brands, function was matched by form. The Vespa was a beautiful, if modest, machine and its beauty was quickly recognized by fashion photographers and film directors. For instance, the Vespa had a key supporting role in the 1953 cinematic masterpiece *Roman Holiday*, with the young lovers played by Gregory Peck and Audrey Hepburn weaving through the streets of Rome.

Vespa's design credentials have since been recognized by various museums such as the Guggenheim and Le Centre Georges Pompidou, which have both housed Vespas within their design collections. There is even a Vespa Museum in the Italian town of Pontedera entirely devoted to the vehicle's history, a history that has seen it swing from being a symbol of Italian romance in the 1950s to the 1960s and 1970s, when it became associated with rebellious youth movements such as the Mod culture in Britain. The Italian postmodern theorist and author Umberto Eco was among those who noted the change in the Vespa's image. He said that the Vespa had come to be linked with 'transgression, sin and temptation'. This is an identity that has been preserved over the years and probably explains why artists and designers such as Salvador Dali and Dolce & Gabbana have wanted to work with Vespa to create customized scooters.

In *Cool Brand Leaders* (Knobil, 2003) the editors note that everything associated with Vespa is now officially cool, even the logo: 'The Vespa logo is in itself a design classic, and now can be found on clothing and accessories enabling everyone to buy into the Vespa legend. The brand ensures that everything that bears the logo must be of the same high quality, with a style combining practicality and beauty, with a touch of that indefinable essence of Vespa.'

It is that 'indefinable essence' – combining design, function, history and popular culture – that helps Vespa remain unique. Over 100 different Vespas have emerged since Corradino D'Ascanio rolled the first model off the production line 60 years ago, but a Vespa today does not look that removed from a Vespa in 1946.

By keeping to the same design principles (maintaining roughly the same shape and elements such as the round headlight and wing mirrors), Vespa has stayed a strong brand in people's minds. Indeed, the history and symbolic quality of the brand are contained within the design of every single Vespa scooter.

Secrets of success

- *Historical significance*. As the first scooter, the Vespa is a brand with historical significance, as it helped keep Italy on the move through dire economic times.
- *Style*. As with many other major Italian brands (Armani, Ferrari, Lavazza, Lambretta, Ducati, Diesel, Dolce & Gabbana), style seems to be contained in Vespa's DNA. It is this style that has helped turn it into a symbol of romance and youth culture.
- *Design*. The chic Vespa look has been preserved by a consistency of design, which means a Vespa can always be identified before you spot the logo.

Fact file

Website: www.vespa.com

Founded: 1946

Country of origin: Italy

Brand fact 1: In the first ten years, one million units were produced.

Brand fact 2: It is one of the great icons of Italian style and elegance, and with currently more than 16 million units produced, is well known throughout the world.

Brand fact 3: During the sixties and seventies, the vehicle became a symbol for the revolutionary ideas of the time.

71 Converse: the heritage brand

Before there was Nike or Adidas or Reebok, there was Converse, which was founded in 1908 as the Converse Rubber Shoe Company. Its iconic basketball boots eventually became known around the world, with a 90 per cent share of the basketball market by the 1960s. Although it is no longer seen as a sports performance brand in the same way as Nike or Adidas, it keeps its basketball associations through sponsoring street basketball events.

The brand has remained true to its original designs, and is loved by fans of retro clothing. It has broadened its associations with fashion design by expanding into clothes and by working with designers such as John Varvatos (who used to be in charge of Ralph Lauren menswear).

Perhaps Converse's biggest influence on brand history is celebrity endorsement. In 1915, basketball legend Chuck Taylor set the way for Michael Jordan and Tiger Woods by becoming the first-ever endorser of a sports shoe brand, paid to promote the Converse All Star shoe.

Today, it continues to sponsor basketball stars, such as Dennis Rodman. But the advertising campaigns nowadays also emphasize the heritage and history of the brand – the most recent campaign featuring Rodman was called, fittingly enough, 'The Heritage Factory'.

Secrets of success

- *Endorsement.* From Chuck Taylor to Dennis Rodman, Converse has always used basketball stars to endorse its shoes. It was also the first company to name a shoe after a player with the launch of the Chuck Taylor All Star in 1923, over 60 years before Nike's Air Jordan.

- *Heritage*. Converse is now one of the coolest heritage brands around, and retains a retro appeal by continuing its original products, such as the Converse All Star.

Fact file

Website: www.converse.com

Founded: 1908

Country of origin: USA

Brand fact 1: Introduced in 1917, the All Star soon led to the creation of the Chuck Taylor All Star, a shoe that became the staple of basketball players worldwide for more than 50 years.

Brand fact 2: The original 1923 canvas and rubber classic Chuck Taylor All Star have sold more than 750 million pairs sold in 144 countries.

---

72 Volkswagen: the longevity brand

Volkswagen has an interesting history. The brand, literally meaning 'the people's car', was originally operated by a Nazi organization called the German Labour Front (Deutsche Arbeitsfront). The company got off to a good start, soliciting the help of Ferdinand Porsche to design the first Volkswagen car, which was produced at the Wolfsburg factory. However, during the Second World War, the factory was destroyed in air raids.

After the war the factory and the car it produced were revived. Volkswagen benefited greatly from the post-war aid given to Germany in order to help its beleaguered automobile industry. When the company was handed back over to the German government in the late 1940s the company really began to soar.

The problem for Volkswagen was that its main product was a strange-looking small car with a roundish appearance. The car sold well in Germany, but export sales were initially slow – partly because of the car's unconventional appearance, and partly because of the Volkswagen brand's Nazi associations.

But then, in 1959, everything changed. Volkswagen commissioned the legendary US advertising agency Doyle Dayne Bernbach to help market the odd-looking vehicle. They decided to call it the 'Beetle', a name that highlighted the car's visual difference from the low, long, horizontal car designs that were popular at the time. The new name also provided valuable distance from the company's past (previously it had been sold solely under the name 'Volkswagen').

This was the key moment for Volkswagen. Its ugly duckling was now widely admired as a quirky, iconoclastic design classic that became the bestselling imported car sold in the United States.

In 1960, the German government sold most of its stock to the public, and in 1965 the company had grown big enough to purchase Audi (it would go on to acquire SEAT and Skoda).

However, the Beetle wasn't strong enough to support the company single-handedly, and in 1974 Volkswagen was nearing bankruptcy. It bounced back by launching more up-to-date models such as the Rabbit, which was the predecessor to the Golf. The Golf proved to be another classic Volkswagen model because, like the Beetle, it is a well-built car matching small scale with big personality.

What makes Volkswagen almost unique in its industry is that, with models such as the Beetle and the Golf, it has created cars that don't really date. A Beetle today has exactly the same silhouette as a Beetle in the 1950s. The Golf is also not a car that you can easily pin a year to. Such consistency of design and personality has meant that the resale value of Volkswagen cars is among the highest in the industry. It also means that unlike, say, Renault it does not need to launch innovative new models every few years in order to sustain its sales. It can simply update its old models with variations, such as the highly popular New Beetle Cabriolet and New Golf.

When Volkswagen has made mistakes – and it certainly has – it is when it tries to change its identity by producing large, powerful cars. When it sticks to what it's good at and concentrates on its timeless success stories and new models that conform to Volkswagen values, it can't be beaten.

Secrets of success

- *Personality*. As cars become ever more bland and homogeneous, Volkswagen continues to produce cars with distinctive personalities.
- *Quality*. Quality is an essential attribute for any car brand and – ever since its early work with Ferdinand Porsche – Volkswagen has maintained an image that signifies quality and reliability.
- *Longevity*. Volkswagen cars imply longevity not only because they are reliable, but also because many of the car models have evolved into classics that don't need to be completely overhauled in order to stay up to date. The shape of the Beetle is as timeless and instantly recognizable as a Coca-Cola bottle.

Fact file

Website: www.volkswagen.de

Founded: 1938

Country of origin: Germany

Brand fact 1: Volkswagen is Europe's number one car maker.

Brand fact 2: The Beetle has been in production in various forms since 1938, interrupted only by the Second World War.

Brand fact 3: From 1968 to 1997 a white Beetle with racing numbers and stripes named Herbie played a starring role in The Love Bug series of Disney comedy films.

CHAPTER 13

Consistent brands

Most brands act like teenagers. They are always trying to get attention with a wild new look or responding to the pressure of their peers with a worrying change of direction. Walking into a supermarket therefore becomes as disorientating as walking into a teenage party. Everything seems new and brightly coloured and unfamiliar, as products competitively scream their slogans from the shelves with bold letters and exclamation marks.

Some brands, however, act in a different way. Rather than panic themselves into a makeover every couple of weeks, they stay consistent with their original identity. Such consistency leads to familiarity, which in turn leads to trust. These brands aren't after the cheap thrill of the opportunistic purchase. They want to build long-lasting relationships and promise to stay faithful to their core values.

Coca-Cola, the world's most valuable brand, is also the ultimate consistent brand, as the slogan 'Always Coca-Cola' makes clear. Although its image has evolved over the decades, it has conserved the central characteristics of its brand – the 'secret formula', the red-and-white identity, the swirly letters of the Coca-Cola logo.

It is this consistency, more than the quality of the product itself, that generates love for the brand. After all, Coca-Cola's one moment of inconsistency – when it came up with an apparently better-tasting formula and called it 'New Coke' – was the largest mistake in the company's history.

73 Coca-Cola: the ultimate brand

Coca-based drinks did not start with Coca-Cola. In1863, a drink emerged that popularized the use of coca leaves for non-medicinal use. It was called 'Vin Mariani', a coca-based wine formulated by Angelo Mariani that became hugely popular among high society within Europe. Famous authors, poets, musicians and even royalty celebrated the wine. The legendary French engineer Frédéric-Auguste Bartholdi remarked that, had he drunk Vin Mariani earlier in life, he would have built the Statue of Liberty a few hundred metres higher. Even the Catholic Church was behind the coca-based drink; Pope Leo XIII was a big fan, and drank it daily.

The secret to Vin Mariani's success, with hindsight, was less down to the alcohol and more attributable to the coca. In Vin Mariani there were two ounces of coca leaves concentrated into the mixture. This meant that some wines contained over 10 milligrams of cocaine per fluid ounce. So Vin Mariani wasn't just tasty. It was addictive.

Twenty-three years after its conception, just when Vin Mariani was reaching its peak in Europe, a pharmacist in Georgia called John Pemberton came up with another coca-based drink called 'Coca-Cola'. In his version of Vin Mariani, he replaced the wine with sugar syrup, added cola nuts and a combination of seven 'natural flavours' that still remain a well-guarded secret, and marketed the product as a brain tonic. Although the drink was non-alcoholic, it originally contained cocaine.

The name 'Coca-Cola' was not the inspiration of Pemberton. It came from his bookkeeper, Frank Robinson, who now has the most recognizable handwriting on earth, being the basis of the brand's logo itself. However, while Robinson may be able to take credit for the name and logo, it was Pemberton who was responsible for the early rise of the brand.

The first year though was not exactly promising. Pemberton had arranged to sell his tonic at a soda fountain in an Atlanta pharmacy for five cents a glass. Despite the potentially addictive qualities of the drink, sales stagnated at six glasses a day, which wasn't even enough to cover production expenses. In other words, Coca-Cola was no Vin Mariani.

However, John Pemberton had one thing over his European counterpart, Angelo Mariani – a marketing brain. While precious little money was invested in the Vin Mariani brand, Pemberton understood the power of advertising right from the outset. The first advert for Coca-Cola appeared in *The Atlanta Journal* three weeks after the drink was invented. So whereas Vin Mariani was soon about to all but disappear, Coca-Cola grew steadily on the back of advertising. During the first two years this emphasis on advertising was overseen by Pemberton but then in 1888, only weeks before he died, he sold the rights to a local entrepreneur and fellow pharmacist (and future mayor of Atlanta), Asa Candler.

Candler officially formed the Coca-Cola company in 1892 and registered the trademark the following year. By 1895, he had achieved his expansion plan, as bottled Coca-Cola was now on sale in all US states. Bottling plants were opened at the turn of the 20th century, and throughout that century Coca-Cola was to grow into the world's most recognized brand, even without the aid of cocaine, and despite the threat of its expanding rival, Pepsi-Cola.

So, the Coca-Cola brand is a brand success story. Maybe it is even *the* brand success story. It is available in 196 countries. It has spawned other successful brands such as Fanta and Diet Coke. It is consistently ranked as the world's most valuable brand, with a brand value reaching $50 billion.

Could it possibly go wrong? Well, yes. It could. After all, no brand can live for ever. In many ways, the values that have made it so strong are now working against it. For instance, a brand that symbolizes the United States to such an extent is bound to be unpopular among certain sections of society in the Middle East. Indeed, a number of Muslim-backed alternatives, such as

Quibla cola, have seen sales rocket in markets where Coca-Cola has declined since the Afghanistan and Iraq wars.

The brand has also been under fire from health officials, who have highlighted the drink's switch from sugar to high-fructose corn syrup. It has therefore been linked to skyrocketing US obesity rates, second as a target only to McDonald's.

What the future of the brand will hold ultimately depends on the future of the market. If the rise in health consciousness increases any further, the Coca-Cola brand could be in trouble. And unlike other brands, it is not in a position to evolve with the market. As the unwelcome reception of New Coke proved, Coca-Cola drinkers want their brand unchanged or not at all. 'Always Coca-Cola' could end up being wishful thinking.

Secrets of success

- *Advertising.* Right from the start, as much money has been spent on the brand as the product (Coca-Cola was certainly one of the first companies whose marketing costs outweighed those of production).
- *Self-belief.* If one brand exudes self-belief then that brand has to be Coca-Cola. This confidence has shone out from its slogans. Slogans such as 'The Great National Temperance Drink' (1906), 'Six Million a Day' (1925), 'The Real Thing' (1942), 'What You Want is a Coke' (1952), 'Coke Is It!' (1982) and 'Always Coca-Cola' (1993) exude the ambition and self-belief of the brand. And as any dating coach will tell you, confidence is attractive.
- *Authenticity.* Coca-Cola has, since the Second World War, billed itself as 'The Real Thing'. Although cola drinks existed before, such as the alcoholic Vin Mariani, and although Pepsi-Cola started less than a decade after its Atlanta rival (in 1894), Coca-Cola has always been viewed as the most authentic cola drink on the market.
- *Continuity.* Apart from one major blip in the 1980s when it came up with the ill-fated idea of New Coke (which I covered

in some detail in *Brand Failures*), Coca-Cola has always kept a consistent identity. This was established during the long reign of Robert Woodruff, who was company president from 1923 to 1981, when Roberto Goizeta took over the reins. In fact, the company has seen only 10 CEOs in its long history.

- *Youth appeal.* From its infancy, the Coca-Cola brand targeted young people, even placing adverts in Atlanta school reports in the 1880s and 1890s. Later on, in 1931 it famously hooked up with Father Christmas for one of the most famous celebrity endorsements of all time, with an illustrated Santa swigging back from a Coca-Cola bottle.
- *US identity.* Throughout the 20th century Coca-Cola's image was all-American, from early posters featuring legend Ty Cobb, to welcoming back US astronauts with a large branded banner. During the Second World War, the company even sent supplies to US troops overseas at the request of President Eisenhower.
- *Aesthetic.* More than any other consumer product, Coca-Cola understands the power of its aesthetic. In 1915, the company held a competition to design a Coca-Cola bottle. The winning

---

Fact file

Website: www.coca-cola.com

Founded: 1886

Country of origin: USA

Brand fact 1: In the first year the company sold about nine glasses of Coca-Cola a day.

Brand fact 2: Coca-Cola has become the most popular and biggest-selling soft drink in history.

Brand fact 3: Coca-Cola is the best known product in the world.

entry was the curvaceous glass bottle that many consider to be one of the best commercial design objects of all time, and which is making something of a comeback in various places around the world. The simple red-and-white branding of the cans (which were introduced in 1955) is another indication of the company's emphasis on aesthetic quality.

74 Nivea: the continuity brand

Nivea, the first mass-market skincare product, was invented in Hamburg in 1911. Before Nivea's arrival, skin cream was an upper-class luxury used by the privileged few. The result of over 20 years of scientific research, Nivea was the first oil-and-water-based cream, meaning it could last a lot longer than the creams based on animal and vegetable fats that had gone before.

It arrived at a time when women were becoming newly conscious of their looks. The birth of cinema, the growth of advertising, and other symptoms of mass industrialization had led not only to more beauty-minded consumers, but also to a new 'product democracy' where previously luxury goods were becoming available to all classes.

Nivea (a name taken from the Latin for 'snow') promised both to beautify and to purify the skin, at a reasonable price. This clear product promise was matched in 1924 with an equally clear brand identity. In what is often referred to as the first major re-branding exercise in history, the deep blue tin with the bold white Nivea logo was created to make the product easy to recognize.

The visual identity has remained roughly the same over the years. And so too have the brand's values. Nivea is still a brand associated with high-quality, reasonably priced, mild and gentle skin care. Although Nivea has extended its brand beyond its original blue-and-white tub, its ranges (Nivea Visage, Nivea Hand, Nivea Soft, Nivea deodorants, Nivea body and Nivea soap) stay completely true to these values.

This consistency has led to a brand that people are loyal to and feel familiar with. It has so far proven to be a brand that not only has meant exactly the same thing throughout the decades, but also travels well internationally. Indeed, even outside Germany, in many of the 160 countries where it is sold, consumers believe Nivea is a local brand, so universal is its appeal.

Secrets of success

- *Consistency.* Since it was re-branded in the 1920s it has remained remarkably consistent, both visually and in terms of the purpose of its products.
- *Cross-culture appeal.* The Nivea brand is never lost in translation. Its simple promise of gentle skin care is understood and welcomed almost everywhere.
- *Visual identity.* Colour psychologists may now be able to tell us that Nivea's visual identity works because blue is the colour of friendship and loyalty and white is the colour of cleanliness

---

Fact file

Website: www.nivea.com

Founded: 1911

Country of origin: Germany

Brand fact 1: Nivea is Germany's fifth most valuable brand, behind Mercedes, BMW, Volkswagen and software giant SAP.

Brand fact 2: Since 2002 its brand value has exceeded US $2 billion according to Interbrand.

and purity, but in the 1920s Nivea's re-branders probably just thought it made a good impression. They were right. Eighty years later, it still looks the same.

75 Hard Rock Café: the memorabilia brand

When the very first Hard Rock Café opened its doors in June 1971, it offered a new type of dining experience.

The novelty of the experience wasn't based around the food or the service, but around a theme – rock 'n' roll. This theme gives the brand its unifying identity, an identity evident in every aspect of the restaurants from the music and the classic all-American menus, to the collection of rock 'n' roll memorabilia that decorates each venue. Each restaurant doubles as a 'living museum' boasting some 60,000 pieces of rock 'n' roll history (guitars, posters, gold discs, lyric sheets and so on) owned by the company. The memorabilia, which has a value of over $30 million, rotates from restaurant to restaurant so each Café continually has new pieces on display.

The formula has travelled well, as there are now over 100 Hard Rock Cafés in around 40 countries, with restaurants everywhere from Los Angeles to Kuala Lumpur.

It pioneered the concept of 'eatertainment', which has been less successfully imitated by the likes of Planet Hollywood and Fashion Café. No other company has found a theme as popular and successful as rock 'n' roll. After all, rock 'n' roll is uniquely at home in a dining environment (think of 1950s diners where people came to listen to Chuck Berry and Elvis Presley), whereas weight-conscious models and film stars aren't the most obvious restaurateurs.

Secrets of success

- *Original idea.* 'There's nothing like an originator,' Hard Rock's marketing director, Steve Glum, told the *Detroit Free Press* in November 2003. 'Other concepts kind of thought they could take our playbook and change the name, take out music and put in whatever. We've got something people can connect to, music and memorabilia.'
- *Tourist appeal.* By being a 'living museum' based in tourist locations, Hard Rock Café has gained obvious appeal among tourists who want the familiarity of a well-known brand. The famous Hard Rock Café T-shirts, boasting the name of the city where they were bought, add to the tourist appeal.

Fact file

Website: www.hardrock.com

Founded: 1971

Country of origin: USA

Brand fact 1: There are over 100 Hard Rock Cafes in over 40 countries.

Brand fact 2: The brand owns over 60,000 pieces of rock 'n' roll memorabilia including Jimi Hendrix's guitar and John Lennon's glasses.

---

76 Clarins: the expertise brand

Jacques Courtin-Clarins never planned to be an entrepreneur. In the 1950s, he was a carefree young physiotherapist helping to massage away the circulation problems of his Parisian patients. It was only when a number of women told him that the massage technique he had invented to help their circulation had also improved their skin's appearance that a light bulb flashed above his head.

In 1954, he opened a beauty salon where he charged people to receive the special massage technique he had developed. At first, he used standard massage oils, but he soon realized that he could make a more effective range using plant oils. The oils proved as popular as his massage treatments, so he decided to sell them for home use. The Clarins skincare range was born.

Steadily, and under Courtin-Clarins' leadership, the brand has grown to earn the trust of women (and now men) worldwide. The brand loyalty Clarins enjoys is a result of many factors, but principally its expertise. This expertise is evident in the products themselves, which are still the result of intensive botanical research. It is also evident in the form of the sales staff – the 'Clarins Specialists' – who are trained by the company, and who can provide free one-to-one skincare consultations. It is further emphasized by the product's subtle branding – the understated white-and-red packaging, scientific language and French translations all add to the sophisticated, high-quality image of the brand.

Fact file

Website: www.clarins.com

Founded: 1954

Country of origin: France

Brand fact 1: Massage oils were the first Clarins product range.

Brand fact 2: All Clarins packaging includes descriptions in French, highlighting its Gallic identity.

Clarins has now successfully applied the expert image it created through women's skincare into other complementary categories such as cosmetics products and male skincare ranges.

The strong consumer trust and loyalty created by consistent marketing and expertise have led to global success and a presence in over 150 countries.

Secrets of success

- *Expertise.* At every level of the brand – from research and production right through to sales – Clarins develops and promotes its expertise.
- *Subtle marketing.* Clarins does not go for over-the-top, abstract advertising messages. Its marketing is more subtle – such as the bilingual product cases accentuating its French heritage.

77 Campbell's soup: the uniformity brand

Campbell's soup is a brand icon. The condensed soup was first produced in 1860 by the Joseph Campbell Preserve Company. The company had originally been formed by a fruit seller called Joseph Campbell, in partnership with a tinsmith called Abraham Anderson. Anderson, however, failed to share his partner's grand vision and sold out to Campbell a mere four years after they had founded the company.

With hindsight – particularly the hindsight of Anderson's future relatives – this was a mistake. The company (which has now evolved into the Campbell Soup Company) has grown steadily over the decades.

Immortalized by Andy Warhol in a series of images painted in 1962, the Campbell's soup can must be one of the most instantly recognizable consumer products in the world. Why did Warhol choose to devote himself to painting so many of these red-and-white soup cans (on one canvas he painted 200)? According to the art critic Robert Hughes in *The Shock of the New* (1991), 'Warhol loved the peculiarly inert sameness of the mass product; an infinite series of identical objects – soup cans, Coke bottles, dollar bills, Mona Lisas, or the same head of Marilyn Monroe, silk-screened over and over again.'

Sameness is indeed one of the secrets of Campbell's success. Whether the tin is tomato, chicken noodle or cream of mushroom (the three most successful Campbell's soups), the packaging is absolutely identical except for the words 'tomato', 'chicken noodle' or 'mushroom'.

The logic behind the uniform design is simple. Consumers aren't buying a tomato soup; they are buying a Campbell's soup. The brand becomes instantly recognized and instantly trusted.

This logic has helped propel Campbell's soup into the position it's in today, with an 85 per cent share of the condensed soup market in the United States and 10 per cent of the total prepared soup market outside the United States.

Secrets of success

- *Uniformity*. Andy Warhol saw Campbell's soup as an archetypal symbol of uniformity and mass production. This sameness has helped to create one of the strongest visual brand identities there is.
- *Tough love*. Campbell's soup has had a series of tough-minded CEOs, such as David Johnson, who took over in 1997. He embarked on a series of factory closures and fired hundreds of managers. 'The competition is always plotting to kill you,' said the battle-hardened Johnson. 'You have to work harder.'

- *Convenience.* Condensed soup is a convenience product. The strong visual identity Campbell's created adds to this convenience. It is the perfect product for consumers to choose while they are caught in what psychologists have called a 'supermarket trance'.

- *Difference within.* According to Robert Hughes, Warhol was fascinated with 'the way advertising promises that the same pap with different labels will give you special, unrepeatable gratifications'. This is wrong in the case of Campbell's soup, which admittedly offers similar products but behind identical labels. Warhol may have recognized the hypnotic effect of a supermarket aisle crammed with rows of the same soup can.

Fact file

Website: www.campbellsoupcompany.com

Founded: 1869

Country of origin: USA

Brand fact 1: Campbell accounts for 85 per cent of all condensed soup in the United States.

Brand fact 2: It became a brand icon in 1962 when Andy Warhol used their imagery for one of his most famous artworks.

---

78 Budweiser: the targeted brand

Budweiser is the world's largest beer brand. When someone walks into a bar in the United States they are almost twice as likely to ask for a 'Budweiser' than any other brand. In some places, the word

'Bud' has even taken over the term 'beer'. Budweiser is one of those brands – like Coca-Cola or Levi's – that is somehow synonymous with the United States. Indeed, its US adverts are transmitted across the globe, creating one of the most uniform brand identities.

Yet, however all-American its image is now, Budweiser's heritage stretches a lot further east than New York. The history of the 'King of Beers' reaches back to 1876, and the Austro-Hungarian Empire. The small town Budweis – now called Ceske Budejovice and located in the Czech Republic – was the inspiration behind the name. Anheuser-Busch (the brewing company that still owns the brand) knew that Budweis had a brewing tradition, and probably also knew of the local beer, Budejovicky Budvar, which had been brewed there since the 13th century.

Today, Anheuser-Busch probably harbours a secret wish it had never used the name. Budvar beer is not only increasingly popular around the globe (and is the number one brand in the beer-loving Czech Republic), but it is also legitimately entitled to call itself 'Budweiser' in 42 countries. The Czech beer has even played about with the Budweiser slogan, calling itself 'the Beer of Kings'. Anheuser-Busch has tried to solve the problem by dangling money in front of the Czech company. So far though, the company hasn't decided to bite, and has proudly hung on to the name.

Fortunately for Anheuser-Busch, the world's best advertisers haven't been quite so reluctant to take the money. Indeed, if any brand has been built on advertising, it is Budweiser. Although it has only been a global brand since the 1980s (when it first ventured beyond the US market), it has managed to become a fixture of consumer culture almost everywhere.

Obviously a good distribution network has helped, but it's the marketing people who have turned Budweiser into a brand legend. Firstly, there have been the slogans: 'The King of Beers'; 'This Bud's For You'; 'True'. Simple. Powerful. Effective. Then there have been the TV ads: the oil-workers; the belching frogs (Bud Weis Er); the belching couch potatoes yelling 'Wassup' down the phone; the far-too-honest best man speech (for the 'True' campaign). Almost every ad campaign they've run in recent years has been a word-of-mouth hit.

On top of media advertising, there have been some cleverly considered, if expensive, sponsorships. Budweiser is a brand that knows its core audience. It also, more importantly, knows where to find that core audience: on the sofa, in front of the TV, watching sport. It's seen at the World Series and the Superbowl. In 1998, the company spent $32 million on sponsoring the World Cup. On every big occasion when you see beer-drinking sports fans, you are likely to see Budweiser.

But still, the brand cannot be complacent. It has a lot of competition from Miller and Heineken. The brand has been criticized for failing to conquer a younger market, a market it badly needs if it is going to remain on top.

Alarm-bells aren't ringing just yet though. The competition still hasn't found a way to steal the 'King of Beers' crown. Miller in particular has kept itself out of the running by diluting its brand with far too many brand extensions (Miller High Life, Miller Lite, Miller Lite Ice, Miller Reserve and Miller Genuine Draft to name but five). Of course, Budweiser has also extended its line (with Bud Lite and Bud Ice, for example) but it differs from Miller in that everyone knows what a regular Budweiser looks like. (If you don't, it's the one with the red-and-white label on the brown bottle. Just thought I'd clear that up.)

Budweiser's main competitive threat seems to have passed. In the 1970s, Miller High Life was fast eating into Budweiser's market share. Miller got within 20 per cent, before its line extensions went haywire. (It is ironic that Budweiser actually *followed* Miller down this rocky path, launching Bud Lite soon after Miller had come up with its own Lite brand.)

Now Heineken is the main global threat to the King of Beers, but still remains a long way off. Each year, more than 50 per cent more Budweiser is produced than Heineken.

So while people are still drinking beer (which, given the radically fluctuating diet patterns of the West, might not be a total certainty), people will still be drinking Budweiser. The King of Beers will keep its crown for some years yet.

Secrets of success

- *Targeting*. Budweiser has always known its audience and it has reached this audience through carefully scheduled TV advertising and sports sponsorship.
- *Consistency*. Aside from the belching frogs, Budweiser has been consistent in promoting its masculine and all-American brand values.
- *Global reach*. Since 1981, Budweiser has bombarded the international market from every angle. The results have been good in every country. Well, apart from the Czech Republic.

Fact file

Website: www.budweiser.com

Founded: 1867

Country of origin: USA

Brand fact 1: Budweiser is the most successful alcohol brand in the world.

Brand fact 2: Its financial value is over four times that of its nearest rival Heineken.

CHAPTER 14

Advertiser brands

In our factory, we make lipstick. In our advertising, we sell hope.

(Charles Revson, former chairman of Revlon)

Of course, most of the brands mentioned in this book advertise their products. However, this section is devoted to those pioneers of advertising who have fundamentally changed or revised the way marketing messages are communicated.

The cases show how advertising has switched from a straight-forward focus on products (Kraft), towards a more transcendental approach – where art (Absolut), sexual imagery (Calvin Klein), music (The Gap) and political attitudes (Benetton) are adopted to elevate the brand identity into an altogether different sphere.

This has inevitably broadened the divide between marketing and manufacturing or the brand and the product. Some of the most radical contemporary advertisers now acknowledge this divide by adding a sense of irony into the mix.

Diesel, the final example in this section, has pioneered a form of self-referential advertising that comments on the over-inflated claims of brands that promise to improve or add meaning to our lives simply by selling us a pair of jeans.

79 Kraft: the household brand

Kraft is now one of the world's largest food manufacturers. Through various acquisitions and infinite line extensions, it now owns various other leading brands, including Nabisco, Philadelphia cream cheese and Maxwell House coffee. However, the reason it has been able to acquire such an arsenal of familiar names is largely down to the success of the Kraft brand itself.

Kraft's success is chiefly due to innovation. In 1916 James Lewis Kraft patented his brand of processed cheese and, in doing so, invented a completely new category. The convenience associated with Kraft was enhanced further with the introduction of sliced processed cheese in 1950.

Kraft's product innovations were matched by an imaginative use of marketing. In 1919, it became the first cheese company to launch a national advertising campaign, with its first ads appearing in US women's magazines.

Kraft was also innovative with its use of sponsorship. It gave its name to one of the most successful radio shows in US history, Kraft Music Hall, which began in 1933 and was eventually hosted by Bing Crosby. The show transferred to TV in 1958 and remained on air until 1971, with Perry Como as its long-running host.

Kraft was also the sponsor of Kraft Television Theatre, which started in 1947 and was the United States' first live drama series, and also the first commercial network programme on TV. The ads that interrupted the drama are now a significant piece of advertising history. They showed a pair of anonymous female hands cooking with Kraft products. As they were shown to an audience completely unused to TV advertising, they became one of the most effective campaigns in history and ushered in the advertising blitz that occurred on TV screens in the 1950s and 1960s.

Its later TV ads were also effective, and became the blueprint for how companies could tie their brand to a product category. An example was the slogan 'America spells cheese K-R-A-F-T'.

Kraft's real innovation wasn't processed cheese. It was an advertising and sponsorship strategy that showed how powerful broadcast media could be used to get inside the consumer's psyche. Kraft wasn't just something used for cooking. It was something associated with the most popular TV and radio programmes, and interwoven into the fabric of daily life. The brand of processed cheese showed how a household name no longer needed to be confined to the kitchen cupboard. It could become truly a part of the entire household. So if ever you want someone to thank or blame for the branded clutter broadcast into your living room, you can start with Kraft.

Secrets of success

- *Room to succeed.* By patenting processed cheese in 1916, JL Kraft found room to succeed in the crowded cheese market.
- *Pioneering advertising.* Kraft also found room to succeed by treading new marketing ground. By pioneering new forms of advertising, such as radio sponsorship and TV ads, the brand found new and powerful ways to reach consumers.

Fact file

Website: www.kraft.com

Founded: 1916

Country of origin: USA

Brand fact 1: Kraft was the first product advertiser on US television.

Brand fact 2: Kraft now makes more money from line extensions than its core brand.

---

80 Absolut Vodka: the advertising brand

If ever you are in doubt about the power of advertising, consider the case of Absolut Vodka. Its first advertising campaign began in 1981, and it has been running almost continuously ever since, wilfully blurring the distinction between art and advertising. During that time, sales of the vodka have rocketed.

The campaign, originally devised by two young junior assistants at the US advertising agency TBWA (who never got the credit until years later), is based on a simple, two-word formula: 'Absolut Perfection', 'Absolut Magic', 'Absolut Clarity' and so on. Above the text there is always a picture of the distinctive, bulky Absolut bottle. Each ad always promotes a different attribute of the brand. For example, Absolut Clarity had a magnifying glass over the part of the bottle with the words 'Country of Sweden', therefore emphasizing a major point of difference with other vodkas (it is one of the few not to be made in Russia).

Before the campaign started, Absolut was selling 10,000 nine-litre cases a year in the US market. By 1985, the brand was the leading imported vodka. Since 1994, Absolut has been placed in the top 10 international premium spirits brands. Over the course of the campaign, worldwide sales have soared from 10,000 nine-bottle cases to almost 8 million cases today. There are 400,000 bottles of Absolut produced every day.

This rapid growth is incredible for an alcohol brand. 'Liquor is one of the most difficult areas in which to create a new consumer brand,' says Donald Mitchell, a Massachusetts-based management consultant and former executive at Heublein, the makers of Smirnoff Vodka:

> The hurdles are many... Most people are not very experi-
> mental in the liquor they will try. You cannot go door to door

dropping off samples like soap powder. Distribution is very expensive and hard to acquire. Establishing profitability with a new brand can take many years, and there are many failures. As a result, the market leader in most categories is still the market leader today. For imported spirits, the country viewed as the most 'legitimate' historical source always dominated the imported category.

According to critics of Absolut, the role of advertising has been over-played in the making of the brand. Luck, they argue, was also on the brand's side. After all, the most 'legitimate historical source' of vodka was Russia. But in the late 1970s and the 1980s the political situation, and President Reagan's notorious depiction of the USSR as the 'evil empire', made things hard for Russian brands such as Smirnoff and Stolichnaya. Absolut's Swedish origin was therefore a brand asset, rather than a handicap.

However, this does not diminish what the Absolut advertising campaign has managed to achieve. Indeed, it was not the only non-Russian vodka on the market – by 1982, Absolut had passed a major Finnish competitor that had entered the international market 10 years earlier. Also, Absolut carefully accentuated its country of origin via the campaign itself, as I've already discussed. In addition, Absolut's advertising campaign helped to get the vodka sold in all the right places. For example, in the early 80s it became the top tipple at New York's celebrity-packed nightclub Studio 54.

The campaign was so strong that Absolut would have succeeded whatever its origin. Marketing and advertising have managed to give brands a power that is stronger than geopolitics. After all, the United States is not very popular in many areas of the world, but it still has many of the most desired brands. We are now living in an age where people are more likely to tattoo the Nike swoosh on their arm than their national flag. Absolut's success is due to branding, not political coincidence.

Is this success likely to continue? If the advertising continues to stay as artistic and imaginative there is only one answer. Yes, absolutely.

Secrets of success

- *Difference.* 'To surprise and delight' is the stated brand aim on the Absolut website. When Absolut advertised in *Playboy*, the ad was called 'Absolut Centrefold', and the bottle was stripped naked of its lettering, wore Playboy bunny ears, and came complete with a list of measurements and interests. Another delightful surprise was Absolut's Christmas gift to readers of *New York* magazine – a pair of designer gloves by Donna Karan enclosed within a December issue.
- *PR.* In 1985, Andy Warhol, who two decades before had inadvertently turned Campbell's soup into a brand icon, was commissioned to do a painting of the Absolut Vodka bottle. This not only blurred the advertising/art line, but also the distinction between PR and advertising, as it received immediate attention from the world's media. The popular vodka overnight metamorphosed into pop art, and an international brand icon.
- *Art.* Absolut's promotional campaigns blur the line between art and advertising. Absolut has also spent money on art commissions and hosted exhibitions, such as 'Absolut Glasnost', a collection of works by 26 Soviet artists timed to coincide with Gorbachev's historic 1990 visit to the United States, which appeared in the US magazine *Interview*. Gorbachev was given the first copy.
- *Innovation.* Innovative marketing is the key to Absolut's success, and explains why it is the only brand to have won the two most prestigious awards in the US advertising business – the Effie and Kelly awards. It is also one of the three brands included in the American Marketing Association's Hall of Fame. The others are Nike and Coca-Cola.

- *Extremes.* Suitably for a product with a 40 per cent alcohol content, Absolut isn't scared of going to the extreme. It once created a towering ice sculpture of the Absolut Vodka bottle high in the Swiss Alps.

Fact file

Website: www.absolut.com

Founded: 1879

Country of origin: Sweden

Brand fact 1: Absolut's first advertising campaign began in 1981. It is still running.

Brand fact 2: In 1985 Absolut blurred the line between art and advertising when they commissioned Andy Warhol to paint the bottle.

Brand fact 3: All Absolut Vodka is produced in Ahus, Sweden.

Brand fact 4: The largest export market is the US where close to 73 million litres were sold in 2003.

---

81 Benetton: the colour brand

In the 1990s, Benetton was one of the world's controversial brands. Unlike other companies – whose wholesome advertising often masks the unhealthy reality of the products – Benetton was working the other way around. Its inoffensive products, including its trademark colourful jumpers, were being promoted through some of the grittiest advertising the world had ever seen. An unsettling series of images – such as blood-covered babies, a child soldier and a dying AIDS patient – was created by photographer Oliviero Toscani. The images seemed more fitting to photo-journalism than to any advertising campaign.

People complained in their thousands. What had such graphic images got to do with Benetton clothes? On the face of it, nothing. Toscani himself said the connection was 'guts'. Benetton was a gutsy brand that hadn't relied on the safety net of market research to launch its products. There is another connection too. As with the multicultural, multi-ethnic images it uses for its 'United Colors of Benetton' campaigns, Toscani's photographs had a global feel, depicting as they did issues of global significance.

And ironically, the images had far more emotional and social power within the context of advertising than they would have had in the editorial context of a newspaper. Indeed, the most shocking thing about the adverts was the small green rectangle with the words, 'United Colors of Benetton'. We were not shocked by the sight of a dying AIDS patient. Upset, maybe, but we see equivalent images on the news all the time. The real shock was that the images were being used to promote a brand – and not a non-profit, charity brand either.

In an official statement, Benetton explained itself as follows: 'Benetton believes that it is important for companies to take a stance in the real world instead of using their advertising budget to perpetuate the myth that they can make consumers happy through the mere purchase of their product.'

Even Benetton's less shocking campaigns can be seen as political. The race politics of Asian and white and black children holding hands may be more straightforward and less challenging than the shocking realism of Toscani's campaign, but it has as little to do with clothes (except through the double meaning of 'United Colors').

As with many companies, Benetton's advertising messages often outweigh the significance of the products. And in so doing, they have not only generated controversy (and therefore extra sales), but they have also questioned the role of branding and advertising itself. Are there lines to be drawn and, if so, where should we draw them?

We already know the answer to the second question. Global brands are political, whether they want to be so or not. When they deal with issues of free trade and fair trade and working conditions, the decisions they are making are political ones. It is impossible to make money out of society without having an effect on society, whether that effect is good or bad.

Obviously, this effect is often to do with the manufacturing process. With Benetton, however, more weight (in terms of people and money) is placed on marketing. They do not come under fire for their factory conditions because most of the work is done by software-operated machinery. And machines are yet to have their own trade unions, although it may only be a matter of time. Benetton's giant factory, just north of Venice, employs a mere 19 people yet produces millions of items of clothing every year.

Benetton adverts may detach themselves from Benetton products, but in a sense the company as a whole has managed to detach itself from the production process through sophisticated machinery. Benetton is moving towards a state of pure branding, where almost all employees work in the stores (the three-dimensional environment) or on branding and advertising.

In other words, Benetton is about advertising as much as it is about products. In fact, Benetton is increasingly a media brand as well as a clothing company. As well as making sure its advertising images stay in our heads, through continuous print media and billboard campaigns, it also publishes its own magazine, *Colors*. And so the medium really has become the message.

To say that Benetton's advertising has nothing to do with its products is therefore to miss the point. With global brands like Benetton, advertising isn't about selling products; it's about selling the brand itself. The pink sweaters and the 'United Colors of Benetton' images both serve the same purpose: to support the brand.

By elevating its advertising into the realm of progressive politics, it has also elevated the brand. We can say that certain images should be confined to news reports and should be beyond branding, but in saying that we are forgetting that newspapers are brands themselves, brands that are financed to a large degree by advertisers such as Benetton.

We may feel, along with Naomi Klein, that Benetton is part of 'a new paradigm that eliminates all barriers between branding and culture, leaving no room whatsoever for unmarketed space'. But to feel that we must believe that culture was somehow once isolated from the world of commercial realities.

When the Benetton family commission avant-garde Italian photographers such as Oliviero Toscani, is it really any different from when the wealthy and powerful Medici family in the Italian Renaissance commissioned Michelangelo to produce works of art to boost their status? Has there ever been a pure 'space' between culture and commerce?

With brands such as Benetton, along with Calvin Klein and Absolut Vodka and numerous others, the line between business and culture does indeed evaporate. But it also evaporates every time a book is published or a Picasso is sold in an auction house.

Benetton is surely as entitled as any other business or any other individual to embrace culture and politics. It has only experienced controversy because it was the first brand to broaden the scope of advertising in this way. The irony is that the controversy only served to elevate Benetton's brand even further, making it one of the most successful advertisers – and, in case we forget, clothing companies – on the planet.

Secrets of success

- *Cultural embrace.* Benetton is a brand with a cultural significance. Its advertising campaigns have had soft and hard political and social messages, giving the brand a status and power its clothing ranges alone could not provide.

- *Courage.* Benetton's bright-coloured clothing may seem a safe bet now, but it was less safe when the company started in the 1960s without any market research. Such courage has spilt over into Benetton's advertising campaigns.
- *Brand emphasis.* Arguably Benetton understands the significance of branding and advertising better than any other European company. In recent years, it has cut its production costs and increased its marketing spend.
- *Micro-marketing.* In his classic business text, *Marketing Management*, Philip Kotler singled out Benetton for its outsourcing strategy and its ability to 'micro-market' to individual retailers 'on a quick-response, just-in-time basis'.

Fact file

Website: www.benetton.com

Founded: 1965

Country of origin: Italy

Brand fact 1: Benetton's 1990s advertising campaigns using Oliviero Toscani gained more column inches than any previous advertising campaign in history.

Brand fact 2: The brand was founded with no market research whatsoever.

Brand fact 3: The company produces more than 200,000 items of clothing a day.

82 Calvin Klein: the sex brand

Calvin Klein does not sell sex directly. He is a fashion designer, not a pimp. Clothes are the product. Sex is just the brand identity, implied through advertising. In the 1970s it was Brooke Shields causing a stir in Calvin Klein jeans ('Nothing comes between me and my Calvins'). In the 1990s it was Mark 'Marky Mark' Wahlberg and his six-pack wearing a bulging pair of Calvin Klein boxer shorts.

The sexually provocative, and often controversial, images have remained the same. It works not only because it generates a huge amount of PR, but also because it gives a dangerous edge to classic, minimalist clothes that on their own look relatively 'safe'.

Furthermore we may not all have the looks of Brooke Shields or Mark Wahlberg or Kate Moss, but these are images we can all buy into. For a designer brand, Calvin Klein is relatively affordable. And even if we can't afford the clothes we can always afford the various aftershave and perfume ranges.

However, Calvin Klein's advertising isn't successful simply because of its sexual message. It is the ambiguity of that message that lends it power. Calvin Klein blurs boundaries of age, gender and sexuality. According to Lisa Marsh, author of *The House of Klein: Fashion, controversy, and a business obsession* (2003), Calvin Klein has introduced 'the idea of ambisexuality'. It is no coincidence that one of Calvin Klein's favourite models is Kate Moss, famed for her 'androgynous' look. After all, this is the brand that first introduced unisex perfume, with its 'One' and 'Be' fragrances. The Marky Mark boxer shorts campaign was also classic Calvin Klein: the boyish face and the man's body; a heterosexual male in a stereotypically homosexual image.

When the brand was accused of child pornography it wasn't because it was truly exploiting children, but because the ages of the models used weren't instantly clear. Indeed, it isn't the sex that makes Calvin Klein controversial. It's the ambiguity.

However, it's also this ambiguity that makes Calvin Klein such a powerful brand. By deliberately failing to distinguish between ages, genders and sexual preferences, it has prevented itself from becoming tied to one particular market. It is therefore no coincidence that it is the most universal, and wealthy, of all designer fashion brands.

Secrets of success

- *Sex*. If ever you doubt that sex sells, look at Calvin Klein. People buy designer clothes to make them feel sexy. It is no surprise that Calvin Klein, the most overtly sexual of fashion brands, is so popular.
- *Ambiguity*. Some global brands blur distinctions of culture and ethnicity to ensure a universal appeal. Calvin Klein blurs distinctions of age, sexuality and gender.

Fact file

Founded: 1968

Country of origin: USA

Brand fact 1: Calvin Klein invented the world's first unisex perfume 'One'.

Brand fact 2: Over a decade after the famous ads featuring Mark Wahlberg the Calvin Klein logo remains the most desired for male underwear.

---

83 The Gap: the easy brand

Advertising has always been important to The Gap. In the late 1990s, Gap ads with the trademark white background and dance routines became one of the visual signifiers of the decade. The style of these ads was so influential that it spilt over into pop videos and even, it has been argued, into blockbuster movies like *The Matrix*.

Like every other aspect of The Gap, its advertising is very carefully controlled and mostly created by in-house teams rather than external ad agencies. This control is evident throughout The Gap, and has helped turn it into an 'experience' brand, in other words a brand whose identity is not simply marked by the products it sells but by the stores themselves. The company's US website states that it you walk into a Gap store you are literally walking into a brand. There are strict rules regarding the layout of the stores, to create a uniform identity across the globe. Also, all Gap clothing is private-label merchandise made specifically for the company. There is complete control over the 'Gap look' from the design board to store displays. Nothing is left to chance.

This control, both of the stores and the clothes, ensures every customer knows what to expect from The Gap, namely easy clothes that are never exceptional. They are not the type of garments that create a stir on the catwalk. In fact, that is almost the point. The Gap is always a safe bet. Gap khakis or jeans with a polo-shirt are casual and comfortable, and never embarrassing to wear. The key thing is choice. Practically every item it makes will come in a wide range of colours. Consider one of their most famous catch-lines: 'Every color – only Gap'. This was a clever reverse echo of Henry Ford's 'Any color they like as long as it's black' statement about his Model T car.

However, there is a problem with being a safe bet, especially when the bulk of your market is under 35. The problem is simple. Safe isn't cool. The first 'crisis of cool' happened in the early 1980s. Since 1969, the year The Gap had been founded, the chain had steadily grown across the United States, partly via the numerous new shopping malls that were cropping up all over suburbia.

In 1983, the brand was radically made over. This was when the crisp, blue-and-white Gap logo first came into being. The company also started to make more of its own clothes, alongside Levi's jeans, which were sold in Gap stores right up until 1991. That was the year when The Gap's brand became really focused, and sold only Gap clothes.

Since then, it has managed to stay fresh by launching sub-brands such as Gap Kids, Gap Body and Baby Gap, in addition to the two other brands owned by the company – Banana Republic and Old Navy Clothing. In total, The Gap operates approximately 4,000 stores.

Of course, there have been blips. In 1994, business analysts were referring to The Gap as a 'mature business', one well past its prime. It then confounded its critics by doubling revenues between 1996 and 1999.

At the turn of the new century, however, it was already starting to hit another 'crisis of cool'. Newer, European rivals such as the Spanish brand Zara and the Swedish brand H & M were making fast inroads into the market by selling clothes at lower prices and often with a faster turnaround. (For instance, while The Gap was restocking its shelves every six weeks, Zara increased its release cycle to every fortnight.)

But The Gap fought back. It recruited Madonna and hip-hop star Missy Elliott for a high-profile advertising campaign and became cool all over again. Groundbreaking advertising and safe, comfortable clothes may seem like an unlikely mix, but it is one that is working. The 'gap' in the market may not be as wide as it once was, but The Gap's appeal remains vast.

Secrets of success

- *Ease.* The Gap is easy: easy to shop, easy to wear, easy to identify with. The brand never falls into the trap of looking like it's trying too hard. As LL Cool J once rapped in a Gap ad: 'How easy is this?' The question was rhetorical.

- *Advertising.* According to Naomi Klein, 'the Gap... is as much in the culture-creation business as the artists in its ads'. The true potential of advertising was finally realized with The Gap's Khakis Swing ads: white backgrounds, retro dance routines and swing music. These weren't adverts capitalizing on trends, but actually creating them. The company has always taken its advertising seriously, and been prepared to spend money on it. In 1998, the year of the Khakis Swing ads, the company spent $419 million on advertising.

- *Narrow identity.* If The Gap wants to do something new it will create or buy a new brand, such as Banana Republic or Old Navy, rather than dilute the core brand's identity.

- *Hands-on style.* According to *Business Week*, CEO Millard Drexler (who has been CEO since 1995) strolls into a different Gap store once a week and chats to consumers and employees in a 'constant drive to improve the company's products and services'.

Fact file

Website: www.gap.com

Founded: 1969

Country of origin: USA

Brand fact 1: Originally the Gap sold names such as Levi's, rather than its own branded goods.

Brand fact 2: The Gap owns the clothing brands Old Navy and Banana Republic.

Brand fact 3: It is now the most successful clothing company on the planet.

84 Diesel: the ironic brand

Diesel is now one of the leading fashion brands in the world. It is also one of the most cutting-edge, puncturing the over-inflated sincerity often found in fashion advertising through marketing campaigns based on irony and satire.

Its identity is global, and it now has a presence in over 90 countries. Although the company is based in Italy (founded by Renzo Rosso and Adriano Goldschmied in 1978), it does not have the same uniquely Italian image of brands such as Armani or Dolce & Gabbana. The global image is deliberate. Even the name 'Diesel' was chosen because it means the same thing in almost every language.

Although the brand achieved some early success, the key year was 1985. That was when Renzo Rosso bought out the other Diesel partners to take control of the company. Under Rosso, the company grew and expanded, taking its range of men's clothes overseas and, in 1989, entering the womenswear market.

It was during the next decade, however, that Diesel became a fashion phenomenon. In 1991, it embarked on a global marketing strategy and came up with the slogan 'For Successful Living'. This was, of course, intended to be ironic. Jeans and T-shirts are not, as far as we are aware, the secrets of a successful life. The slogan, which now sits within the Diesel logo itself, represents the brand's irreverent attitude towards advertising and marketing in general.

As Diesel is aimed at a media-savvy (and often media-cynical) audience, its marketing is pitch perfect. The tongue-in-cheek consumerist values it preaches are not to be taken at face value. For instance, one recent campaign included posters with the headline: 'The Global Diesel Individuals Market Research Survey'. And underneath there would be some bizarre – and we assume entirely fictional – piece of market research, such as: 'Global number of Diesel Individuals who dream of participating in Miss or Mister

Universe: 55'. This is advertising as satire. And the joke is on advertising (and market research) itself.

Diesel adverts are the future. This is where advertising has to end up eventually. In the 1950s it was possible to argue sincerely that a product could improve your life. Now, we have been bombarded with far too many of these promises, and the value of our lives hasn't necessarily increased in line with the number of products we own.

Consumers, in other words, are not stupid. And Diesel doesn't try to patronize their intelligence. Instead, it lets them in on the joke. In an age saturated with marketing images (we encounter literally thousands every day), Diesel's stand out because they wittily acknowledge their status as marketing images. They don't pretend – like so much other brand imagery – to be beamed down from some higher plane.

Although the marketing industry was originally offended by Diesel's irreverent, postmodern take on advertising, it has changed its tune. Just as Eminem won a Grammy after slagging the record industry off, so Diesel has received awards from an industry it is revolutionizing. The Cannes Lion, Epica and various other advertising festivals have consistently awarded Diesel with top honours.

But Diesel's success isn't just down to intelligent advertising. It is also a result of producing high-quality and innovative clothes that, like its advertising, don't conform to the normal rules of the fashion industry. Diesel is hard to pin down. It is neither high fashion nor high street. It does its own thing and, as such, appeals to independent-minded fashion lovers the world over.

Secrets of success

- *Irony.* Diesel's self-aware advertising campaigns work by sharing a joke with its customers. According to social commentator Nick Compton, Diesel is one of a wave of 'New Trash' brands that 'offer inverted commas big enough to live, love and laugh within'.

- *Anti-cool.* Diesel has succeeded where Levi's has failed. Rather than try too hard to be cool, as Levi's has done with its sincerely hip advertising, Diesel deliberately advertises a kitsch, uncool, 1950s-style ethos, which paradoxically makes it even cooler. This is what Naomi Klein has referred to as the 'uncool-equals-cool' aesthetic.

- *Passion.* A sense of humour doesn't equal a lack of passion. The opposite, in fact. As Renzo Rosso has maintained, 'Diesel is not my company; it is my life.' And for once, no irony was intended.

Fact file

Website: www.diesel.com

Founded: 1978

Country of origin: Italy

Brand fact 1: The brand is based in over 80 countries with over 200 stores.

Brand fact 2: Until 1989 Diesel only sold menswear. It now targets women and children as well.

Brand fact 3: Tom Cruise and David Beckham are two of Diesel's many high-profile fans.

CHAPTER 15

Distribution brands

Successful brands depend on successful distribution. After all, brands strive to be seen and get noticed. If they are not distributed successfully they remain almost invisible.

However, the brands in this section haven't just succeeded at distribution; they've revolutionized the very concept. The one thing all these cases have in common is that they made things easier for the customer.

Avon pioneered the concept of personalized home shopping over a century before the rise of the internet. Hertz came up with the idea of car rental, making cars more freely available, and has since built up a distribution network of over 7,000 locations. Domino's Pizzas enabled people to have pizza sent straight to their door. Dell changed the way computers would be distributed by selling tailor-made products direct to the customer. Amazon pioneered the concept of affiliate marketing and showed how companies could distribute their brand, as well as their products, via the web.

The example of Amazon shows how the emphasis of distribution has shifted away from products towards brands. Whereas brands used to be supported by the visibility of the products in real-world locations, for today's online companies products are hidden in warehouses. Rather than relying on people seeing the products through the physical distribution network, brands based in cyberspace need to spread their identity through different means, through links with other members of the virtual community.

This reminds us that distribution is now a dual process, where the distribution of products is second to, and at the service of, the distribution of the brand.

85 Avon: the resilient brand

To some people, Avon might still seem like a bit of a joke. For many, it might still conjure up images of over-groomed, 1950s-style sales reps with fixed smiles and even more fixed hairstyles knocking on the door and saying 'Avon calling!'

But while Avon still might not be the most sophisticated or hip of beauty brands, it remains one of the most profitable. In fact, it has a brand value higher than Chanel's. Although it is well over a century old, the 'housewife's favourite' is surviving and thriving in these post-feminist times.

Avon has been successfully overhauled over the past few years, into a brand appealing to younger women as well as its core older market. It has adapted well to our celebrity-obsessed, interconnected age by signing up glamorous female role models such as the actress Salma Hayek (the 'face of Avon') and tennis stars Venus and Serena Williams.

The 'Avon calling' image is fading fast as the company has shifted its focus from door-to-door sales towards the web. There are still thousands of sales reps or Avon ladies (there are 500,000 sellers in the United States alone), but the average age has got younger as Avon has launched a sub-brand called Mark aimed at the youth market. Instead of calling on bored housewives, these younger reps infiltrate parties, dorm rooms and English classes, selling to their peers.

Door-to-door sales are also still doing well. As Faith Popcorn and Lys Marigold explain in *EVEolution: Understanding women*

– eight essential truths that work in your business and your life (2001), home selling still works just as well among women with careers as it does among housewives. After all, working people are increasingly starved of time and energy. So time-saving, hassle-free services work as well as they always did.

Indeed, it could be argued that they work better than ever because the rise of the internet has taken the stigma out of home services and extended the concept of shopping away from a social or community experience towards a more isolated, individual one.

Also, Avon has tightened up its act since the appointment of Andrea Jung as chairman in 2001 (Avon's first female leader). It has got rid of its more old-fashioned 'soap-on-a-rope'-type products and has launched new ranges such as Avon Wellness, devoted to health products. It has abandoned the visual clutter that used to be the hallmark of its advertising in favour of a slicker and cleaner identity. Its products may still be cheap, but its marketing has definitely gone upmarket.

While other beauty companies suffered during the early years of the millennium, Avon has grown stronger. It has endured the economic meltdown in Argentina, a global recession and the loss of a major business partner (Sears), yet the profit margins got higher. In fact, because of its cheap products and wide global distribution network (3.4 million sales reps across 148 countries), Avon not only braves but often benefits from an unstable economic environment. It looks like the fixed smile is here to stay.

Secrets of success

- *Resilience.* Avon's home-selling sales structure has helped make it one of the most resilient of beauty brands, and it has been one of the few to grow stronger during turbulent market conditions.
- *Adaptability.* Avon has adapted well to the internet era by encouraging its reps to sell via the web. It has also been able to adapt its image to a younger, more glamour-conscious market.

Fact file

Website: www.avon.com

Founded: 1886

Country of origin: USA

Brand fact 1: Avon is ahead of beauty and skin care brands such as Chanel and Johnson & Johnson in terms of brand value (it is second only to L'Oreal).

Brand fact 2: It has over 3 million reps in 148 countries.

---

86 Hertz: the credibility brand

Hertz, the car rental company, is a truly global brand. It has a presence in over 140 countries, with thousands of outlets based in approximately 7,000 locations. It remains head and shoulders above its nearest rival, Avis, partly because it has been leading the category for so long. Indeed, Hertz has been operating in one form or another since 1918 when Walter Jacobs began renting Model T Fords to customers in Chicago.

The idea of car rental was a completely new one, but it gained instant acceptance. When the company was acquired by successful businessman John Hertz in 1923 it was already a success, generating $1 million a year. Hertz gave the business the self-explanatory title, the Hertz Drive U-Self System, so people knew exactly what the company was for. Today, although the name has been reduced to Hertz, everybody still knows what to expect from the brand.

It is remarkable that Hertz has retained such clarity when you consider how many different owners the brand has had. In 1926, it was acquired as part of John Hertz's business empire (which also included the Yellow Cab and Yellow Truck and Coach Manufacturing Company) by General Motors. In 1953, it was bought from GM by the Omnibus Corporation, which tightened the operation by getting rid of the coach business and concentrating solely on car and truck rentals. In 1967, it became a wholly owned subsidiary of the RCA Corporation. In 1985 it switched to UAL Inc, and in 1987 it switched again to Park Ridge Corporation, a company set up by Ford Motor Company and Hertz management for the sole purpose of buying Hertz. In 1988, Volvo became part of the equation, joining Ford and Hertz management as a major investor. In the 1990s the Park Ridge Corporation fully merged into the Hertz Corporation and became a wholly owned subsidiary of Ford. In 1997, Ford sold a 20 per cent stake and Hertz became a publicly traded company, listed on the New York Stock Exchange. But in 2001 Ford ended the game of corporate pass-the-parcel by reacquiring Hertz's outstanding stock, thus placing the brand firmly back in Ford's hands.

It is testimony to the Hertz brand that so many diverse owners and vested interests haven't managed to dilute its brand identity. Obviously, having been the first to enter the car hire market it had a natural advantage. Early innovations such as the 1926 introduction of a company credit card helped establish Hertz as the natural leader of the category. And once you are the leader, brand awareness becomes automatic.

'What makes a company strong is not the product or the service,' writes marketing guru Jack Trout. 'It's the position it owns in the mind. The strength of Hertz is in its leadership position, not the quality of its rent-a-car service. It's easier to stay on top than to get there.'

Of course, this is a slight over-simplification. Poor service and a chronic case of unreliability could easily knock any brand off its leadership perch, especially today when the internet and mass media provide greater access to such information. But being the leader gives a brand an obvious advantage. The dominant 'position it owns in the mind' (to borrow Jack Trout's phrase) means that Hertz becomes the world expert in car rental. This means the company gets a lot of free PR without even having to try, as any media story on car hire is likely to mention Hertz, just as any story on fizzy drinks is likely to mention Coca-Cola.

You lead the market for long enough and you become the market. So Hertz doesn't just operate within the car hire category. It *is* the car hire category.

Secrets of success

- *Credibility*. Hertz is the most credible car hire firm in people's minds because it is the oldest and the most popular. Hertz would have to start making some major mistakes to dent this reputation seriously.
- *Continuity*. Hertz has been passed around the business community so many times you would think the brand would be getting a bit dizzy. But it isn't. It has stayed focused on what it does best, even with the occasional offshoot, and therefore remains the number one car rental brand.

Fact file

Website: www.hertz.com

Founded: 1918

Country of origin: USA

Brand fact 1: Hertz remains the most popular car-hire brand in the world, ahead of rival Avis.

Brand fact 2: The first Hertz hire cars were a dozen second-hand Model T Fords.

Brand fact 3: Today, it has a presence in 140 countries.

87 Domino's Pizza: the home-delivery brand

Like many other leading brands, Domino's Pizza came up with something new. The something new in this case was home-delivery pizza. By inventing the business category, they led it from the beginning.

Not that it was a smooth ride. When 23-year-old Thomas Monaghan bought a pizza store called 'Dominick's Pizza' in 1960 with his brother James, he had no intention of building a global brand. He simply wanted to make enough money to enrol at the University of Michigan School of Architecture. He had little knowledge of the restaurant industry.

His brother James left in 1961 and a second partner left in 1964. Various financial hiccups sent Monaghan back to square one, but he was determined to carry on. In 1965 he changed the name to 'Domino's Pizza' and looked for a unique selling point. Having conducted some informal customer research, he knew there was no point simply competing on price or quality as that would place him in a saturated market. What people really wanted was pizzas delivered to their door. Obviously, to offer such a service Domino's would need to be fast. Over the next two years Monaghan developed an efficient order system and a speedy method of making pizzas. The pizza-delivery guys were even told to run to the door when they got out of their delivery vehicles.

In 1967, he introduced a 30-minute delivery pledge at his new store near the University of Michigan. With 20,000 students on one campus, word of mouth spread rapidly enough for Thomas to expand and sell his first franchise.

But more obstacles were to follow. A fire destroyed the company's central office in 1968, and Domino's hit major money problems as it continued to expand. By 1970, there were 42 Domino's Pizza stores, but the company was weighed down with $1.5 million of debt owed to more than 1,500 creditors, leading to over 100 lawsuits.

However, during the 70s Monaghan fought back, and his long-term strategy based on intensive staff training started to pay off. Indeed, in 1980, 9 out of 10 Domino's Pizza franchisees had begun their careers in the company in the lowest-level jobs.

The company suffered a five-year legal battle with Amstar Corp, the maker of Domino Sugar, after Amstar had brought a trademark infringement lawsuit against the pizza firm. However, in 1980, the federal court ruled that Domino's Pizza did not infringe on the Domino Sugar trademark.

With this obstacle overcome, Domino's was free to expand. In 1981, Monaghan decentralized his company's operations, a masterstroke that led to a rapid growth in the number of new stores, bringing the total to 582 across the whole of the United States by the end of that year.

During the 1980s, the brand went global, opening stores in Canada, Australia, Japan, the UK and South America. By 1990 there were over 5,000 Domino's stores and 1,000 franchises.

Following Monaghan's retirement in 1998, Domino's Pizza has continued to grow, with annual worldwide sales approaching $4 billion generated from over 7,000 stores and over 140,000 employees.

This is remarkable when you consider the failed partnerships, the hundreds of lawsuits, the devastating fire, the trademark dispute, the debt situation and all the other hurdles the brand has had to overcome. Obviously, Monaghan's dogged grit and determination had something to do with it, but it is also due to the two unique factors that set Domino's apart.

The first is people. Unlike a lot of fast-food operations, Domino's has always invested a considerable amount in its workforce. Monaghan believed in devoting resources to employee training even when his company was drowning in debt. This training included establishing a week-long new employee orientation programme. Domino's also has a promote-from-within policy, so that most managers and franchisees started on the lowest rung of the company's ladder. Obviously, if employees are offered a career path rather than simply temporary and part-time jobs, they become more devoted to the brand, and service levels improve.

The second key to Domino's current world-leading status is innovation. Not only did it invent the market within which it competes, but Domino's has kept ahead by consistently treading new ground. Among Domino's various innovations are:

- *Pizza boxes*. In the 1960s Domino's invented the sturdy, corrugated pizza box, designed to maintain heat and prevent moisture from weakening the cardboard. Tom Monaghan claims this was one of the fundamental innovations responsible for the growth of Domino's.
- *The spoodle*. The spoodle, as its name implies, is a cross between a spoon and a ladle. It was invented in 1985 to help reduce the time spent saucing a pizza.
- *The pizza screen*. This is a mesh tray that helps a pizza cook more evenly than on a wooden or stainless steel tray.
- *The car-top sign*. Domino's delivery cars have a 3-D sign on top of them, promoting the brand. They were the first company to come up with the 3-D sign on the top of a car, something that is now used by taxi firms, driving schools and other businesses.
- *Fibreglass tray*. Domino's was the first restaurant company to use a fibreglass tray for handling dough.
- *Hot bags*. In 1998, Domino's introduced their patented HeatWave hot bags, which use an electric heating mechanism to keep pizzas hot during a delivery.
- *Pizza distribution*. Domino's stores save the time needed to make dough, grate cheese and prepare toppings by a distribution system that supplies prepared ingredients.

Such innovations have kept Domino's ahead of what is now a quite crowded market. Also, as the first to arrive in the market, Domino's still holds a natural advantage. Think of home-delivery pizza, and Domino's is probably the first brand that comes to mind.

Secrets of success

- *Market creation.* Like many other successful brands, Domino's created an entirely new market, in this case home-delivery pizza.
- *Determination.* Thomas Monaghan overcame remarkable odds to turn Domino's into a success. It is largely due to his unflinching determination that the brand is here today. Lawsuits, debt, fires, trademark infringement – none were a match for his ambition.
- *Marketing.* From its 3-D car-top signs to the branded fridge magnets (with telephone number) it gives out with each pizza, Domino's knows how to spread the word.
- *Motivation.* Staff training and a promote-from-within policy ensure employees remain motivated.
- *Distribution.* Through its network of 18 distribution centres, Domino's supplies its stores with products ranging from dough to pizza boxes.

Fact file

Website: www.dominos.com

Founded: 1960

Country of origin: USA

Brand fact 1: Domino's was the first brand of home delivery pizza.

Brand fact 2: In the 1960s it invented the pizza box.

Brand fact 3: Today, it has over 140,000 employees working in over 7,000 stores.

Brand fact 4: Dominos makes and delivers nearly 6 million pizzas a week.

- *Local ownership.* Domino's franchise system teaches local business people about Domino's, and helps them set up franchises in their home countries. So Domino's Pizza Mexico is a Mexican company and Domino's Pizza India is Indian. This means Domino's can adapt to local cultures a lot better. For instance, in China, Domino's pizza is more popular in the morning and at lunch time. And in Brazil, cinnamon and banana is one of the most popular toppings.
- *Tangible benefits.* When Thomas Monaghan first decided to have a 30-minute delivery pledge, people were shown a simple and tangible benefit of the brand.

88 Dell: the direct sales brand

In 1983, an 18-year-old called Michael Dell enrolled as a pre-med student at the University of Texas. He wasn't interested in the course and would later admit that he was only doing it to please his parents.

His real interest was computers. While other students were hunched over their books or out partying, Michael was in his room dismantling and upgrading IBM PCs he'd bought from local retailers. Once the computers were upgraded, he went out and sold them to other students, university staff and local businesses. The first month's revenues were a staggering $180,000.

It didn't take Michael long to realize that he could keep more of that money if he bought the components separately and made the computers himself. Once he'd made his own PCs he then went about selling them, at a price 15 per cent lower than other, less comparable, computers.

The following year, he officially set up the Dell Computer Corporation and started placing the word 'Dell' on the products.

Then, in 1985, he started to tailor computers for the needs of specific customers. Those customers could ask for exactly what they wanted and didn't want in their computer, as easily as if they were selecting toppings for a take-away pizza.

So by the mid-80s the two central elements of the Dell brand were in place, namely computers that could be phone-requested and delivered to the doorstep (rather than bought in a shop), and computers that could be made to order. This was the key combination that not only made life easier for computer buyers, but also helped cut company costs, as no shops or dealers were required and it made sure there were no spare parts being wasted. (Dell only ordered what was required, based on what each customer had asked for.)

Once these two elements were in place, there was no stopping the Texas-based company. By his 28th birthday, Michael Dell was the CEO of a Fortune 500 company (the youngest in history).

Today, Dell is the leading direct-sales computer vendor, and one of the biggest PC manufacturers on the globe. The internet has helped Dell, as it has become the perfect medium for direct sales. As well as PCs, Dell also produces servers and third-party software. However, the company has experienced the occasional brand failure – such as the 1999 launch of the web PC.

Tracing further back, there have been other banana skins in the brand's path. For instance, it started selling PCs in PC superstores rather than just through its own distribution channel. Michael Dell later called this decision a 'huge mistake'. However, such mistakes have helped the company stay focused on what it does best: that is, sell direct.

Secrets of success

- *Focus.* 'We sell direct,' says Michael Dell in *Lessons from the Top* (Neff and Citrin, 1999). 'And that clarity has proven to be just awesome. It kept us running off in five different directions. We became incredibly focused.'

- *Harmony.* Dell unifies production and distribution. 'The reason this company is successful is because we've got these things working in harmony in a way that nobody has ever been able to achieve before,' says Dell.
- *Self-awareness.* Dell is a brand well aware of its own identity. It is not Apple, and so doesn't try to create the most aesthetically pleasing computers. Dell is about function and value and what the company calls 'problem solving'. It is not a style or luxury brand, and has never tried to be.

Fact file

Website: www.dell.com

Founded: 1984

Country of origin: USA

Brand fact I: Dell is the world's number one direct sales computer vendor.

Brand fact 2: Most of its products are sold to businesses and governmental bodies (only around 10 per cent of its systems are sold to consumers).

---

89 Amazon: the e-shopping brand

Amazon has succeeded where thousands of others have failed. It has managed to become a leading global brand that is based on the internet. Unlike the e-brands that were quickly sucked into a cyberspace black hole (Boo.com, for instance), Amazon understood that you couldn't stand alone. The internet, if nothing else, is a network. And Amazon knew that to achieve success on the web you had to become a network.

What Amazon did was take the central distribution strategy of the real-world brand colonists – Nike, McDonald's, Coca-Cola – and apply it to the virtual world of cyberspace. The strategy was simple. Be everywhere. Be seen by everyone. Become a part of the scenery. For Amazon to become the leading cyber-brand, Amazon founder Jeff Bezos understood that Amazon's brand imagery would have to be as omnipresent as the Nike swoosh, the McDonald's golden arches or the Santa Claus red and white of Coca-Cola. Amazon would have to be everywhere on the web, always only a few mouse-clicks away.

Yet while Bezos's strategic objectives were the same as other global brand builders, his tactics had to be different. The internet had not completely rewritten the marketing rulebook (as many late-90s commentators had thought), but it had made sure that the rulebook now needed a serious update in order to be relevant to a new, interactive media age.

Coca-Cola, and the rest, had achieved their omnipresence in two ways. The first way was distribution: the physical products out on the high street or on the shelves of the supermarket. The second, and arguably the more significant, was advertising. This was the modern alchemy that had, for over a century, managed to turn a product into a brand: base metal into gold. Advertising had become, by the 1990s, almost synonymous with branding. While the product told us that Coca-Cola was a brown-coloured, sugary, fizzy drink, the adverts pointed out that Coca-Cola was in fact something far bigger. Coca-Cola, the brand, meant love and magic and happiness. It meant Father Christmas. Its apparent aim wasn't simply to quench the consumer's thirst, but also (in the words of one of its many theme tunes) 'to teach the world to sing'. Advertising managed to turn Coca-Cola into an icon to be worshipped. An icon that promised eternity. Always Coca-Cola. An icon that didn't have to explain itself, which didn't need to be questioned. It simply was.

The problem for an internet brand was that the distance between the consumer and the company was a lot narrower. After all, the internet was characterized by information and interaction. The advertising used to build previous global brands had been about the exact opposite.

Information had always been chiselled away into a three-word slogan: 'Just Do It'; 'the real thing'; 'I'm Lovin' It'. Budweiser's whole brand identity could now be distilled in one four-letter word: 'True'.

And as for interaction, well, no chance. Advertising had always been communicated via one-way media: billboards, TV, radio, event sponsorship. Consumers became audiences. They sat down, they shut up, they listened, like submissive Victorian schoolchildren. When they saw a Nike billboard, the only way they could interact with it was to draw a comedy moustache on Michael Jordan's face. Interaction was therefore an illegal activity. Consumers were, in short, outside the brand message.

The internet, of course, changed all that. Suddenly, consumers had a voice. They could post their opinions about brands on message boards for other people to read. They could form discussion groups with other aggrieved customers. People from Britain could now join forces with people from North America, Australia or the Indian sub-continent. Brands, once in control of their own message, were now having their slogans undermined by an unending supply of customer information.

The global brand had met its match in the form of the global consumer. Anti-sites, such as Microsucks.com and McSpotlight. org, were set up to counteract the promotional jargon of the leading brands. The Davids and the Goliaths now had a level playing field. The message for internet brands was simple: inform and interact, and if they wanted to become omnipresent they had to think differently.

And think differently was what Amazon did. In 1996, when Amazon was still a tiny online bookstore, Bezos came up with his big idea: affiliate marketing. Other sites would sell Amazon products, promote the Amazon brand, and take a commission for every sale. The incentive for the participating sites was simple: a higher income for roughly the same amount of work.

The incentive for Amazon was equally clear. It was casting a far wider net than it could have done by sitting back and waiting for customers to type in its URL. The beauty of Amazon's affiliate marketing scheme was in its relevance to almost every website. Business sites could sell business books; kids' sites could sell Harry Potter; pet sites could sell books on understanding the psychology of your springer spaniel. And these sites could make money from every sale (at a commission rate of 3.5 per cent) without having to worry about handling stock. By the end of the 90s, the number of Amazon affiliates stretched well into six figures. Amazon was everywhere on the web.

Amazon's affiliate scheme is only half of the marketing equation, however. The genius of Amazon is that it combines both these things together on its site. Instead of just getting a standard bit of blurb about each book, customers can provide their own reviews (along with a star rating) to inform other customers about each product. Word-of-mouth publicity is therefore contained within the site itself. Customers inform each other and get the opportunity to interact on message boards, in a giant online consumer community.

Today, Amazon is no longer simply a bookstore. It sells DVDs, toys, hi-fis, CDs, software, kitchen equipment and even holidays alongside Harry Potter. Today, it has broadened its brand identity to represent safe and convenient online shopping.

It has applied the same formula in each local market, so that whether customers are based in Dallas, Seoul or Paris they know exactly what to expect. The Amazon list of associates keeps on expanding, along with the brand's revenues, even though now most customers visit the site direct.

Amazon shows that any brand wanting to become big on the web needs to weave a successful marketing web of its own. It also needs to understand that the internet is a democratic medium.

Ultimately, Amazon succeeds by making the customer the star of the show.

Secrets of success

- *Inclusion.* At Amazon, customers are not voiceless entities who only buy products. They can sell products (such as used books) or offer reviews of items for other shoppers. This is peer-to-peer marketing at its purest.
- *Networking.* Amazon doesn't see networking as an expensive lunch followed by an exchange of business cards. For Amazon, networking means creating a literal network of thousands of websites all clicking through to Amazon web pages.
- *Information.* Amazon customers are told all the details they need to know before buying a book or CD or whatever it is they are interested in. They are told the price, when it will be delivered and what other customers have thought of the product, and are even offered a list of similar items.
- *Focus.* Although Amazon has occasionally dabbled with TV advertising campaigns, it generally keeps the focus on reaching its customers more cost-effectively via the internet and through viral marketing.

Fact file

Website: www.amazon.com

Founded: 1996

Country of origin: USA

Brand fact 1: Amazon.com is the world's most successful online retailer.

Brand fact 2: At a party in 1996, Jeff Bezos came up with the idea of affiliate marketing. There are now millions of Amazon affiliates on the web.

CHAPTER 16

Speed brands

Do not squander time, for that's the stuff life is made of.

(Benjamin Franklin)

In the 1995 hit movie *Speed* Keanu Reeves finds himself on a bomb-strapped bus with Sandra Bullock and a load of panicking passengers. If the bus falls below 50 miles an hour the bomb will automatically detonate. Keanu needs to think fast. It is rush hour. One wrong turn on the Los Angeles freeway and it's goodbye bus. Eventually, Keanu saves the day and successfully shows off his biceps by climbing under the bus and dismantling the bomb while the vehicle speeds around an empty airport.

Speed is not only the finest moment in action movie history, it is also a telling metaphor about the pace of the modern world. We are all, metaphorically speaking, on that bus. After all, this is an age of interactive technology, of rolling news coverage and unseen threats (all three are literally depicted in the film, by the way).

This impacts on business too. A fast society creates a need for fast brands. If a brand can't keep up or find its clear patch of freeway, it is over. Every brand needs to make a decision about how it responds to the increasing speed and danger within its market. Is it Keanu, searching for clear road? Is it Sandra, following each new direction? Or is it one of the passengers at the back of the bus hyperventilating into a brown paper bag?

This section is devoted to brands that have used speed to their advantage, beating their competition by offering a fast turnaround of products or fast access to information.

90 Reuters: the objective brand

Reuters is the original speed brand. Created over a hundred years before the multimedia and the internet ushered in the information age, it was the forerunner to the fast-paced data and content providers of today.

In the 1850s, before it became known for news gathering, it sent stock market information from Belgium to Germany via carrier pigeons. Pigeons were replaced by bicycle messengers and the telegraph. Julius Reuter then moved to London to set up the Reuters agency, which expanded into all types of news reporting.

Reuters built a reputation for fast, accurate and objective information, which newspapers proved willing to pay for (the first of which was the British daily *The Times*). Through Reuters, news from around the world could appear on the front page of a newspaper within a matter of hours.

Today, although the company is still best known as a news agency, most of its business has returned to the provision of financial data. Sophisticated technology may have replaced the carrier pigeons but the values of speed and accuracy remain the same.

The 21st century has not been kind to the Reuters brand – sharp rivals such as Bloomberg now provide rolling financial data via TV but, in a world where long-trusted and objective sources of information are becoming ever more important, it is likely to remain one of the leading infobrands.

Secrets of success

- *Trust.* Trust is important for any brand, and even more so for an information provider. Whether it is reports from Iraq or stock market data, Reuters always supplies trustworthy information.
- *Branding.* With a product as intangible as information, the brand reputation becomes everything. The Reuters principles of accuracy and objectivity have become the model for all infobrands, from market research companies such as Forrester Research to Reuters' rival, Bloomberg.

Fact file

Website: www.reuters.com

Founded: 1851

Country of origin: UK

Brand fact 1: The first Reuters service used carrier pigeons to send stock market information.

Brand fact 2: Today financial information services accounts for over 90 per cent of its business (the rest being news reports).

Brand fact 3: It now has 427,000 professional users.

---

91 FedEx: the 'first' brand

FedEx delivers 5 million shipments every business day. It is the world's leading delivery brand, worth billions of dollars.

It is, like 'Hoover', one of the few brand names that doubles as a verb. To 'FedEx' something now means to send an overnight shipment.

It has become synonymous with the service it offers, partly because of its long list of firsts. FedEx was the first transportation company to:

- dedicate itself to overnight package delivery;
- offer next-day delivery by a guaranteed time;
- offer Saturday delivery;
- offer time-definite service for freight;
- offer money-back guarantees and free 'proof of performance'.

It is these firsts that helped FedEx achieve yet one more – in 1983 it became the first US business in history to reach the $1 billion mark in less than a decade, without the help of mergers and acquisitions.

Its brand values of reliability and punctuality are now so well known they have even been the basis of a movie. In Robert Zemeckis's 2001 blockbuster *Castaway*, Tom Hanks is a FedEx worker who ruled his life by the clock before a plane crash stranded him on a desert island.

Today, FedEx is the perfect brand for our fast-paced times, now serving almost 100 per cent of the US population and millions of customers worldwide.

Secrets of success

- *The law of the first*. FedEx has proved the law of the first by leading the way through innovations such as guaranteed next-day delivery.
- *Speed*. FedEx is a fast brand suited to the fast pace of the internet age.
- *Promotion*. From its central role in *Castaway* to its PR stunts with Amazon (delivering new instalments of Harry Potter on the day of its release), FedEx is never short of positive publicity.

Fact file

Website: www.fedex.com

Founded: 1973

Country of origin: USA

Brand fact 1: FedEx is the largest express transportation company.

Brand fact 2: FedEx is now a verb. To 'FedEx' means to send something by express delivery.

Brand fact 3: FedEx delivers over 3 million packages every day.

---

92 Zara: the speed-to-market brand

Amancio Ortega might not be the most famous man in fashion. He might not be as well known as Calvin Klein, Tommy Hilfiger, Jean-Paul Gaultier or Dolce & Gabbana, but he is a hell of a lot richer. In fact, he is the second-wealthiest man in fashion, behind only Bernard Arnault, head of luxury goods conglomerate LVMH (Louis Vuitton Moët Hennessy). The multibillionaire, who regularly makes the upper regions of *Forbes* magazine's rich list, is also the wealthiest man in Spain.

Ortega, who has a fortune of over $9 billion, is the founder and president of Inditex, the parent company for the fashion chain Zara, which makes most of its profit. Ortega is not a flamboyant entrepreneur. He is about as far removed from Richard Branson as you can imagine. He never does interviews and hates having his picture taken.

The same sceptical approach to publicity is evident in Zara itself. Its headquarters aren't based in Madrid or Barcelona, but hidden away in the Galician port of Arteixo La Coruna. There are no Zara press offices outside Spain, and the one based in Arteixo La Coruna is reluctant to provide much information. Unlike other fashion brands, Zara does not send out samples of its clothes for magazine photo-shoots and it spends little on advertising (in 2002 its marketing budget was under 1 per cent of the company's total expenditure).

And yet, Zara is an incredibly popular brand. From its 1975 launch to its present status with stores dotted around the globe, the Zara brand has grown largely through word of mouth. Its secret is to make catwalk styles affordable, adapting rather than copying labels such as Prada and Christian Dior and getting them out into stores as quickly as possible.

Zara succeeds through speed. By producing most of its products in-house, it is both the supplier and retailer. Its speed-to-market time is therefore faster than rivals such as The Gap and H & M. New products arrive in stores every few days, not just once a season, and it manufactures more than 11,000 different products a year. This not only makes Zara the most up to date of high-street stores, but it also means shoppers keep coming back for more, in case they miss anything. This fast, ever-changing stock turnaround is also popular with the high-fashion brigade. The deputy editor of British *Vogue* has admitted that 70 per cent of her wardrobe comes from Zara.

Its fast-fashion formula is also fuelling fast growth as the company seeks to expand further away from the European market it now dominates. The company is successfully proving that it is possible to build a global brand around products rather than promotion.

Secrets of success

- *Fashion.* Zara is referred to as a fashion-conscious equivalent of The Gap, catering for a similar market but with a European edge.
- *Limited marketing.* Some brands, such as Gucci and Rolex, limit distribution to increase demand. Zara limits its marketing activity, playing hard to get with the media, so rumours and word-of-mouth publicity end up filling the information void. Even its new stores are completely hidden behind boardings until the day they open.
- *Repeat custom.* The average clothes store in Spain expects customers to visit three times a year. Fans of Zara, on the other hand, return 17 times a year, owing to the ever-changing ranges of clothes.
- *Response.* Zara responds quickly to consumer behaviour. If a style doesn't sell well within a week, it is withdrawn from shops and replaced with a new design.
- *Cost.* Zara replicates high fashion but makes it affordable. Its low inventories and minimal advertising spend help keep prices down.

Fact file

Website: www.zara.com

Founded: 1975

Country of origin: Spain

Brand fact 1: Zara's marketing budget is often less than 1 per cent of the company's total expenditure.

Brand fact 2: It is the fastest changing global fashion brand, making over 11,000 different styles of garments a year.

- *Control.* As Zara produces much of its own stock completely in-house, it cuts out the middleman, retaining more control and therefore getting its products in stores faster than its competitors.

93 Hello Kitty: the cute brand

Mickey Mouse was the first cute cartoon character to unleash a global brand, but he wasn't the last. The Japanese Hello Kitty character shows that 'cute power' is here to stay. The white cartoon cat with the giant head and wide-open eyes is a phenomenon and, even considering it comes from the land of brand extensions, it has been stretched beyond most others. There are Hello Kitty toys, stationery, mobile phones, bracelets, stereos, watches, handbags, televisions and pop-up toasters.

For grown-up Hello Kitty fans there are even Hello Kitty Daihatsu cars, imprinted with the cute feline's face, diamond watches and coffee makers. According to the US book *Hello Kitty Hello Everything!* by Marie Moss (2001), you can have a Hello Kitty wedding, complete with branded china and silver spoons, crystal wine glasses, place cards and Hello Kitty bride-and-groom dolls. You can even have the ceremony at Puroland in Japan, a theme park devoted to Hello Kitty and the other characters licensed by the Sanrio company.

In 2004 Hello Kitty turned 30. That is quite an age for a cat, but even older for a cult brand in Japan, where youth market trends come and go very quickly.

However, Sanrio moves equally fast. Each month, the company launches 500 new Hello Kitty products and gets rid of 500 old ones. The company changes the Kitty range to match not only different trends but also different locations. For instance, in Japan there are 200 'localized' Kitty dolls representing the identity of each region, which also makes them into perfect souvenirs for tourists.

The thing that really sparked the Hello Kitty boom in the 1990s, though, was when it crossed over into the adult market. That was the decade when adults started to feel confident about buying into childhood brands. Think of the millions of adult Harry Potter readers, for instance. Hello Kitty provides a route back to childhood that also manages to make its fans look chic – Sarah Jessica Parker, Mariah Carey, Drew Barrymore and Tyra Banks are just four of the glamorous celebrities who own Hello Kitty merchandise.

According to Ken Belson and Brian Bremner, authors of *Hello Kitty: The remarkable story of Sanrio and the billion dollar feline phenomenon* (2003), the brand is the archetypal example of Japanese *kawaii* (roughly translated as 'cute') culture, a culture that deliberately provides a sentimentalized and idealized version of reality. Hello Kitty's version of reality has a deliberately feminine slant – signifying a life of tea parties and making friends.

Once this is considered, the millions of Hello Kitty extensions make sense. Unlike the extensions of other diversified brands, these extensions only serve to strengthen the core identity. After all, like many of the strongest cult brands, Hello Kitty doesn't just offer its fans a way to help define their personality, but also provides them with an escape route out of reality into a completely branded world.

Secrets of success

- *Cuteness.* In a world of increasingly harsh and ugly realities (wars, terrorism, recession), cuteness is becoming a powerful brand attribute.
- *Lifestyle.* Hello Kitty's millions of products enable fans of the cute cat to create their own branded lifestyle.
- *Speed.* The Hello Kitty brand keeps its faddish customers happy by radically updating its range every single month.

Fact file

Website: www.hellokitty.com

Founded: 1974

Country of origin: Japan

Brand fact 1: The cute kitten is the main attraction at the Puroland theme park in Japan.

Brand fact 2: It is now possible to purchase a fully branded Hello Kitty wedding.

94 Google: the search brand

In 2002, the internet search engine Google was named 'Brand of the Year' by readers of Interbrand's Brandchannel.com, outranking Coca-Cola and Starbucks.

This achievement was remarkable for a number of reasons:

- Google had only been going since 1998.
- It had never advertised on TV.
- It relied mainly on word-of-mouth publicity.
- It had almost no brand visual imagery on its site, apart from the Google name itself.
- It had never hired an advertising or marketing firm.

Google is a global brand like no other. Indeed, it feels strange even to use the word 'brand' when referring to it, so conditioned are we to thinking that branding is something that surrounds a product or service with glossy advertising. With Google, branding isn't what surrounds the service. It actually *is* the service.

The Google brand and the Google search engine are one and the same thing. There is no fatal gap between perception and reality, which the Nikes and Starbucks have been accused of having, because everybody's perception of Google is based on their experience of using it.

And this experience couldn't be simpler. Even virgin users know what to do when arriving at the home-page for the first time. They see the name 'Google', they see the search box, and little else. They type in what they are looking for and, a split-second later, they have the results in front of them. The extreme complexity of the software leads to the most relevant search findings on the web, and most users find what they are looking for on the first page of results, which are presented straightforwardly against a blank white background.

Obviously, Google is a free service for web users. It makes its money elsewhere – chiefly from advertisers. These fall into two groups. There are the larger ads that are displayed at the top of the search findings, which form Google's 'Premium Sponsorship' scheme, and there are the ones that are in isolated boxes, underneath the header 'Google Ad Words'. Both sections are shaded in blue to make it easy for the user to distinguish between page search findings and the objective results.

This two-tier advertising model enables Google to generate income from small as well as larger advertisers. However, while advertisers are the chief source of income, they are not allowed to dictate the look and feel of the site. There are no logos or corporate imagery. There is just plain text and a link through to the relevant website.

So far, Google has stuck to text-based ads clearly separated from the main results, and the company's stated aim is still to provide the most objective results on the web, keeping the site 'clutter-free and focused on search'. Indeed, the company argues that its stripped-down approach to web advertising works in its advertisers' favour.

'The momentum of our advertising relationships is a strong validation of the high quality and appeal of our service,' says Sergy Brin, Google's co-founder and president. At the end of 2000, advertisers at Google were already witnessing an average click-through rate four to five times higher than the industry standard for web banner ads.

Google is seen as the archetypal 'neutral' search engine model – as all of its advertising remains independent from the main index. Google should, in some respects, put off its paying customers. After all, it affords them little space, separates them from the main index and forbids their corporate imagery. The reason advertisers are undeterred is partly because Google is by far and away the most popular search tool on the web. People trust Google, and this is something companies want to buy into. Ironically, if Google gave more space and more visual control over to its business customers, the adverts – and the search service itself – wouldn't be as effective.

Although Google has branched into general-purpose portal services, such as a news section and shopping comparison tool, it has so far managed to remain clutter-free. Whether the pressures of the commercial environment will end up forcing Google to add more stuff to the site remains to be seen. At the moment, Google seems to realize that simplicity, usability and minimalism are the holy triumvirate that keep web users coming back.

Secrets of success

- *Word of mouth*. The internet has made society more tech-nologically connected than ever before. This connectivity has helped Google become one of the most successful word-of-mouth hits in history.
- *Ubiquity*. Google is everywhere on the web, as it is used by a variety of other major websites to provide search listings. It also has various international sites to appeal to a global, multilingual audience.

Fact file

Website: www.google.com

Founded: 1998

Country of origin: USA

Brand fact I: In July 2004 Google suffered from a computer virus that ground the search engine to a halt. The virus coincided with Google's flotation on the UK stock exchange at a value of £20 billion.

Brand fact 2: Google remains not only the most popular search engine, but also the most visited site on the web.

- *Experience.* The experience is the brand. Google views its brand from the outside in and keeps the focus firmly on the user's experience. It doesn't think of advertisers first and visitors later. It knows that, by keeping the number of visitors at a high level, advertisers will automatically be interested.
- *Technology.* Google shows how technology should be used. It deploys incredibly complex software to create an incredibly simple website. Even the most computer-illiterate users have few problems.

95 CNN: the information brand

We are surrounded by information. Saturated by it. This is, after all, the information age: the age of multimedia, the internet and satellite technology.

The problem now isn't getting hold of information; it's trusting it. We need to know where the information is coming from, before we believe it. For this to happen, information needs to be branded, which leads us to CNN – the archetypal information brand. What MTV did for the music video, CNN has done for news coverage. It single-handedly defined the concept of rolling news, broadcasting often live coverage from across the globe, 24 hours a day. As the first channel of its kind, it has remained the most viewed, despite competition from Fox News, MSNBC, CNBC and numerous others (including the Middle Eastern equivalent, Al-Jazeera).

The value of CNN was first fully realized during the first Gulf War, when people around the world tuned in for live, on-the-spot information. Since then, it has proved its worth during the 9/11 terrorist attacks and the conflicts in Afghanistan and Iraq. CNN has been viewed as a 'spare tyre' according to the company's vice-president of strategic marketing, Molly Battin: 'If there was a problem or emergency, people knew they could turn to it and count on it but they didn't need it on a daily basis.' In the 21st century, CNN has decided to become more than a 'spare tyre', by launching sister networks such as CNN Headline News and CNN fn (for financial news), catering for more targeted markets.

CNN has also been instrumental in adapting TV coverage for the internet generation. The network now uses what it calls 'multi-element screens' and 'news wheels' (rolling text headlines across the bottom of the screen), which means that as many as three news stories can be broadcast simultaneously from one channel. Such techniques were quickly adopted by rivals.

Its global reach has proved slightly more difficult to imitate. With a 212- country reach and with studios in all major continents, CNN remains the most global and therefore the most advertiser-friendly of all news brands.

CNN, as the most recognized name in global news coverage, is seen as the most authentic. Like Coca-Cola, it is 'the real thing'. Of course, truly objective coverage from any one source is impossible. But CNN's information-packed screens and 'Breaking

News' headlines are strangely addictive. This is information on amphetamines, rarely slowing down or giving us time to absorb the information. The result is that we are constantly fed information without ever being fully satisfied. As a result, news-hungry viewers around the world stay tuned to the never-ending coverage, waiting for the next headline.

Secrets of success

- *Pioneering approach.* CNN changed news broadcasting with its 24-hour rolling coverage, and it continues to pioneer new formats.
- *Reach.* CNN doesn't just report from everywhere in the world, but it is watched from everywhere as well.
- *Urgency.* Rolling news coverage is, by its very nature, an urgent type of broadcasting. Where McDonald's gave the world fast food, CNN gave us fast news.

Fact file

Website: www.cnn.com

Founded: 1890

Country of origin: USA

Brand fact 1: CNN has the widest global reach of any TV station in the world.

Brand fact 2: CNN's website was the most popular news site in the aftermath of the 9/11 attacks in 2001.

---

96 Hotmail: the viral brand

The internet brought with it a new type of promotion: viral marketing. This was basically word of mouth intensified by the interconnectedness of new technology.

Hotmail, the free web-based e-mail service, provides the ultimate example of viral marketing. By automatically including a line about its service and a web link at the end of every message it helped deliver ('Get your free e-mail at Hotmail'), Hotmail ensured that customers were passing on the message just by communicating with their friends. Without actually mentioning it, people were endorsing the service just by using it.

In its first 18 months, with almost no advertising, the brand had over 12 million subscribers. Even now that the brand is owned by Microsoft, very little is spent on marketing. But Hotmail keeps on growing virally by turning every single e-mail into a marketing tool, and every single user into a brand ambassador.

Fact file

Website: www.hotmail.com

Founded: 1995

Country of origin: USA

Brand fact 1: Hotmail is the most successful brand to be built on viral marketing.

Brand fact 2: The 'Get your free e-mail at Hotmail' line is still included on Hotmail messages, generating new customers every day.

Brand fact 3: Hotmail now has more than 8.5 million subscribers.

Secrets of success

- *Incorporated message.* With Hotmail, the service and the marketing message are incorporated together, making every user spread the word.
- *Viral marketing.* People have a wider network of e-mail contacts (friends, colleagues etc) than via any other medium. Hotmail, as an e-mail service, could tap into the widest and most immediate of 'technosocial' networks to create a marketing virus, where friends told friends told friends without even thinking.

CHAPTER 17

Evolution brands

Brands change all the time. Old brands update their image. Expensive brands introduce cheaper products. Fattening brands launch healthy versions.

Most of the time these new directions fail. They cost the brand lots of money and serve to confuse the people they are aimed at.

Sometimes though, evolutionary change makes sense. For example, when the Bacardi company was forced to leave Castro's Cuba in 1960, it moved its headquarters to the Bahamas. Its brand identity then shifted from Cuban to Caribbean.

When the shift in identity feels like a natural evolution, rather than a desperate bid for short-term sales, it tends to work. HSBC's migration towards a unified identity made sense as part of its strategy to link its subsidiaries together. Intel's decision to create a consumer brand coincided with its inability to trademark its microchips.

However, Samsung's recent reinvention is perhaps the most remarkable case of brand evolution. It has shifted from being a rather tired, indifferent technology company, to a leading industry pacesetter that has got Sony shaking in its high-tech boots.

The factor all these cases have in common is that they each represent a step closer towards a solid identity, rather than a step away from it. Brand evolution should therefore not be something that confuses people, but something that actually brings the brand into clearer focus.

97 Bacardi: the Caribbean brand

Bacardi is the bestselling spirit brand in the world. The rum it produces has remained almost unchanged since 1862, when the Spanish immigrant Don Facundo Bacardi Masso started making it in a small tin-roofed distillery in Cuba.

It wasn't the best of working environments, as Masso had to share the premises with a colony of fruit bats, which lived in the rafters. This is where the Bacardi bat logo comes from. It had been originally suggested by Masso's wife, Dona Amalia, who thought it would be a useful way of distinguishing the rum. She was right. Within months it was known in Cuba as 'el ron del murcielago' – the rum of the bat.

However, it was the quality of the spirit that really set it apart. Maso had spent years trying to find a way to make a lighter and more refined rum than the strong and rough-tasting rums that had gone before. He eventually arrived at Bacardi's distinctive secret formula. This quality was recognized through various awards, beginning with the medal it received in the Madrid Fair of 1877.

Bacardi's popularity grew steadily, decade by decade, both in Cuba and abroad (it was the first spirits company ever to manufacture its products outside of its native country). It kept the same identity, and the same taste, and left it for customers to use it in different ways – such as in cocktails (pina coladas and mojitos) and mixed with Coca-Cola.

The Bacardi company had to leave Cuba in 1960 when its assets were seized by Castro's regime. New facilities were set up in the Bahamas, Canada, the United States and Spain, helping its global reach. By the end of the 1970s, Bacardi was the most popular spirit brand in the world.

Recent years have seen a slight shift of identity for the brand. Following the Bacardi company's consolidation into Bacardi Limited in the 1990s, which included establishing its headquarters in

Bermuda, Bacardi now accentuates its Caribbean identity through its advertising. It has also launched successful sub-brands such as Bacardi Breezer, enabling the brand to achieve a younger identity without tarnishing the core product.

Secrets of success

- *Uniformity*. The strict determination to make sure the rum was exactly the same wherever it was produced helped its global expansion.
- *Adaptability*. Bacardi is easily adapted to different tastes as it is easily mixed with soda drinks and cocktails (including the world's most popular cocktail, the pina colada). It has also adapted to today's club-orientated drinking environment with the small-bottle sub-brand Bacardi Breezer.
- *Secrecy*. Like Martini (which merged with Bacardi in 1992), Bacardi updated a traditional drink with a new and secret formula. This secrecy has not only stopped imitators, but it has also added to the mystery and legend of the Bacardi brand.

Fact file

Website: www.bacardi.com

Founded: 1862

Country of origin: Cuba (now Bermuda)

Brand fact 1: Bacardi was the first spirit brand to make its product outside its native country.

Brand fact 2: Bacardi's shift in identity from 'Cuban' to 'Caribbean' began in 1960, when the company's assets were seized by Castro's regime.

Brand fact 3: Bacardi is the most financially successful spirit in the world, with a brand value of over US $3 billion.

98 HSBC: the acquisition brand

HSBC is one of the largest banking and financial organizations in the world. It is also Britain's most successful company.

Evolving from the Hong Kong and Shanghai Banking Corporation (hence the initials), which has its origins in the 19th century, HSBC has adapted to the global market through the creation and acquisition of subsidiaries. The strategy, which started in the 1950s, peaked in 1992 with one of the largest bank acquisitions in history, the purchase of the UK's Midland Bank. It soon added various other financial institutions, such as Credit Commercial de France and The Republic New York Corporation, to its ever-expanding shopping list.

In 2003, the acquisition strategy stepped up a gear with the controversial purchase of the relatively downmarket US consumer finance group Household International for $14 billion, which represented the brand's need for a substantial US presence in line with the bank's global ambitions. It also reflected its desire to be seen, primarily, as a consumer-based company. 'Two-thirds of every economy in the world is based on consumer expenditure,' HSBC chairman Sir John Bond told trade publication *The Banker* ('HSBC's killer move', 6 October 2003) at the time of the deal. 'And the more you can get your organization to sit astride that, frankly, the better for your business.'

Unlike many other giant organizations that acquire established companies, HSBC has opted for a uniform brand identity. The aim has been to make the name and logo as well recognized as possible throughout the world, so that each local subsidiary has the psychological power of a global brand.

Repetition leads to familiarity leads to trust. The more a bank is recognized abroad, the more confidence it inspires back home, a paradox reflected by the slogan 'the world's local bank'.

Secrets of success

- *Global presence, local approach*. As with its main rival Citibank, HSBC is a global brand that operates as a local retail bank around the world.
- *Acquisitions*. HSBC shows that, for companies with a big enough budget, the best way to enter a new market is to buy a company that is already there.
- *Brand migration*. When HSBC became a fully uniform brand in 1999, it was after a long and slow migration of each local business towards the HSBC identity. The typeface, colour scheme and hexagon logo arrived at different stages before HSBC stood alone as an independent brand. By that time, customers were fully prepared for the new image.
- *Uniformity*. The name and visual identity has become the same throughout the world, lending strength to its banks in each local market.

Fact file

Website: www.hsbc.com

Founded: 1865

Country of origin: Hong Kong (now UK)

Brand fact 1: HSBC is the second biggest bank in the world, behind only Citibank.

Brand fact 2: HSBC is Britain's most valuable brand.

---

99 Intel: the educating brand

Ever since 1971, when it gave the world the first microprocessor, Intel has been about innovation. Of course, for a producer of computer ingredients (boards, systems, software, as well as chips), innovation is almost essential. However, its innovations don't just affect its products. They also involve the brand itself.

For the Intel brand the key year isn't 1971 but 1991, when the Intel Inside programme was launched. This was the first time a computer component brand had communicated directly to PC buyers, rather than to PC manufacturers.

The reason why Intel decided to become a consumer brand was partly a result of legal issues. In the late 1980s the courts had ruled that its microprocessors, given numbers such as the 386 and 486, were not trademark protected. That meant that rivals could use the same numbers on similar chips and steal Intel's market from under its nose.

Intel therefore decided to shift the emphasis from the processor numbers to the Intel name itself, and boost awareness of the brand among computer buyers themselves.

The media were sceptical. The idea that a pure technology company could become relevant to consumers in the same way that brands such as McDonald's and Coca-Cola were seemed laughable. After all, most people just wanted to use a computer. The perception was that people didn't want to think about components buried inside that they couldn't even see. In 1991, most consumers wouldn't have even known what a microprocessor was, even though it was the thing that actually powered their computers.

Intel therefore decided to look at other brands that had managed to become household names despite only providing a part of a finished product. Brands like Dolby, Teflon and NutraSweet provided obvious examples. Intel realized success depended on two factors: cooperative marketing (working with PC makers and licensing them to use the Intel logo) and building a strong identity in the consumer's mind.

The first job was to get the computer makers on board. It did this by setting up a cooperative fund. Intel took a percentage of the purchase price of processors and put it in a pool for advertising funds. So long as computer manufacturers used the Intel logo, Intel offered to share the costs for PC print advertising. By the end of 1991, 300 companies had signed up to the programme.

Intel also started its own independent advertising campaign. Owing to a lack of consumer knowledge, Intel was educating people about microprocessors as well as promoting its brand values. As a result, awareness of Intel grew around awareness of microprocessors, and the brand became associated with high-quality innovative technology and reliability.

With its Intel Inside trademark, the advertising campaigns have fundamentally changed the way people view their computers. As the Intel website boasts: 'today many personal computer users can recite the specification and speed of the processor, just like car owners can tell you if they have a V4, V6 or V8 engine'.

Fact file

Website: www.intel.com

Founded: 1968

Country of origin: USA

Brand fact 1: Intel was the first computer component brand to advertise directly to consumers.

Brand fact 2: The 'Intel Inside' slogan was created in 1991 to safeguard the brand against imitators.

Brand fact 3: Intel is currently the fifth most valuable brand in the world.

The brand is now consistently ranked as one of the 10 most visible brands in the world. Not bad for a company selling a largely unseen product.

Secrets of success

- *Customer education.* Product innovation was followed by equally pioneering advertising, which not only educated consumers but led to the growth in technology advertising in the 1990s.
- *Mutual benefit.* Through Intel's cooperative marketing programme, both Intel and computer makers have a mutual benefit in promoting the brand. Intel's advertising is also cited for helping create more PC demand.

100 Samsung: the rising brand

South Korea's electronics company Samsung is the fastest-growing big brand in the world according to the world's leading brand consultancy, Interbrand. Its brand value doubled from $5.2 billion at the end of 2001 to $10.8 billion by 2004. It is now, in terms of value, one of the top 25 brands in the world, and is fast catching up with its main rival, Sony.

So how has Samsung evolved from being a boring, nondescript brand into its current position as *the* global brand to watch? Well, firstly, it has gone upmarket. Over the past few years it has shifted towards 'designer' technology products such as flat-panel TV monitors and ultra-thin DVD players. It has also successfully entered new markets such as mobile phones, by offering premium-priced products. This has helped give Samsung an aspirational edge it never had before. It has also led to higher profit margins.

Secondly, it has switched from being a brand sheep to a brand shepherd. Whereas it used to follow the market, its wholehearted embrace of digital technology has placed it at the leading edge. It has successfully promoted its digital credentials through a massive advertising campaign, promising to provide a 'Digit All Experience'.

Perhaps most importantly, however, Samsung has made the all-important move towards brand-centric mentality. Since it was launched in 1969, Samsung has spent most of its time promoting and advertising specific products. As a result, there has often been a lack of a coherent identity. At the start of this century, Samsung changed its strategy towards a more holistic approach. It now launches international campaigns aimed at boosting Samsung's entire reputation, rather than specific product ranges. Everything is now geared towards the brand, and it invests more heavily in raising its global profile, such as through sponsorship of the Olympic Games.

With a mission to have the premium market share for at least 50 different types of products, and with the digital revolution only just beginning, Samsung's fast rise is far from over. So how about a bold prediction for this bold technology brand? Okay, how's this? By 2010, Samsung will be one of the top 10 most valuable brands in the world.

Secrets of success

- *Brand focus.* 'Samsung has successfully made brand building the key focus of its marketing strategy including product development, selection of distribution channels, channel marketing, as well as external and internal communications,' says Jan Lindemann, global managing director of Interbrand.
- *Leadership.* Samsung used to have a rather lacklustre image as a 'follow-the-crowd' kind of company. However, its new image as an ambassador for digital technology has turned it into an industry pacesetter.

Fact file

Website: www.samsung.com

Founded: 1969

Country of origin: South Korea

Brand fact 1: Samsung is the fastest rising brand on Interbrand's 'List of the Top 100 Brands'.

Brand fact 2: Between 2002 and 2003 its brand value jumped up by 31 per cent to US $10.89 billion.

Brand fact 3: Samsung literally means '3 stars' in Korean.

The last word

So what makes a brand successful? It's a difficult question and, as this book has revealed, one to which there are a lot of different possible answers. As I mentioned in the Introduction, it is precisely the lack of conformity that makes these brands successful.

However, there is one factor each brand has in common – clarity. A clear brand message combined with a clear point of difference is evidently the key to a successful brand.

Of course, the day-to-day realities of business and marketing are far from clear. They are a complex fog of economic factors and human judgements. Each new product or service inevitably comes out of that fog, and risks adding even more confusion to a world already saturated with brands. Consumers can now come in contact with more brands in a single day than their 1930s equivalents would have seen in a whole decade.

To break through the clutter, a brand inevitably needs to have a clear message. That does not mean it has to stand for only one type of product; it means that the values and image represented by a brand should be consistent and easy to identify.

Branding is the language of business. It is the way a business communicates with the world outside. While brands are usually the result of complicated business decisions, that complexity should never be reflected in the brand itself. The job of a brand is to speak to the market in a clear voice.

The brand may have been a result of weeks of complicated meetings and managerial decisions, but consumers choose brands in a matter of seconds. Their perspective is very different from that of the brand manager. They are not on the company payroll. Their jobs are not devoted to the brand. They just want to make a quick decision. And to help them, a brand must be communicated clearly.

The process of branding is therefore very like the process of writing. A good brand, like a good novel or poem, is capable of translating complex human thoughts into simple language. To be successful, it must also communicate something new or different with that language. As William Wordsworth said of writers: 'Every great and original writer... must himself create the taste by which he is to be relished.'

Likewise, every great and original brand must also create the taste for which it will be appreciated and, ultimately, loved. While a brand's success can be inspiring, it can never be copied. This ensures that, while they may be related, no two members of brand royalty will ever look or act the same.

References

Ballard, JG (1996) *Cocaine Nights*, Flamingo, London

Belson, K and Bremner, B (2003) *Hello Kitty: The remarkable story of Sanrio and the billion dollar feline phenomenon*, John Wiley & Sons, Tokyo

Cohen, B and Greenfield, J (1997) *Ben & Jerry's Double-Dip: Lead with your values and make money, too*, Simon & Schuster, New York

Critser, G (2003) *Fat Land: How Americans became the fattest people in the world*, Houghton Mifflin, Boston, MA

Fernandez-Armesto, F (2003) *Ideas that Changed the World*, Dorling Kindersley, London

Freud, S (1900) *The Interpretation of Dreams*, Macmillan, New York

Godin, S (2000) *Unleashing the Ideavirus*, Do You Zoom, New York

Gray, J (2002) *Straw Dogs: Thoughts on humans and other animals*, Granta Books, London

Haig, M (2003) *Brand Failures: The truth about the 100 biggest branding mistakes of all time*, Kogan Page, London

Hofman, H (1994) *Search for the Real*, MIT Press, Cambridge, MA

Hughes, R (1991) *The Shock of the New: Art and the century of change*, Thames and Hudson, London

Klein, N (2000) *No Logo: Taking aim at the brand bullies*, Picador, New York

Knobil, M (ed) (2003) *Cool Brand Leaders: An insight into Britain's coolest brands 2003*, Superbrands, London

Kotler, P (1993) *Marketing Management: Analysis, planning, implementation and control*, Pearson Higher Education, New Jersey

Levine, M (2003) *A Branded World: Adventures in public relations and the creation of superbrands*, John Wiley & Sons, New York

Lindstrom, M (2003) *Brand Child: Remarkable insights into the minds of today's global kids and their relationships with brands*, Kogan Page, London

Love, JF (1985) *McDonald's: Behind the arches*, Bantam, New York

Marsh, L (2003) *The House of Klein: Fashion, controversy, and a business obsession*, John Wiley & Sons, New York

Moss, MY (2001) *Hello Kitty Hello Everything!: 25 years of fun!*, Abrams, New York

Neff, T and Citrin, J (1999) *Lessons from the Top: In search of the best business leaders*, Doubleday, New York

Ogilvy, D (1983) *Ogilvy on Advertising*, Orbis, New York

Pinker, S (2002) *The Blank Slate: Denying human nature in modern life*, Allen Lane, London

Popcorn, F and Marigold, L (2001) *EVEolution: Understanding women – eight essential truths that work in your business and your life*, Hyperion Books, New York

Ragas, M and Bueno, B (2002) *The Power of Cult Branding*, Random House, New York

Ries, A and Ries, L (1998) *The 22 Immutable Laws of Branding*, Harper Collins Business, New York

Strinati, D (1995) *An Introduction to Theories of Popular Culture*, Routledge, London

Torekull, B (1999) *Leading by Design: The Ikea story*, tr. J Tate, Harper Collins, New York

Trout, J (2001) *Big Brands, Big Trouble: Lessons learned the hard way*, John Wiley & Sons, New York

Walton, S and Huey, J (1992) *Made in America: My Story*, Bantam, New York

Index